# The Homecoming Seasons

# OTHER BOOKS BY JAMES P. MACGUIRE:

*London and the English Countryside*
*Campion* (with Christopher Buckley)
*Beyond Partisan Politics*
*Miracle in East Harlem: The Fight for Choice in Public Education* (with Seymour Fliegel)
*Dusk on Lake Tanganyika and Other Poems*
*The Rockaway Hunting Club at 125* (with Dr. Benjamin Allison)
*Newman and the Intellectual Tradition*
*The Catholic Shakespeare?*
*Modern Science/ Ancient Faith*
*The Catholic William F. Buckley Jr.*
*Catholicism and the American Experience*
*Real Lace Revisited*
*Worlds Within Worlds: A Father's Poems and Prayers*
*International Religious Freedom: The Rise of Global Intolerance*

OCTOBER 11, 2022

FOR ANGELA AND TOM —
WONDERFUL NEW FRIENDS,
THANKS TO TREDDY!

# The Homecoming Seasons

## An Irish Catholic Returns to a Changing Long Island

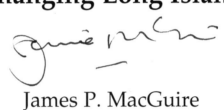

James P. MacGuire

HAMILTON BOOKS
*an imprint of*
ROWMAN & LITTLEFIELD
*Lanham • Boulder • New York • London*

Published by Hamilton Books
An imprint of The Rowman & Littlefield Publishing Group, Inc.
4501 Forbes Boulevard, Suite 200, Lanham, Maryland 20706
www.rowman.com

86-90 Paul Street, London EC2A 4NE, United Kingdom

British Library Cataloguing in Publication Information Available

**Library of Congress Cataloging-in-Publication Data Available**

Names: MacGuire, James P., 1952- author.
Title: The homecoming seasons : an Irish Catholic returns to a changing Long Island / James P. MacGuire.
Other titles: Irish Catholic returns to a changing Long Island
Description: Lanham : Hamilton Books, an imprint of Rowman & Littlefield, [2022] | Includes index. | Summary: "The Homecoming Seasons: An Irish Catholic Returns to a Changing Long Island is James P. MacGuire's poignant memoir of returning to his childhood hometown on the South Shore of Long Island to raise his own family, re-encountering its natural wetland beauty, his late parents' now older friends, and making new ones in a community undergoing transition. The quarter century that the book details is filled with life, death, triumph, and loss, and chronicles, above and below its surface, a fragile yet ultimately resilient world"—Provided by publisher.
Identifiers: LCCN 2021059191 (print) | LCCN 2021059192 (ebook) | ISBN 9780761873303 (paperback) | ISBN 9780761873310 (epub)
Subjects: LCSH: MacGuire, James P. | MacGuire, James P.—Family. | Lawrence (N.Y.)—Social life and customs—20th century. | Lawrence (N.Y.)—Social life and customs—21st century. | Irish Americans—New York (State)—Lawrence—Biography. | Irish American Catholics. | Isle of Wight (Lawrence, N.Y.)—Biography.
Classification: LCC F129.L377 M33 2021 (print) | LCC F129.L377 (ebook) | DDC 974.721—dc23/eng/20211207
LC record available at https://lccn.loc.gov/2021059191
LC ebook record available at https://lccn.loc.gov/2021059192

*For PJ and Walker*
*And the many neighbors and friends who supported us along the way*

# Contents

# Author's Note

I hope this memoir of a forgotten little corner of Long Island from childhood through middle age reflects the different modes of consciousness, observation and perception with which all of us are endowed as we progress in life.

I am grateful to my longtime publisher, Jed Lyons, for his continuing support. Thanks, too, to Edward G. Reitler Esq. for his proofreading, copy editing and counsel.

Needless to say, any shortcomings are my own.

JM St. Patricks Day, 2022

# Introduction

In 1994 my mother died. She had been diagnosed with colon cancer two years before and had been operated on successfully. However, in an unusual metastasis, the cancer migrated to her brain. After a period of weakening, in early November of 1993 she collapsed at her home in Lawrence on a Sunday morning. Three of her six sons were with her, and had we not gotten her to the hospital so swiftly she certainly would have perished then and there. In the event she was revived and stabilized and given some radiation treatments to shrink her several brain tumors that had grown so shockingly suddenly. Her quality of life was good for a while. She went out to Thanksgiving dinner at the local country club, and all who saw her said how beautiful she looked. She came downstairs for a few minutes on Christmas Eve to greet family and old friends at her annual cocktail party. And then she slowly declined, finally giving up the ghost on a Mardi Gras night in February.

My mother's house was on Cedarhurst Avenue in Lawrence on western Nassau County's South Shore. It had long been the center of our life, and especially in summers its five bedrooms were usually full of family who loved the superb sports facilities nearby and proximity to the Atlantic Ocean and its expansive beaches.

My mother's road to the little corner of Long Island where she spent the last half century of her life was a winding one. Her grandfather, P.J. Casey, had been a Western Union executive for 67 years until his death in 1927. The company moved him from New York to its Long Branch, New Jersey office each summer so he could supervise the greatly increased tele-graphic traffic in the "Summer Capital." (Seven presidents—Chester Arthur, James Garfield, Ulysses S. Grant, Benjamin Harrison, Rutherford Hayes, William McKinley and Woodrow Wilson had all resided there in the season.

1

P.J. Casey knew them all and liked to recall Mrs. Lincoln's graciousness after the assassination.)

P.J. Casey's wife was Julia Rhoads Casey. My mother remembered her grandmother as a dour New Amsterdam Dutch lady who ate slowly and said little in contrast to her extroverted, Irish jig-loving grandfather, but Julia was well read and had graduated with the first class of women at Hunter College.

Their son, my mother's father, was John Schuyler Casey, called Schuyler. He took his engineering degree from City College and launched into a successful career in construction and manufacturing with the Treadwell Corporation, of which he became CEO. He was athletic, gregarious and a gifted salesman who was accorded life memberships at both the Downtown Athletic Association, where he laid the cornerstone, and the New York Athletic Club, where his name can still be seen in the lobby on a plaque commemorating the clubhouse's completion.

My mother's family had summered on the Jersey Shore but switched to Long Island in the late 1930s after my grandmother had died in a fall from a horse at Eaton's Ranch in Wyoming. Schuyler Casey used John Bierwirth Sr. as his banker for the Treadwell Corporation, and Mr. Bierwirth encouraged him to come to the Five Towns. "If you can get me into the Lawrence Beach Club, I will," Casey replied. And Big Jack Bierwirth did.

My father's family, meanwhile, had originally settled in upstate Johnstown, New York in the early nineteenth century as commerce expanded westward with the building of the Erie Canal. They operated a livery stable there. My grandfather, Dr. Daniel Philip MacGuire, came south to attend Columbia University and then Columbia's School of Physicians and Surgeons before decamping for a further year of study at Heidelberg, then the world's leading medical school. He acquired a fashionable dueling scar there before returning to teach at Columbia and establishing his private practice on East 72nd Street. He married my paternal grandmother, Beatrice Butler, whose father, James Butler, had left behind fifteen generations of Kilkenny farmers to emigrate to America in 1876, worked on farms and later in hotels, and in due course built up the country's second largest chain of grocery stores, the Butler Stores, surpassed only by A&P.

In his spare time, James Butler enjoyed harness racing north of the City with such swells as Cornelius Vanderbilt. Later he operated a powerful thoroughbred racing stable as well as three racetracks—Empire City (Yonkers Raceway today), Laurel Park in Maryland, and, when racing was banned for some years in America, the Juarez Jockey Club in Mexico across the Rio Grande from El Paso, where his partners were "Father of the Kentucky Derby" Colonel Matt Winn and Harry M. Stevens of hot dog fame, soon to be joined by local chieftain Pancho Villa, whose offer that his army band be installed as the official track band could not be refused!

In his book *Real Lace*, Stephen Birmingham referred to the Butlers and other leading families like the Bradys, McDonnells and Ryans as "FIFs" for First Irish Families. Neither mine nor the other families so-called would have dreamed of referring to themselves in such a pretentious fashion. In fact, I can remember my father's delight when a rather stuffy aunt who had married into the family announced she had hired a genealogist to establish our relationship to the Butler Dukes of Ormond at Kilkenny Castle. After some time, the answer came back . . . well, let's just say no answer came back. Our Butlers were apparently, to use C. D. B. Bryan's delicious phrase, "more felonious than Thou."

At the same time, however, their sense of Irish identity was strong and Catholic faith profound, even when that was not welcomed warmly in the upper precincts of Establishment Society into which they moved.

My father's family had spent weekends and summers at James Butler's Westchester farm, East View, adjacent to Butler's neighbor and friend, John D. Rockefeller at Pocantico Hills. In August they headed north to my grandparent's house in Saratoga Springs for the race meeting there.

My Dad, Philip MacGuire, often called "Big Phil" to distinguish him from my eldest brother, graduated from Yale and volunteered for the Squadron A Cavalry. After Pearl Harbor, however, he transferred to the Army Air Force, and served as a pilot on the Aleutian Island atoll of Attu. When he returned from the Pacific, Lawrence became an attractive option for a family of two young children with more likely to follow. Although my father had grown up on East 72nd Street, the easy commute to his Wall Street office and the family real estate holding company in midtown, the proximity to the water, several Yale friends and the fine sporting facilities were all selling points. An additional incentive was that in those days, thanks to John A. Morris, my father's family still had racing dates at the old Jamaica track nearby, Empire City having been declared too antiquated to house the growing post-War crowds. And so, my parents came, first to White's Lane and then, in 1947 to what would become the family home on Cedarhurst Avenue.

At the time of Mother's death my wife Lanie and I were living on Carnegie Hill in Manhattan. After a peripatetic 15 years of boarding school in Rhode Island, Johns Hopkins in Baltimore, further graduate study at Cambridge, the Peace Corps in Thailand, and running maternal-child health and agricultural developments programs in central Africa, I had returned to New York to work in publishing and television. Lanie was completing her qualification as a Jungian analyst. Our son Pierce was three and enrolled in pre-school at the Church of St. Thomas More.

As that winter turned to spring and spring to summer, we slowly sorted through Mother's things and put her house on the market. It sold quickly to an orthodox Jewish family who liked it, in part, because they could walk to worship. At the same time, we began thinking of where we might best live. Such thought was clarified when in September we learned that another child was on the way, and our apartment was likely to be too small.

Although neither of us had ever contemplated living on Long Island there was suddenly a certain logic to the idea, and an old friend's house in an attractive neighborhood had come on the market. With Lanie's family's help we were able to buy the property, and on the second Friday of November, as the last leaves were falling from the trees, we moved to 7 Stable Lane.

The Village of Lawrence is in the westernmost part of Nassau County, bordering the Rockaways section of Queens, only an hour's drive from midtown Manhattan. Stable Lane is a small street in a tiny subsection of Lawrence called the Isle of Wight. Originally, laid out on the village's southern shore as a summer colony in the 1880s and sometimes referred to in those days as "Lawrence-by-the-Sea," many of the street names have anglophile associations such as Albert, Victoria and Oxford Place.

Stable Lane is a smaller road near the entrance to the Isle of Wight where horses from the once extensive but now redeveloped Williams estate were tended. There are only three houses on Stable Lane, one of which, opposite us, was converted from the eponymous purpose it once served. The other two were Cape Cod cottages, built side by side in the early Fifties. Ours was one of these.

# Chapter 1

# The Isle of Wight

The Isle of Wight is a neck of land of about forty acres located on the north shore of East Rockaway inlet, or Reynolds Channel as it is also known. About ten acres is high land with an elevation of about ten feet. The rest is salt marsh.

When the glaciers melted and receded from the ocean the Isle of Wight was born. Thousands of years after that the Atlantic Ocean embroidered it with a string of sand islands that appeared and disappeared, joined and separated, were pierced with inlets and then washed away. Thousands of years later still the Indians came, spending their lives fishing, hunting and trapping (mink, muskrat, rabbits, squirrels, and possum), and transforming the gaudy shells that washed up on to the beach into wampum, used as Indian money as far west as the Mississippi.

The sea was full of fish and the woods were full of game, and the Rockaway Indians loved to fish and hunt. They raised corn, beans and tobacco and their few cows grazed in the meadows. Their houses were built of reeds, cut from the low land bordering the shore and were covered with bark from the trees. A hole was left in the roof to let out the smoke from the fire by which they cooked and kept warm. The women did the work while the men made wampum from choice seashells. They loved games both of skill and chance and would play dice by the hours, using shells as counters. They had frequent gatherings by the shore at which huge quantities of shellfish were consumed. As long as the next meal was provided for, they had no worries. Hunting, fishing, games and clam bakes. All of this still goes on, though the Indians be long gone.

Then the white man came. Early in the 1600s the Dutch settled New Netherlands and the English settled Massachusetts Bay. Their colonial policies were fundamentally different. Through the patroon system the Dutch established small semi-feudal settlements principally in the Hudson

Valley region. The British created a chain of self-governing, semi-independent communities under a town meeting form of government. The British population grew more rapidly, primarily through immigration, whilst the Dutch population remained relatively stagnant. Therefore, while the Dutch were confined to the Hudson Valley the British were spreading to Rhode Island, Connecticut and across to Long Island. A collision was inevitable.

In 1643 a group of colonists from Massachusetts and Connecticut settled in Hempstead. It was a long way from New Amsterdam to Hempstead over a deep sandy wagon track and across the Hellgate rowboat ferry, and even more uncertain and dangerous by sea in a sailboat. The last thing the English settlers wanted was to be governed by the Dutch and the last thing the Dutch wanted was a fight with the British, but no one could disguise the fact that the Hempstead settlement was clearly in Dutch territory. So the settlement's leaders, the Rev. Robert Fordham and John Carman, negotiated a deal. On November 1, 1644, the Dutch governor of New Netherlands William Kiefft, granted them a patent "with their heirs, executors, successors covering a tract of land from the East River to the South Sea, embraced between parallel lines drawn north and south from Hempstead Bay on the east and from Matthew Garretson's Bay on the west."

In 1664 the British seized New Netherlands and renamed it New York. In 1685 Governor Dongan regranted the inhabitants of Hempstead their patent. The Hempstead population increased, but land in the middle of Long Island was considered infertile. Only the "necks" were fit to pasture cattle. There was good farm and grazing land on these, and most of the necks could easily be enclosed by building a fence from the head of the bay or one of the tributary streams on one side to the bay or stream on the other.

On March 14, 1659, a Town meeting appointed a committee to lay out the ground for fencing and enclosing Rockaway. On April 17, 1659, an order was made naming 47 persons to carry out the fencing. 539 panels were required of a three-rail fence or about 7,000 feet. Among the persons named were Thomas Hicks and Adam Mott. On February 22, 1667, Mr. Seaman, Mr. Jackson and Mr. Blew Smith were selected to lay out all of the common meadow at Rockaway. On December 25, 1678, at a town meeting held on that day, the allotments were made. There were 41 allotments. Among them were John Carman, "Mr. Hix," Adam Mott, Mr. Seaman, Mr. Jackson and Mr. John Smith Blew.

One of the smaller necks in Rockaway was called Hick's Neck, and Thomas Hicks had a plantation there. The Hicks family burying ground still exists at the easterly edge of the Village of Lawrence boundary. Adam Mott owned one of these properties and on January 26, 1692, conveyed it to his brother Joseph, by a deed in which he described it as follows:

"A certain parcel of meadow ground lying and being situated at ye south meadows on a neck known by ye name of Hick's neck bounded on ye east by ye meadows of Nathaniael Persel and west by meadows of William Jecocks and north by ye woods and south by ye cove or water, that parteth ye beach and quantity of acres nine in more or less as it was first laid out."

This was the Isle of Wight.

Captain Jacob Hicks was a son of Thomas Hicks. He was a leading and wealthy inhabitant of the town of Hempstead, a captain of the Queens County militia, justice of the peace, and a church warden or vestryman of the Hempstead church. When his father died, he inherited the plantation. When he died in 1802 his lands at Rockaway passed to his sons Stephen and Jacob. Although Captain Jacob Hicks was strong and wealthy his descendants were weak and poor. The ownership of the land he had carefully assembled became scattered, and it was not until 1856 that Alfred N. and Newbold Lawrence came out from New York in search of land to develop and began to reassemble the Hicks properties. At almost the same time a syndicate of families living at Wavecrest (Far Rockaway) and keeping their boats in Bannister's Creek, acquired the upper portion of Hick's Neck and began to develop a summer colony called Ocean Point (later "Cedarhurst").

The Isle of Wight was laid out in 1881. Lots were sold on "Lawrence Beach" and a summer hotel called the Osborne House was built by the water, where Oscar Wilde stayed in the 1890s.

It did not remain Lawrence Beach for long, however. Nature intervened.

Along the Long Island shore, because of a back eddy from the Gulf Stream and the angle that the shore makes to the prevailing wind, the ocean "sets" to the west and each wave leaves the beach slightly to the west of the point where it arrives. The westerly set is particularly pronounced in times of easterly storms.

The effect of the set is to prolong the westerly ends of the sandy ocean islands and eat away on the east thus moving the entire island gradually westward or eroding it entirely. If the island is so firmly fixed that it cannot erode, a point or peninsula is formed at its westerly end that grows larger and larger. Eventually the peninsula loses stability. A September hurricane or a winter storm breaks through at its weakest point. A new inlet forms which makes the peninsula an island. The westerly end of the new island continues its westerly movement until it meets and joins the shore thus closing the old inlet from the sea. A shallow bay forms behind it with its mouth open eastward where the new inlet flows. The new inlet works gradually westward, and the sequence is repeated.

The westerly end of the Long Beach where Brockleface Gut formerly lay, and Woodmere Bay flowed southward into the ocean and was still Town land. In front of the Isle of Wight and separated from it by a narrow bay that opened easterly into the inlet lay the ocean beach that the Lawrences owned. On this beach were the bathhouses and casino of the Lawrence Beach Association.

To the horror of the Lawrences, the inlet moved westward eating away the easterly end of the outer beach and extending westward the west end of Long Beach. Year after year the inlet's westerly movement continued until the Lawrence's ocean beach was gone, and Long Beach extended in along the peninsula some three miles to Edgemere.

In a vain attempt to apply the principles of the English law of waters and watercourses, the Lawrences contended that they owned to the sea, just as the allotments of 1678 (whose title they had perfected) stated; that the changes in the beach were simply stages in a cycle that had repeated itself over and over again for thousands of years; that the new peninsula was simply the emergence in a temporary unstable form of the outer islands and that in the natural sequence of events the ocean would break through, a new inlet would form, and the peninsula would become an island again. But the law of erosion and accretion was applied in the Town of Hempstead's favor, and by this time the Lawrences had run out money to take the case to the Court of Appeals.

In the years that followed Man intervened over Nature. The new outer beach, now called Atlantic Beach and joined to the mainland by drawbridge, became so fixed in its peninsular form by groins, jetties, bulkheads, fill and the construction of streets and massive buildings that the natural cycle has ended forever.

While for the Lawrences this was a tragedy, for the Isle of Wight community it had its compensations. The Isle of Wight became an isolated settlement, hard to find, that few people knew existed. The Isle of Wight Corporation had bought up all the available land in and around the Isle of Wight in order to protect their Ocean Avenue (now Sage Avenue) homes.

In the early years people moved to their Isle of Wight cottages for the summer. Most of them had no heat and many only primitive kitchens. There was a Casino where Dick and Mary Payne now live, where most residents took their meals. In the 1890s there was also a hotel, the Osborn House, where Oscar Wilde once stayed (on the same trip that he visited Walt Whitman in New Jersey).

Richie Tilghman has many fond memories of pre-World War II life on the Isle of Wight: Selling "Sea View Seaweed;" Manning Barr's daughters Nancy, Cynthia and Polly; Richie's older brother George ran the day camp on the IOW, and Richie gave tennis lessons on the court, long gone, on the ball field. Other Tilghmans were Billy, Jim, San and Sally ("the most beautiful girl on Lawrence Beach" and later a longtime classics teacher at Brearley and music lover, married to Allen Wardwell). George Fiske was his best friend. Brother Billy challenged Richie to a fight. Bucky Smith trained Richie, and he won giving his brother a bloody nose. They played baseball on the roof of the Pardee-Reitler house. One night the boys jumped off the dock at the CYC and swam buck naked to the Barr's dock. "We learned a lot from the Barr sisters." The Tilghman's father was headmaster of Morristown Prep and died during WW II. Their house on Edward Bentley Road, *Driftwood*, is now owned by Sally Tilghman's sister-in-law, Helen Dubois.

As time passed the Isle of Wight owners grew older. Some moved away; others died, and their IOW stock was in the hands of their estates. An effort to develop the Isle of Wight and liquidate their holdings was made in 1938 with no success. Four Square (built by Edward Bentley and now owned by Price Blackford) and the Lynch's house (where the Sipps now live) were built at that time but because of the Depression there were no takers. The stockholders were unwilling to put up any money to pay the carrying charges. Unpaid taxes accumulated.

Before World War II and during it, Daniel H. Cox and his family were the only Isle of Wight residents. John Koehne and W. Manning Barr came down in the summer. In 1945 Koehne discovered that the marshland on which the Isle of Wight sewage disposal facilities were located had been sold for taxes. This meant that shortly the Isle of Wight would become uninhabitable and Koehne's investment and summer home would be lost. He called Manning Barr and lawyer Edward Bentley in a huddle and opened a bottle of V O. Several huddles (and bottles of Canadian whiskey) later a plan was formulated for the restoration of the Isle of Wight. The owners' association was transformed into a strong property owners' association of which every owner of property became automatically a member. $25,000 was subscribed for, to redeem the delinquent property to be repaid out of the proceeds of the sale of the Isle of Wight Corporation's land. The Association acquired all of the Corporation's property, including marshland and nearly all the three quarters of a mile of waterfront and the unsold lots. All of the property in the Isle of Wight was placed under deed restrictions which obligated the owners to pay the amounts needed to pay the carrying and other costs. Land was sold and new interest was aroused. The waterfront was frozen and preserved. Continuance of the sewer was assured. The Isle of Wight was saved, and a new generation moved into it following World War II.

The 1,000 acres of Hick's Beach marshes were threatened once more in the fifties. This is a beautiful area, depicted by Louis Auchincloss in his story "Collaboration," where here and there can be seen small rises, breaks in the flat pattern of swampy lands. These high land areas, now covered with bayberry and short trees, are the remnants of dunes that were thrown up when the ocean broke on these shores before the buildup of Atlantic Beach. Until the fifties one could gather all the clams and oysters one wanted, and the Lawrence-born, *New Yorker* writer A.J. Liebling proclaimed the sweetness of Rockaway oysters. Pollution has now destroyed their beds. Blue claw crabs, once great in number, are now severely reduced due to pesticide, oils spills and sewage. In the fall baby bluefish and snapper crowd the creeks at high tide feasting on the spearing, those little fish with silver lines on their tails. Small bass, weakfish and eels also frequent the creeks, cornering and snapping up smaller fish in the shallows.

The bird life is amazing, especially considering the proximity to Kennedy Airport and the Big City smog. In half an hour in the summer, egrets—blue, yellow and black crowned, as well as green herons—can be seen. More furtive are the clapperrail and marsh wren—noisy fellows; both love the tall grasses and reeds. In the spring and fall the meadow hawk, a harrier, can be seen gliding and swooping over the marsh looking for rodents, his favorite prey. All kinds of shore birds—from small sandpipers to the larger yellow-legged snipe—are there, scampering along the banks of the creeks at low tide. Ducks and brant, a small replica of the Canadian goose, rest there too, in flocks, during the fall. In fact, ducks, mostly of the black and mallard varieties, spend all summer with us. Cormorant on the other end prefer to bide in winter. On the inland border of the marshlands where the willows grow and small brush abounds, orioles, red-wing blackbirds, grackles, goldfinches, a variety of warblers and that long-beaked, fat and stumpy fellow, the woodcock, gather.

The entire Hicks beach area was once owned by people from Philadelphia. Around 1885 they dreamed of building a racetrack on these marshes. It would not have been easy since there are countless places where a person walking would sink up to his thighs. That neither racetrack nor railroad for racegoers was built proved a blessing, for in the great storm of 1938 and again in the Forties hurricanes whipped waters into raging waves.

Absentee landlords put the land up for auction in 1953. The village was vitally interested, and a group of 40 citizens put up $110,000—the assessed amount—to bid at the auction in the Knights of Columbus Hall in Lynbrook. Alas, when the auctioneer's mallet came down the property had gone to developers for twice that amount. Fortunately, the Health Board was concerned and put severe restrictions on the property and ultimately the Appeals Court of New York State affirmed the village's right to condemn and control land within its limits. Long Island once had tens of thousands of acres of wetlands. Today, thanks to our neighbors' foresight, Hicks Beach in the village of Lawrence represents an important portion of what is left and provides the Isle of Wight a buffer from the waters of Reynolds Channel.

## Chapter 2

# Early Years, 1994–1997

We moved into our new house after dark on a chilly November Friday evening. The heat had been turned off and took a while to come back on. "I knew this house was a lemon," Lanie shouted when her bath water came on cold. In half an hour it was piping hot, and she was assuaged. The view in the morning was enchanting. From the upstairs we can see Reynolds Channel and Bannister's Creek, and the marshes beyond Sue Gatehouse's house next to ours. The air was fresh, the sky was clear, the future bright, however obscure the present, what with a house piled high with boxes ready to be attacked.

Where have I been the last ten thousand years, and where am I going? Genes in pools that have migrated and mutated, metamorphosed and mingled all over the map, so who can say what direction they're headed in now? And yet, isn't it odd that, after so much travel, they might choose to come back home to Stable Lane, two miles from where I grew up, nestled on a point of land overlooking a pond, a marsh, 200 yards walk from water and only ten minutes from the Atlantic Ocean. Duck and geese soar overhead, and yesterday I jogged past a cock pheasant feeding on Mrs. (Nancy) Benkhart's lawn.

When I was a boy, I would ride my bike down here to David Rutter's house, built by his father and the nearest to the Yacht Club (later it was Art and Mary Murray's and a larger house on the property belongs to Caroline Williamson now). We would explore the marsh and once walked the entire length of the dike, the old beach road, back to the Causeway. It's too overgrown with bayberry and other trees to do that now in 1994. Later we begged Seth Robins for rides on his go-kart and played Sunday afternoon soccer on the communal field, retiring for delicious hot chocolate in the Koehne's kitchen. I remember Dad picking me one winter afternoon when it was too cold to ride my bike and drove me home in our Oldsmobile station wagon. The radio was on and the Americans, led by their goalie Jack McCarten, had just won a great upset against the USSR at the Squaw Valley Olympics. That was 1960, and I was eight.

## BACK TO 1994

Former President Reagan has written the country to announce he has Alzheimer's disease and will withdraw from public life.

On the first weekend we moved in Peggy Lovering thoughtfully came to the door to give Lanie the flowers from the altar at Trinity-St. John Episcopal Church in Hewlett, a touching welcome. The Catholics likewise sent me an initial communique from St. Joachim's in Cedarhurst—a request for money. And so, our spiritual journey on the South Shore of Long Island began!

By the second weekend the house moved out if its inchoate chaos as insurgent Republicans led by Newt Gingrich solidified their control of both houses of Congress for the first time in 40 years.

The sun porch, especially, took shape, as did the playroom. Mrs. Thornley (Joan) Hart is moving back into the city full-time from her beautiful place at the end of Longwood Crossing and kindly sent two arial photos of the Isle of Wight from their first house out this way (now Sonny and Babs Staniford's). They appear to be taken in the early fifties, and I try to identify houses that were once here but have now been torn down and remember families I once knew but have long forgotten: Mom's friend, Lucy Doolan, an artist and golfer; her bridge buddies, Sis Wright and Burr and Helen Freeman; the Pardees, Putnams and Wades, all gone now.

After another full day's unpacking, I walked to the end of Sage Avenue out onto the Little Beach to watch the sun set, the sweet, salty stink of low tide offset by high clouds and dazzlingly clear yet soft, painterly light.

I sensed the slowness of life, difficult for someone who has always wanted to hurry it up and frightened of sitting still. Parenthood changes that. Some things simply cannot be rushed, and in this place, it is possible to exult in the slow unfolding of the crimson-skied sunrise, and the endless hours it takes to wash and feed a squirming three-year-old, the grass still growing and the marsh reeds bending in the breeze. A man rows into the rising creek in a catamaran, ripples recede to his stern and the tide flows, still no sign of cold. The year yearns to end yet lingers.

### First Christmas

By mid-December, the cold came, and now with the trees completely bare one can see the waste, branches broken, limbs down, life everywhere scattered 'round. A grey morning in Lawrence, Pierce is watching TV in the next room, Lanie still sleeping heavily as pregnancy takes its predictable toll. Much left to do in the house but even more on the grounds—trees, bushes and flowerbeds long untended. It seems incredible that 13 months ago Mother was still with us, impaired but very much alive.

I decorated the Christmas tree after the Hunt Club Carols last night. Bill Miller was a jolly Santa Claus. I saw Maria Dessanti there, sister of Nick Benvin, the Club's longtime manager, in whom Mom had first confided her sickness so that Maria could drive her to Sloan-Kettering for tests. Mother knew the secret would be safe with Maria whereas others would inevitably gab. She started to cry as I greeted her. I did the same, and there we were, embracing amidst the happy throng.

Pierce was flu-stricken all weekend but enjoyed the pre-Christmas excitement, shopping for a tree, hanging ornaments, finding his special racing car present in the garage. His mother almost killed him, but he burst around the Isle of Wight in it like a banshee.

Before Christmas there was a procession of bright and seasonally mild days. Duck hunters lay on the bottom of their boats and in blinds on Crooked Creek, decoys strung out, birds overhead, dogs tense, BOOM. The yellow sky goes orange, then red, and the blackness looms. The year's shortest day, but too busy and blessed with oncoming life to let the darkness hold sway.

The Friday before Christmas we had a shakedown cruise cocktail party with neighbors Sue Gatehouse, Tyler Mullally, the MacMillens, Margie and Tim Carpenter, the Wielers and their boisterous boys. Sue is a single lady and Tyler twice widowed. The MacMillens are two of my parents' oldest friends, dating back to Saratoga before the War, after which they moved to Long Island. Tim Carpenter and Dad were at Yale together, and he grew up with my Butler cousins in Bedford. His first wife, Aunt Kitty, was my mother's best friend until her too early death from leukemia, and his second wife, Margaret, is one of the most civic-minded ladies in the community and my mixed doubles partner. Her parents, the Owens, were dear friends of my parents', albeit a bit older. Posey and Mom played bridge. Steve and Dad played tennis and supported each other in AA. It was a great group.

Pierce fell asleep in his pew at the Trinity-St. John children's service on Christmas Eve. The MacMillens asked us for a drink to continue my mother's 30-year-old Xmas Eve tradition. I hung stockings with P.P. and Lanie, then went to Mass with my brother Pierce. Christmas Day itself was very joyous, opening presents, lunch at my brother Schuyler's, Pierce loving his cousin Casey.

Gaggle of geese, duck in flight, sun going down, over the winter-browned marsh, rose colored sunset, frost in the dawn, the hard months ahead, and nothing to do but take stock and plow on. On New Year's Eve we had a quiet dinner *a deux*, and then a good long stare into the flickering fire as the year wound down. A good year for Pierce, a sad year for the rest of us, although Mother continues to exert her influence. The new house, for example, could not have happened without her and Lanie's love for each other, so in a sense it was her final gift.

New Year's Day David and Margaret White brought Little Margaret out and we walked and rode tricycles to the Little Beach and the yacht club. Ann Thornton's dog Tovy raced up the shoreline after duck who feinted him ever farther into the water. Pierce rang the Yacht Club bell while a cop on his beat slept in the squad car. There was a deafening roar from beyond Reynolds Channel. Construction? Traffic? No, an acoustical phenomenon, the heavy air acting like a lens to bring the crashing noise of the surf on Atlantic Beach almost in our very door. The next day I drove across to Long Beach, looking out over the bridge to see the vast network of wetlands making up the South Shore, marsh and scrub, water swirling and eddying.

Pierce awoke with a cry on Wednesday night: "I'm *frowing up*," whereupon he promptly did, and came to sleep with us. Brave little fella. On the weekend his virus had spread to us, and we joined him in sickness, which he much enjoyed.

## 1995

### Winter

1/20: This was the first year the Internet was entirely privatized, with the United States no longer providing public funding.

Heaviest rainstorm of the year, a black day with slivers of lightning in the sky (This week they discovered that lightning goes upward from storm clouds in blue and green shafts, even as the white ones descend).

The unexpected rewards of investing so much time these last four years in what from a bachelor's perspective would have seemed useless activities: changing diapers, bathing or just holding Pierce. A child's giggle at a shared joke as he emerges from a night's sleep is a greater treasure than gold.

On Friday night Pierce saw me come downstairs with a jacket and necktie on.

"Why are you wearing a jacket?"

"Because I always wear a jacket when Mr. and Mrs. MacMillen come to dinner."

"Then I want to wear a jacket, too." And he donned his parka. Later he followed Mac into the loo and asked, "Do you need *pwivacy*?"

"No."

"Oh." And they stayed in there together.

1/25: Rose Kennedy was buried yesterday at 104.

"The most important element in human life is faith. If God were to take away all his blessings—health, physical fitness, wealth, intelligence—and leave me with just one gift, I would ask for faith . . . for with faith in Him. . . . I believe I could suffer the loss of my other gifts and still be happy." (*Times to Remember,* 1974)

Late January light on all three sides of our bedroom windows. Beautiful morning makes a man want to sing, to celebrate the subtle shades of winter's progress and spring's approach, as seen in the heightened yellow of the willow. The nerve-jangled noise of Manhattan seems a universe, not a mere eighteen miles off. And, at evening, the sun setting off the Atlantic Beach Bridge, its orange glow highlighting Bannister's Creek, the birds flying overhead in the hard, blue sky, the first stars shining, makes one wish he was on the empty water, steering a broad reach, heading for our eternal home.

Can we ever know the mind of another? It would seem unlikely since one's own mind is so many ways sundered into an uneasy alchemy of good intentions and sheer spite. The painful paradox of human striving, and if we admit that God brings good from evil must we not also concede the possibility He can extract evil from good? Who can explain it? Who can understand?

*I have often thought . . .*
*I have?*
*Not really, to be honest,*
*Never might be too harsh,*
*Seldom would be more like it . . .*

And then of course one must grapple with the quality of one's thought. Not a pretty picture. We aspire to build cathedrals in our minds (having long since lost the will to do so in our cities) but "the mind has mountains," as Gerard Manley Hopkins wrote, and many snares.

2/15: First anniversary of Mother's death. I will also associate it not by date but by the fact it was Shrove Tuesday. "Joan didn't need another Lent," Father Luke said. "The rest of us do." I certainly do.

2/16: It's difficult to believe four years have passed since Pierce's birth. Last night he called his older (by three days) cousin, Casey, and the two chatted away at length, little people with their own thoughts and words, hopes and fears. Had Lanie and I not plunged in, where oh where would I be now? He came into the shower this morning, and I said "Happy Birthday."

"Sing it to me!"

Later, after Lanie gave him a candlelit bran muffin he said, "Mommy, it's been a beautiful morning." He sang, "You Are My Sunshine," all the way to school on the bus and loved hosting his class to cupcakes.

P.P. last night during the *Newshour:*

"Dad, what are they talking about?"
"Crime."
"What's crime?"
"It's when bad guys hurt people or take their money, so they're talking about
    the best way for the police to protect us."
"Do they protect little boys?"
"Yup. And little girls, too."
"But little girls don't have bosoms."
"Well . . . "
"But Mommy has big bosoms!"
His father's son.


2/19: I saw Treddy Ketcham, another old Yale and racquet sport friend of
Dad's and one of the last of the bachelor clubmen, in the Hunt Club bar for
lunch after he had gone to Church, an infrequent occurrence. "It was the 50th
anniversary of Iwo and I figured I owed God that much."

3/1: Lanie and I met at Christmas of 1989 as we were walking into a party
at Bill and Robin Hubbard's off Lexington Avenue. She was and remains
beautiful with rose-colored cheeks and a vivacious laugh. In those days I had
left publishing and was a fellow at a think tank, the Manhattan Institute, writing a book on school choice, *Miracle in East Harlem*, which Random House
published to modest success. It became clear to me that I could not support a
family writing full time, and after some fits and starts I joined forces with an
old friend, Web Golinkin, and his partner, Joe Maddox, in launching a new
cable television network dedicated to timely, actionable health information.
We wrote a good plan, Allen & Co. found us some seed money, we created
a strategic content partnership with Mayo Clinic, and the Providence Journal
Company became our lead investor. If all goes well, we could launch by early
1996.

Snow dusted the South Shore at the end of winter: Snow glistening on the
bird feeder, on the post and rail fence. And then it rained. When it rains the
wind blows and water hits the glass panes, and the house shakes gently as a
distant cat cries. Next morning is a grey mild March day. No sign of spring
yet, but there will be, some day.

Spring segues in, not so much a break as a slow transition. So much to
tend in the garden—ilex, ivy, crabapple, yew, cherry, wild strawberry, holly,
hydrangea, forsythia, wisteria, crocuses, daffodils, primrose, clover.

3/19: First breakfast outside in our courtyard. Birds running riot—robins,
sparrows, nuthatches, cardinals all around the yard, nibbling at the ivy, where
we saw sprays of insects last night.

And during the days of deprivation, I often looked up into the hills for support and remembered first courting Lanie, her brown hair shining in the wind and eyes asparkle beside the fire, when life itself seemed full of hope that could overcome any hardship, and in this way, I stumble towards the future that sometimes holds infinite dilemmas, towards a dawn that seems phantasmagorical yet may still be real.

And the rain came down, the first drab, irritating bit of Spring. On the ride into New York, I look at the faces on the outbound train, finding a community all my own, just where I started: The scholar studying the Talmud, the girl with the reddish hair and the black velvet hairband, the old man shuffling up the aisle.

## Spring

Penny Coe shows me her cornelian cherry, yellow in spring and red berries in fall. Also, her crab apples and the cedars of Cedarhurst (*Juniperus Virginius*). Mother of my childhood classmate Elice, she is still the mayor of our village, sagely presiding over the village's demographic transition from mostly reform to orthodox Jews. Her emphysema gets a bit worse each year and she sometimes takes oxygen, but still appears doughty and determined. She had the village maintenance men put up a sign to watch for children at play when the Lindenthals and we both saw hot rodders careening through Sage Avenue. And she and Tony ("No Baloney") gave us a lovely cherry tree as a housewarming present. Crocuses climb and bulbs pop up. Yellow pansies, camellias and lilies follow.

In April, we gave the second of two cocktail parties announcing our arrival. Old friends of Mom and Dad's mostly—Sylvia Lynch (their first babysitter after the War), Helen Corroon (Sylvia's twin, though she claims to be seven years younger!), Sandy Whitman, the Bierwirths, Baldridges, Finches, and Jim Hellmuth. Our generation is a bit thinner but includes the Hinckleys, Blackfords, Donna Johnston and Jane Hardman. Sylvia and Helen were called the "Maitland Twins" and were considered hell raisers in their day. My brother Kevin was old Jim Maitland's driver one summer. Sylvia Whitman was Mom's longtime bridge partner, and her slyly witty husband Sandy grew up in what became my cousins' the Roach's house. He is retired from shipping and Jack Bierwirth just retired as CEO of Grumman. His wife, Marion, is from Atlanta, and therefore a southern ally for Lanie. Nancy Baldridge is Jack's sister and one of Lawrence's most gifted gardeners. Her husband Bob is just retired from the textile business at Milliken. Years ago, we played squash and tennis, and when I was a boy, he took David Rutter and me snorkeling beneath the Atlantic Beach Bridge.

Pierce is growing ever more independent, escaping the house to visit the Passeggios next door, announcing, "I'm the new neighbor," determined as a lion to be his own man. He has great imagination and can stage conversations between his animals by the hour. He is psyched for Rhoads' arrival though the actual event will be interesting. On an Easter weekend walk up Albert Place blind Katherine Kepler was digging in her garden as we passed. Mom drove her to church most Sundays after Mr. Keppler died. She recognized my voice instantly and said hello, then recounted planting peas on St. Patrick's Day and how Mrs. Chauncey, a decade older than her at 94, had criticized her for doing so on the waning moon. The old wisdom.

The Oklahoma City bombing kills 168 people and reminds us that evil in the world never ceases.

5/3: Lanie is two days late and will be induced on Friday. She looks beautiful, like a primitive fertility goddess, and is very brave but uncomfortable.

On Cinqo de Mayo Lanie called me in her most gloriously high-spirited voice to say everything was a go. She was induced at 2 p.m., began to feel contractions at 7 and between 8 and 8:40 p.m. went from 3 to full dilation. The baby's heart rate lowered precipitously, and Dr. Sailon said, "Let's go." Rhoads was born at 8:52, aided only by forceps and demerol. He cried vigorously and looked quite red, then cooed and slept with an exhausted L., who thinks he looks like Pierce. He weighed in at 7 lbs. 8 oz., slightly cone headed, a little hair. His first day was marked by daisies from Uncle Pierce and visits from Margaret White, Cousin Judy and Rog Renicke, Fawzia Mustafa, Cam and Lydia Wilson. Lanie was exhausted and sore of course, but the spring weekend was lovely, azalea and dogwood in bloom in the park near Lenox Hill. The baby has a low biliruben count, but he sleeps and feeds and yelps and yawns most sweetly. Pierce was playing with our neighbors J.J. and Julia Lindenthal when we came home and cried out, "Oh, a baby!" He cradled Rhoads. Every few minutes he runs into the room to hold him, says how much he loves his little brother, and then goes crashing outside again.

When we got home the tulips were so tall they headed for space, as delicate as a thoroughbred's leg.

Much conflicted though I was, I left Lanie with Bibi, her friend Caroline and those of my own family nearby and caught the last plane to Dallas to make the cable TV convention for America's Health Network's big debut announcement. A line of thunderstorms running north and south 500 miles closed the airport, hail the size of grapefruit in Oklahoma, nature terrible and grand. Lanie understands why I have to go and is irritated at the same time, and who can blame her? Bibi and Caroline pitch in, bless them. A son, two days old when I left, is more than twice that age when I come home three days later.

5/15: Daisies and pansies still in bloom, I planted flowers at the back of the property, an azalea at the side. I potted geraniums for the courtyard and picked a spot for a rose bush given us by Ann and Jim Thornton.

Rhoads is a sweet little pup, very well behaved except when hungry. Pierce calls him "my darling little brother." He has experimented with holding him upside down at least once. He enjoys running around with my childhood classmate Babbie MacLean's son, Shane. Lilies are beginning to pop on the heel of the fragrant purple lilac. Life, which was only just stirring last week, has now exploded in the May mulch. Lanie got her diploma from the Jung Institute this week, a great achievement.

The spring sprung—Lilies of the Valley, each a precious pearl. Even the old rhododendrons bloomed forth, and the pretty marsh flower, *rosa rugosa*. Now a moist summery yellow greenness is everywhere on the lawns and hedges. Pierce goes sojourning forth to collect "capertillars," to show his grandparents, newly arrived from Texas. His grandmother, Johnnie Marie, recoiled at the sight. "No *Gwanma*, they're my *fwiends*."

Last night I went to look at a rose bush out back and froze when I saw an old rabbit. He could not see me but felt me as dusk gathered and a light mist fell. He had been chewing some sweet grass but was now alert to another's presence, but unsure as to who or where it was, until I sneezed, and he fled to the marsh. Then I went to turn on the water in the front garden and frightened a cock pheasant and hen on their stroll. The cock ran for the field, and I chased after him only to find a pair of nestling duck. Later a crow and starling played tag in midair. Paradise.

## Summer

Summer squall. Rhoads begins smiling. Pierce shows signs of insecurity, asking me to sit with him. The new growth at its height: Giverny-like scene of high tide flooding up into Stable Lane from the marsh, raindrops plopping in the spreading puddle, the wild wet green field behind. Pierce takes swimming lessons at the Lawrence Beach Club and repeats Nancy Samuelson's instruction: "REACH! PULL!" Except he says, "POOL." Carl and Nancy took over the job as their summer respite from the Williams College swimming program, just as the Muirs had done before them for half a century. Bob Muir was one of the most beloved men ever to walk or swim hereabouts and coached the Olympic team in Melbourne in 1956. He was a role model of manly goodness for us all and chose the Samuelsons to come after him. We have been blessed.

Dawn and Harry Groener come out for a Sunday night when the lights are low on Broadway, and Harry plays hide and seek around the swing set with Pierce until he laughs so hard he falls asleep on their bed. Rhoads snivels

and struggles to turn over. The house is wreathed in birdsongs from 4 a.m.
on these mornings, and the summer stretches ahead. Last night Lanie stroked
Rhoads tenderly and said with complete conviction, "I could have another
one." Oh Dear. I would love it, but could we survive? Later, she says, "That
was just the hormones talking."

Pierce is rampaging on the beach, he and his cousin Casey climbing into
the dunes chased by Shane MacLean and Russell Aldrich. Russell bops him
with the plastic shovel most unfairly, thinks Pierce, despite P. having shot
R. continually with the air gun. And the red sun all the time setting over the
green grassed dunes. A red bird seems to skate above the surface of the sand.
And sail boats head past on a westerly reach, even as I yearn to fly east, a
full fathom below the fathomable surface of what little we are ever enabled
to know.

7/5: Pierce and I go to fireworks on the beach amid 600 others. Collecting
sand crabs and snails. Later the local *South Shore Record* gossip column,
"Rosalind Reports," included Lanie, Pierce and me in the attendance. "But I
wasn't even there," Lanie protested. "Neither was Rosalind," I assured her.
She's been in a nursing home with Alzheimer's for five years, and my childhood friend Rob Snyder has taken the column over.

7/13: Our Fifth Anniversary. Dinner is graciously supplied by Lumar
Lobster (the $10.95 Clambake) assisted by a good Montrachet. Five years
ago, Lanie and I were sleeping in her 46th Street loft the day after our wedding, when her father called to inquire after our well-being.

"How is Jamie?"

"Well Daddy, Jamie's a little hungover."

"To judge from the liquor bill, he earned it the old-fashioned way." As
indeed we all had at a festive dinner at the old Côte Basque.

My baby brother Peter turned 40, and at the party Becky gave him outside the Thayer's carriage house which they have taken for the season, Jake
Carpenter supplied the illegal fireworks that almost lit the neighbor's new
house up. That night I dreamed I was sleeping with a mouthful of fur and
decided it must be Janet York's dog. When I woke, Pierce had snuggled up
to me in bed, his wild mop of hair against my face.

Leaving Providence airport on business the other day I ran into two old
friends: my old Latin teacher, Father Julian, up from Portsmouth Abbey
to pick up his author friend, Tracy Kidder, coming in from Kentucky; and
Richard Cohen, now president of *Penthouse* and seeking to expand their
global market share. Father Julian had once written of me in his Latin class,
"Only the occasional yawn would reassure me he had not fallen asleep altogether." Rich was always on the make for the next score at Macmillan. Two
of the most disparate personalities imaginable, and I took great pleasure in
making the introduction.

Overnight a spider wove a web around the car, the humidity hovered, and heat grew. Rhoads smiled as he was bathed four times a day while his elders sweated it out, grilling bluefish and sweet corn.

A great photo-op this morning as Lanie suckled Rhoads at one breast and Pierce limped in from his bedroom to cuddle at the other. They slept like that for an hour. A beautiful sight.

Sea birds wander inland, Daddy Long Legs invade the kitchen, ants run riot on the roof and flies overwhelm the porch. Sea anemones blossom and algae blooms on the water.

8/10: Last night Pierce slept in five different beds. A murder of crows sat atop a towering white pine early on a humid morning, clamoring and heckling up a storm, the moon sliver faint in the sky, and torrid sun ascending. The pheasant hen guarded one of her young by the roadside. No breeze under a blazing summer sun.

If not exactly broken, the great heat wave of '95 was interrupted by huge thunderstorms and a soaking rain, followed by a patchy fog and more rain.

Our good neighbors down the way, Dick and Mary Payne, have two beautiful girls, Sara and Lindsay. Lindsay is a gifted athlete who suddenly came down with flu symptoms this week. Debbie Drake recommended she see our childhood pediatrician, Dr. Maisel (The Paynes live in Charlotte but for the summer and did not know a local doctor). Ever diligent, even in his seventies, Jerry took a blood test, thank goodness. It came back shockingly—leukemia. On Jerry's orders Lindsay was admitted immediately to Long Island Jewish Hospital for 28 days of chemo. Childhood leukemia is addressable in this day and age, but she faces a tough fight. The entire community is praying for her.

Pierce became increasingly excited as the time to go to Colorado came. He's handled Lanie nursing Rhoads well enough but last night insisted on sleeping on the chaise longue in our room "so we can all be together." The point being that of course we all should be, a concept alien to those of us in the Spock generation. I drove them to Newark the next morning and he promised to take care of Mom and Rhoads. That night he fairly sang through the phone, "We're at our house in Crested Butte."

Woodchuck smeared across the road, skunk smell swelling in the air. I know the marsh hawk flies higher in the summer sun. Jerry Garcia and Mickey Mantle are dead. I heard Jerry often at the Fillmore in the summer of '69, but the Mick was my hero from childhood, and I suffered with him all along the way. But then there were great moments too, watching him crack one into the upper deck, patrol center field and race around the bases with blistering speed.

I joined the family for one week in Colorado, and, when we got back, the grass had burned white in the Long Island heat. Dawn dew was the closest thing to rain all month. Over Labor Day weekend Pierce jumped off the diving board for the first time. He had balked on Friday with Bibi, then asked me to help him on Saturday. Thereafter he did it 200 times on his own Sunday and Monday. He is asking me more and more about Jesus and God.

## Fall Arrives

In September eBay was founded by Pierre Omidyar, and Sony entered the video game market with the release of PlayStation.

On October 3rd, O. J. Simpson was found not guilty of the deaths of his former wife Nicole and Ron Goldman.

10/18: Swam in the still warm ocean a week ago, but a night of driving rain and lower temperatures Saturday night brought Fall close. I moved mulch and transplanted a chestnut tree Jack Bierwirth gave me. Jack says there were no trees at all on the IOW when he was growing up in the thirties. Leaves are still on the trees but not for much longer. Pierce came down with an allergic rash made worse by scratching; Rhoads is a pink and ever smiling presence.

A sudden silence that comes with the fall ("Every weekend farther we get from summer," Ann Thornton likes to say, "the deeper in the country the Isle of Wight becomes."), crimson and pumpkin predominating the landscape. Rhoads is snuffling through the night with his first head cold. No fever but not comfortable. He gave me a little smile at 4 a.m., and then proceeded to tug my hair playfully for a good half hour until he drifted off again as Lanie slept peacefully beside him. The mysteries of life are nuanced and slow to unfold, requiring the road map that only Grace can supply.

10/29: Rhoads was christened last Friday night. Father Luke talked about an insight he had had during the recent Papal Mass at the Meadowlands. "As I looked around, I was struck by the enormous outpouring of love and reverence for John Paul by everyone there, and it occurred to me that we must always hold faith precious, and whatever faith we have we should be grateful for and realize, 'It's enough.'"

Nion McEvoy and Denis Hector were godfathers, in from San Francisco and Miami. Candace Kelleher was the godmother. Walter and Mary Chatham and other friends came on from town.

11/1: B.R. Trooper (aka Pierce) and I went on his first round of Long Island trick or treating last night. Margaret Carpenter put a good scare into him as the Wicked Witch of the North. Eliza Chauncey, 94, Katherine Kepler, Jane Hardman, Suzy Gatehouse and Tyler Mullally were all welcoming. Pierce was excited and thrilled and slept all night with us after feasting on his candy supper.

The world soggy, humid, ridiculously warm: A last rose of summer grows on our champion climber as it develops its berry-like tips, a suitable way to end the season. The hollies' berries brighten red. Even the despicable trumpet vine turns a brilliant crimson. And the birds—diving cormorants, swan, and more herons walking stiff-legged on the marsh—than I can ever remember.

Rhoads is six months old, a genial little fellow, bright eyed and red cheeked. Especially endearing when one happens to be leaning over him when he wakes. Beautiful smile, and a playful swipe of his hand on your cheek. There is much to learn in interaction with a baby about the need to love and be loved in our mutual helplessness.

First frost on the windshield, outside spigots turned off for the winter, nine mice trapped, birds still passing overhead, and the season slumps toward December's dirge, night coming early now, though the dawn is lit anew (temporarily) courtesy of daylight savings.

11/4: Prime Minister Yitzhak Rabin is assassinated at a peace rally in Tel Aviv.

11/12: The nor'easter hit Saturday just after seven and crashed down on us all night. Ocean Avenue is impassable with downed trees and dozens of willows fallen on the Lawrence Village golf course. We lost electricity but nothing worse. The wind whipped and ripped, but there was a sweetness to the night in that Joe Muskardin celebrated his 40th anniversary at the Hunt Club, where he landed after rowing out with four of his Croatian boat club buddies from Trieste to escape the Iron Curtain and, capsizing, was plucked from the sea by an American destroyer. "How could I spend 40 years in this place? The truth is it's gone so fast, I love all the members, everyone here is my family, and I thank you for giving me the opportunity to live freely, to raise my children decently and for always being so kind to me."

Joey will tend his bees and make his honey in retirement, but on this night he sang old songs (his brother Dario covering for him on the high notes) and claimed his share of dances in the bar after. Earlier I asked him if he were nervous. "I only speak two or three words," he said. He spoke for ten minutes. Later he reminisced to me about coming to the dinette off the kitchen to talk with Theresa and Myra at 50 Cedarhurst Avenue, who with Mother's express approval had a kind of ongoing at home for the help from other houses after supper. "Those girls were my first friends here," he said, and I'm sure it was true.

11/29: My Favorite Pierceisms of late. Yesterday it snowed four inches, and Pierce found a penny at school. This morning he woke up and wondered at the ground's white blanket. "Mommy, it's so beautiful. Do you think a lot of other people found pennies yesterday too?" And then his reassurance when I tell him something he wants to see might be scary: "Don't worry. Daddy, I'll *pre-tect* you."

12/12: Winter whacks us with a succession of arctic days, trees frozen, wind wild, and the inner self vacillating between the primal despair that comes with the darkening earth and a curious peace. Many a winter morning when young I rose about five as I do now to sit with Dad and Paget, our flat-coated retriever, after his morning feed. Whatever it was that woke Pa in the winter dawns, whatever aspect of the manic-depressive chemistry that was, I have it too. Tomorrow would be his 77th birthday.

So much of what I am comes straight from him. He had qualities I could never aspire to—nobility, courage, magnanimity and compassion—and faults and disabilities so devastating I am curious why they passed me by. But real tenderness and manly love as well. I have spent much of the last two years meditating on Mother's death. Sometimes it feels as if Dad is far away. And yet I only have to build a winter fire, sit in my bathrobe before dawn, drive to the beach early on a bright morning, or dream of serving an American twist, and I feel him with me.

12/20: I bought a tree amidst the blizzard, choosing a balsam fir over a Douglas pine this year. It is leafy and healthy and looks fine on the sun porch, filling the house with its evergreen scent. Pierce served as a shepherd at Trinity Church's pageant, and we caroled after. The next morning dawned beautifully, the entire sky scalloped with red clouds to the southeast. Amazing how beautiful just standing on a train platform can sometimes be.

Pierce complains he was not "imbited" somewhere and proceeds on his "sperriment," which consists of dumping large amounts of water where they'll do the most harm. Then he almost breaks his neck crashing down the stairs in a cardboard box. When we heard the noise from the dinner table, I thought, "That's it, but thank you, dear God, for giving him to us for four years." He was fine.

Christmas was frantic, excessive, but fun. Rhoads contemplates all the commotion with great seriousness. Pierce is delighted, excited and irrepressible. I had a sweet moment trimming the tree alone. I felt a surge of closeness to Mom, then glimpsed something/nothing out of the corner of my eye. We had a good laugh, she and I, and Christmas rolled on.

## 1996

Wind roars, whistles, blows, shakes, batters, whips, baffles, buffers, whooshes, lifts the rafters, pours through the windowpane, sweeps the marshes, blows the brant up the shoreline.

Too many gray dawns with the mist rising off the marsh. Not enough vision to see what lies ahead, heightened by a ruined rush hour spent cleaning the throw up P.P. ingeniously placed in an invisible hole between the bucket seat and the floor, utterly unreachable and unlikely to degrade for five million half-lives, redeemed by the sweet memory of waking in the gray winter light, two sons pressed against either side.

1/7: Snow again. One of the worst blizzards in American history hits the eastern states. New York City's public schools close for the first time in 18 years, and the federal government in Washington D.C. is closed for days.

The whirring house, the predawn stillness, rumblings from the animals in their mangers as the black sky blues. Days of digging. Joys of a fifty-foot driveway obscured when one is digging it out.

Pierce and I start a snowman, but it soon turns into a volcano. As he walked by, Bill MacMillen chided us that it could not be a proper snowman unless it wore a necktie, so he went back to his house and donated a yellow one from his attic. Then we headed to the Little Beach to chase the duck. Pierce sat on my shoulders, until I stepped into deep muck and sank three feet, throwing him over face first. He started to sob, then looked at me stuck in the hole in the ground and broke out laughing.

Arctic cold. Between mid-November and early February, the darkness of the morning is only lifted by the occasional splendor of a clear dawn, yet even those emerge late, especially after the solstice, when one waits hopefully, but the light is withheld even later. Presumably, it is light later in the afternoon, but who would know, trapped in meetings or riding subways beneath the East River. But in February the break finally comes, and the sun begins to shine as early as six thirty. Blissful waterfalls of light!

Surely many others have lived through these thoughts before. I sing to my nine-month-old at night and now Rhoads tries to sing back, eyes bright and trusting smile so humiliating. Too young to understand how deeply flawed a father is, too pure of heart to see the impurity stained upon others. Instead, Rhoads is content to flow through life's early chapters, a funny noise here, a bright light there, a sour taste here, his range all the while expanding, but without the complications even a four-year-old like Pierce has begun to face—disappointment, rejection, uncertainty and all the rest.

2/16: I am stuck in Orlando for Pierce's birthday, having given up my hotel room and rental car upon Delta's assurance that the flight would go out into the blizzard. I got an airport hotel and trudged there with my fifty pounds of Indian River citrus. At first, I thought he might cry when I called with the news. His voice thickened, then Pierce steadied himself and said over the line, "O Dad, it's OK." Heartbreakingly brave, and when I got home the next day, I gathered him up.

2/26: High cirrhus clouds this morning, swan flying overhead and the most beautiful sunrise yet over the marsh. Pierce has had a bug for the last week and Rhoads is teething. Lanie cooks a delicious crab casserole for my birthday supper. I packed the computer and my clothes till close to midnight, woke to feed a stirring Rhoads before six, the first streaks of light painted on the eastern sky, and took off for the airport for three months in Orlando and the launch of America's Health Network.

3/18: Lanie is away in Europe, and I am in Orlando. I called and asked Bill MacMillen to drive Bibi to pick up the car once it was serviced. She asked him, 82 and un-child friendly, to hold Rhoads while she went in. And he did it! Must tell his children, who will not believe it.

Lanie shares vestry board notes from her church: "The pastor was given permission to move his psychological practice into the rectory from his office because his practice is *swindling*." Oh dear. The original Malaprop, seeking new pews, begged donations for "beery wenches."

3/25: America's Health Network launched yesterday at 9 a.m. after two and a half years of hope and hard work. Even at 2 a.m. the morning of the launch I felt as if it could be like the scene in *The Sting* where they put on a good show and then take it away. We're on the air live sixteen hours a day with "Ask The Doctor" programs and much more to come. Now comes the hard part, executing an ambitious business plan, but at least we'll have a fighting chance.

4/8: Arrived home to a huge hug from Pierce. More verbally advanced than before. "It's not fair," is a new concept he enjoys transmitting. Rhoads was sleeping but soon woke. Bigger and rounder than I remembered. A beautiful baby in every way. The three of us walked the Isle of Wight. Fiske and Michelle Warren, both doctors, are adding on to their house as are Peter and Incy Brooks. Henry and Corbin Blackford, who gave the boys their video collection as a house present, have a new video game, and Pierce runs into their house to see it. I remember when Mrs. Hollenberg, a bridge buddy of Mom's, owned the house, and my cousin, Mark McCarty, then squiring Mrs. H's grand-daughter Leslie Klotz, jumped from the roof into the pool. Lanie cooks a delicious shrimp dinner. Sunday is the Easter egg hunt, and when Pierce runs past the eggs and into the marsh in his brand-new sailor's outfit I estimate the dry cleaning bill will be close to fifty bucks.

Rhoads is crawling like a locomotive on Easter afternoon, though at times different parts are moving in different directions. He attacks the carpeted stairs. Three steps up, he looks back to make sure I'm watching and then smiles. He crawls and strains, frequently using the banister to push off of, and often landing sideways on his tush. Like all of us, trying to get a grip, find a place in the great world, he gets to the second-floor landing, looks around beaming, and claps his hands in the golden light of our greatest day.

5/5: Rhoads' first birthday: Sweet-tempered, walking everywhere, falling down a fair bit. Sunday he toddled across the beach and was lost in reverie sitting and sifting fine ivory-colored grains through his small fingers. He groans himself awake in the morning and cries, and when I come in, he is trying to sit upright in his crib. He always looks delighted to have company and be lifted out, cheeks flushed. Then, diaper changed and bottle warmed, he glugs it down between Lanie and me on the bed and throws it aside. He turns over, opening his eyes wide to make sure his world around himself is complete, smiles and falls back to sleep. The blessings outweigh every challenge.

5/19: Today the fog cleared, Rhoads rose at 6, Lanie was up watering plants at night and Pierce slept beside me. I played tennis with Bill MacMillen and Jack Bierwirth, whose pheasant we ate last night with an olive marinade and Pommard. We had a beach foray where everyone got wet in the surf, and when the taxi came to take me to the plane, we saw a snapping turtle crossing the Causeway and trying to climb the wire fence to re-enter Sage Pond. Ancient creature, it could be a hundred years old. Could it be a female on the way back from laying eggs? Phil Thornton and Jack Talmage of Ducks Unlimited fame arrived after it fell back on its shell, turned it over with a stick, and held the fence wire up as the slimy, blackened beast slithered under.

Snapping Turtles are aquatic, leaving the water only to lay eggs or move from one pond to another close by. The female buries herself completely and usually lays 20 eggs, perfectly round and white with a thin hard shell. The carapace is oval—not highly arched. It has several sharp notches in its rear margin, pointed outwards toward the tail. Younger Snappers are a dull black; older ones are dirty brown and often encrusted with mud and moss. If food is sufficient, they live in one pond for many years, and maybe for a lifetime. Up to 13" in length and 50 lbs. They eat carrion when they can find it under the water, but mostly they provide their own. Anything they can pull under the surface and drown, no matter how large, is within their diet. Duck and other swimming water birds, like the swan, especially young ones, pay a stiff price. Heron may also be taken because the Snapper in its natural habitat is practically invisible. In a contest between the sharp eyes of a bird and the sharp eyes of a reptile, it is believed that the latter will win. Swimming animals such as muskrat, moles, rats and swimming reptiles such as little turtles and water snakes are also part of its diet. The Snapper hunts by crawling under a mass of water weed and then slowly rises until just the snout and eyes are clear and waits for a passerby. The Snapper strikes at its food, and the head, retracted, is thrown forward at a rate comparable to a rattlesnake's, to seize the victim. One snap of the powerful jaws, edged as they are with horn as sharp as a knife, and out will come a sizeable chunk of meat. Later the turtle will find the remainder of the carcass wherever it fell and feed on that too.

The sky flying down to Orlando was a layered dream etched in coal color cross strokes, the falling sun a crimson orb, and the guy next to me asked if I could close my screen so he could get a better view of "Grumpier Old Men." Upon arrival my only cell phone message was from God knows who: "We're out here at this dog track and want you to know, you're good people, buddy." Thanks.

5/30: I spent Memorial Day gardening. Rhoads is now saying "Hi" and the "CHOO" part of "Ah choo." Flowers are blooming, grass never more green, muskrat munching by the roadside, a baby bunny scampered down the garden wall.

Give me a green field, a climbing hydrangea, and all that lives upon the sapphire sea. Keep my babies and Lanie close to me, in peaceful communion with all the earth and all that is over and beneath it.

Rhoads laughs delightedly as he's carried along the surface of the pool. Last night at the Beach barbeque Pierce ran up and said, "Dad, I've made some new *fwiends*." He was playing with Steve Madsen's boys. That night, after all three MacGuire men had a Father's Day bath together, I put Rhoads to bed. Pierce joined me, waking Rhoads up with his chit chat but never more touching than when he said, "Dad, I love it when you're here." So do I. Remember feeling that way about my father, but not being able to express the emotion. Such emotions were not then expressed.

6/19: Ella Fitzgerald has left us at 79. The Voice of Jazz. WKCR played her non-stop for days, and it was beautiful. As a 17-year-old at the Savoy she would jump down from the band stand to join the dancers in the Lindy Hop.

Pierce raced at the LBC for the first time, although at times forgetting to move his arms. The crowd cheered him on, and he got a big hand at the end. It gave him confidence, and now he's swimming and diving with abandon. It gave his old man a shiver up the spine I hadn't expected. He's growing up.

6/27: Last night was Art Nicol's 50th, a great drinks party at the Racquet Club, lovingly thrown by Peggy. A wonderful family feeling throughout. I saw friends I hadn't chatted to for years, especially Art's cousin, my old Saratoga buddy Jane Jane Clark, standing with Rusty Staub. Arthur almost died two years ago; he looks great now.

Fatigue fills one. Yesterday I went to jog the beach at five, and laid down on the sand instead, the sun beating and breeze blowing over me as I lay, unable to move, not quite able to sleep, a thousand phantasmagoria swarming through my skull, a million deeds undone while working on a thousand start-up business challenges. Will I ever do anything truly creative again?

7/1: Pierce and I went to Mass yesterday. At communion he asked me what the priest and deacon were eating. I considered soft-pedaling the water and wine as a memorial but decided he had best hear it straight from the shoulder. "That's the body and blood of Jesus."

"Yuk," he responded, "That's *gwoss*." To be continued.

7/6: Dolly the sheep, the first mammal to be successfully cloned from an adult cell, is born at the Roslin Institute in Midlothian, Scotland.

7/17: My first cousin once removed, Nicholas Bluestone, was killed in the TWA crash/possible bombing off Long Island en route to Paris. 229 dead, including America's Health Network consultant's Dick Hammer's wife and daughter and Allegra Braga's mother. How can any parent survive such a catastrophe? And poor Cormac, the brother left behind, in shock.

Pierce has a good eye and hits the baseball consistently, although he has yet to admit the possibility that he could ever be out. Rhoads jumps on my chest until he falls and is caught. He tries to count, "one-two-three." Pierce's new word is, "Actually." Also, "I happen to know." As in at a Mexican restaurant, "I happen to know you have coloring here . . ." Crayons and paper materialized and soon he was in the kitchen entertaining all.

Lanie says that Pierce and Rhoads are such diverse personalities. Pierce is always out there testing new ground, whereas Rhoads is content to make his way smoothly through. I was afraid to release his hand at the top of the stairs for fear he'd fall too fast, but no, he just used his legs and belly to navigate slowly and surely downward, and got to the bottom safely, smiling to the last.

8/8: A sad week for the Sauders, Lanie's folks. Lee was diagnosed with aggressive, late-stage Lymphoma, rare, fast moving and likely untreatable. Dr. Jain claims he will bring it into remission. We'll see. Everyone in the family is hopeful, except Lanie. I pray for a better experience than Dad's, as good or better than Mom's.

Pierce woke screaming hysterically, saying he saw "flying saucers and alien caterpillars." Bibi says it comes from cartoons. His latest malapropism, "I want to go to the Summer Sports *Rewards* dinner," so he could claim his reward, which upon so doing he promptly lost.

8/15: Flying home Thursday night, beat, I found myself seated next to an autistic boy, whose only word was, "Hi." He was a sweet child who enjoyed grabbing my paper, and one could really see that the face of Jesus lay behind his spastic struggling.

Labor Day: Lanie is in Texas tending to her ailing Dad. A great 60th birthday party given by Jake and Donna Carpenter for my old tennis partner, Ray York, who was utterly surprised, bit back tears and then insulted everyone in sight for three hours. A happy night. Hurricane Edouard failed to arrive, although the riptide swallowed the sand, wind whipped the gulls and crows, and the ocean was closed at precisely the time of year one most wants to use it. The cricket and cicada calls rose as the hurricane grew near, the light turned eerie, the world turned toward the long amber light of fall. I smell smells that send me back 40 years and don't have time to write them down. So many friends said goodbye as they left the beach this Labor Day afternoon. For us, of course, this signifies the start of the second summer, and then the glorious Fall.

9/8: Pierce is starting kindergarten tomorrow. Last night he was bouncing off the walls, couldn't sleep and kept saying, "Dad, school starts tomorrow. TEACH ME TO READ!"

Steedman Hinckley died of cancer in the spine. A good man. In recent years he had been leading the preservation efforts against Disney in Orange County, Virginia, but he and Ingrid had been stalwarts around here when he was operating his airline and they were raising two beautiful girls, Annelise and Katherine. The Christmas Glogg party and singing of *Santa Lucia* by the Swedish ladies and girls dressed in white and holding candles at the top of the stairs on Barrett Road is a treasured memory.

9/23: Yom Kippur, and so much to atone for. The breeze rose in the night. I checked Rhoads in his crib to see if his feet were cold. He was scrunched up at the foot of his bed, along with assorted toy animals and his spelling blanket. Pierce was awakened to pee, and when I took him to his mother to cuddle I told him I would be home on Friday. "That's what you said last time," he replied sleepily.

"And I came, right?"

"*Wight*," he said and smiled.

As the taxi drove up there was a fresh breeze, and the first light, geese flying overhead in the autumn air.


**The Ghosts of Lawrence**

I see them now in every sea gull soaring in the morning every goose descending to the pond against a blackening sky. I hear them in the cock pheasant's cry and in the chug chug of the boats out on the channel.

I see them in the Wood Mouse, probably the most abundant mammal on Long Island, a beautiful creation, with fur the color of a newborn fawn. Also in the Grey Squirrel, Cottontail, Muskrat, Opossum and Raccoon. I remember garter snakes, salamanders and shoals of fiddler crabs when young, as well as frogs and toads even 10 years ago. Gone now, as of course are the foxes that once were hunted on horseback.

But I know they are there as surely as I know the old snapping turtles sleep in the mud beneath the pond. And I remember so much more. Old Mrs. Kniffin, who became penurious in later years and would ride the beach bus with us and walk to the village, calling in to our house to freshen up en route. One winter she had her gardener feed a fallen tree trunk a little more into the main fireplace every night! And yet she had helped start the Lawrence School, and her son, Howard, was a senior man at Lazard and wonderfully philanthropic himself.

Then there was Mr. Cleven, the Norwegian carpenter who did Mom's work for many years until he retired and John Jankosky came along. One day the McCarty twins grabbed his ladder out from under him while he was on their roof, but they got over that. Mr. Cleven's son, Donald, has just retired as our postmaster. Then there was Harry Piazza, who was called "Saboo," and made his living fishing for eels and golf balls in Woodsburgh Inlet between the 6th and 7th holes; Joe Proscia, the last of the local ice men; Mrs. Roth, who ran the business side of Raeder's pharmacy for her son-in-law, Dr. Pepper;

and Harry and David Sakoff, who kept the stationery store and lugged huge bales of newspapers off the Long Island Railroad trains until they were in their upper seventies. If Mrs. Sakoff wasn't looking, they would always give us free candy, and David reminisced about how he had played the violin, his face lighting up with the memory.

10/6: A good night at The Brook with P.J. O'Rourke speaking and Chris Buckley, Morgan Entrekin, Chris Isham, Steve Smith, George Plimpton, Chuck Whittingham, Stuart Janney, Nathan St. Amand, Avie and Stan Mortimer, Willie von Raab and Mongo Meehan in attendance. My brother Pierce kindly took me. It was civilized, gentlemanly, and fun. "Clinton is doing so well in the polls he's considering dating again," P.J. said. A prophetic voice!

The next day in NYC was slightly overwhelming. On a beautiful clear October sky. Lovely walk downtown on Park Avenue South. I witnessed a gentleman from Pennsylvania who had locked himself out of his car and attracted half a dozen entrepreneurs with different technologies trying to break in. Many consultants were on the sidelines as well. A great New York scene. Then to the TV Food Network for the shocking announcement that Providence Journal had been sold to Belo. And AHN's future? We'll see.

The next morning Pierce and I walked down Stable Lane toward Orient Place, jumping over puddles, laughing and joking, throwing his knapsack up in the air and catching it, chortling, until the bus rolls up and he jumps toward it positively glowing, his delighted grin reflected in Cindy the driver's face as he clambers happily on board, not before running back to give me a goodbye kiss.

And Rhoads is now wheeling in his stroller crying "Doggie!" whenever terrible Tovy comes into view.

10/7: I stopped in Dallas on my way home to NYC to see Lee Sauder. Balder and hoarse from chemo but in good spirits. Thereafter, a too rushed weekend with the kids. I planted a sassafras tree (for tea colors and its three distinctive leaves).

10/19: The season's first nor'easter felled several trees, flooded the lane and many of the IOW lawns. Rhoads has a slight allergy and Pierce the season's first cough. The rain is rinsing through the wetlands and the season's first swans huddle by the shore. The high tide ran water up to the yacht club's parking lot, but the six boats still in the water held fast to their moorings.

The last of the leaves—wild cherries—almost gone, and the chilly winds begin. Gulls crack their clams from up high on docks that will go unswept till spring, and the Grand Central Parkway is like a pastel fantasy in the low November sun.

Greyest of Sundays brightened by waking surrounded by Pierce and Rhoads. Lanie, most beautiful girl, is dressing for church. I drive PP to

Sunday school, then drive to squash. Bill MacMillen gets his glasses broken on the court and face slightly gashed but is not badly hurt. We sip turkey soup with Treddy in the bar and eat pecan pie. The odd thing is that I have always considered the seasonal darkness a creative friend whilst still striving towards the light. Rain soaking, night falling early, time to start packing and prepare to move on.

12/8: It's my time. These last weeks before the winter solstice are never easy, and I do hate the leaving light. A good time for drinking tea, building fires and playing piano in the parlor. And oh! The books I would read if I ever have the time 20 years hence. This time of year has always brought a strangeness with it I have tried to overcome with various saturnalian strategies, but now, with Lanie asleep upstairs and Pierce and Rhoads also slumbering directly overhead, one tried to lie abed but couldn't and so descended, *in media noctus*, to sit, read, scrawl, wait.

A good job and intriguing challenges, yet one still yearns to describe the hidden architecture of the ineffable, and to light the most distant stars.

12/11: My father's birthday is in just two days. The strength of his image burst inside my brain and then dematerialized like an imploding star. While I waited for the cab the airport at 4:30 on Monday morning I heard a noise on the stairs and looked up. Rhoads belly flopped down to join me, experimenting awhile with the shadow his skull made on the white wall, but eventually dropping down to where I could pick him up and hold him as he rattled off various incomprehensible words. When the taxi came and I returned him to his mother's side, he cried most horribly.

I could only think of another small boy descending in the pre-dawn dark to sit beside his bath-robed father in the den reading the paper, feeling safer and more secure since he could share his presence, and how it hurt when he went away, as, alas poor fellow, he so often had to.

Watching *That Thing You Do* without sound on the way to Orlando I realized that the art director's concept was straight out of *Shindig* and *Hullabaloo*, two '60s TV rock shows I hadn't thought of in years. Funny, of my age group in Cedarhurst and Lawrence I should be the only one to return to raise a family. Phil Snyder is up the road living with his mom. Billy Denson a mile farther away doing the same. Fred Heath and Elaine Ubina are at least a generation younger. Where are the rest?

Fred Alexandre went to Princeton and U. Va. Law, worked for DuPont and then tried a year at seminary in Switzerland, whence he has returned to Wilmington. Elice Coe tried acting and now works for a company called "Condomania," in Pasadena. "I didn't know you were in real estate," I said.

"No, Jamie, I sell CONDOMS."

John Carr and his brother Rufus are both house-bound with mental disorders and living on a family farm in North Carolina. Good, sweet-natured friends, and we played touch football and helled around as teenagers and college students with much hilarity. Then it fell apart for them. Drugs played a role, but it's still so sad for them, and their now elderly, wonderfully cheerful parents. Virginia Farr is in Houston, Joanie Herrick on her second marriage, married a naval architect in Fairfield County, Deirdre MacGuire (my non-cousin classmate) living a funky Upper West Side life, Lars Potter doing well renting out oil rigs in Corpus Christi, Debbie McTigue the registrar of the New School, David Rutter selling clothes in Chicago, Ross Savage teaching school in Minneapolis. Petie Horner a mom in Greenwich and sister Sandy dead far too young of leukemia, leaving two kids. Linda Coleman is a nurse and Jenny Whitman a midwife. All kinds of results all over the place.

As the tide rose and our lane flooded an odd old large wing-spanned bird—a great blue heron—stuck by the tidal ditch and fed on fiddler crabs in the puddle before I approached and spooked him into flight.

12/21: Ran around Orlando shopping the last weekend when I wasn't covering for our sick VP of Programming, George Hulcher, at the network, and then, after the last fax left me short of time, dashed for the airport for the trip to the Ranch in Texas. As I drove The Festival of Lessons and Carols came on NPR from Kings College, Cambridge, where I went to so many Evensongs in another life in what seems another millennium, beamed by the BBC on the afternoon of Christmas Eve and heard by a harried traveler on the Bee Line Expressway driving in a Green Breeze en route to an airport where he could fly to Dallas, whence he would drive northwest into the cattle country of Wise County. A few minutes of memory, prayer and recollection, but a treasure just the same.

12/28: The Ranch was cloudy and damp, but Lanie's father, Lee Sauder, looked relatively well and loved having his grandchildren around. Pierce won his grandfather's heart when the jeep they were riding in broke down in the Renshaw pasture and he exclaimed to his grandparents, "Here we are in the middle of nowhere with nothing to eat!"

Back in New York came the terrible news that Treddy is hospitalized and operated on for colon cancer, perforated intestine, peritonitis too. A Yale friend of Dad's and lifelong friend of all of my brothers, Treddy is the last of the bachelor clubman and has made his retirement full by volunteering for all kinds of assignments in all kinds of organizations—St. Nicholas Society, Sons of Colonial Wars, squash and tennis, his many clubs. Always chipper, never downcast, the thought of him sick is painful.

When I get to see Treddy in the hospital he introduces me to his "tentmate, who has the same sort of problem I do." He proves to be a black gentleman whose live-in has stabbed him in the back. I tell him how glad I was to hear his brother and sister-in-law have rushed down from Rhode Island. "They

couldn't wait to move in on me, and in that respect I'm quite glad to be here."
He has a long way to go to get back.

Driving back, I am put in mind of some other Ghosts of Lawrence.
The names of the ghosts—Pete Ashmore, riding her bike in a plaid skirt,
Sis Wright with her coral glass frames, Posie Owen, Dodie Burger, Coco
Monroe, Sip Putnam, Marcelle Timpson, Sylvia, KK, Mopsy Ijams, Edna
Morris, Dot Pardee, Fluffy Lynch, Muffie Ludlow, Hallie Dixon, Pebbles
Stone in her coveralls. What a collection!

Eliza Chauncey, 97, comes for New Year's Eve and says, "The last time I
had caviar was for breakfast on the Aquatania." Would that be in the 1930s?
Eliza was born a Parish, a cousin of the famous decorator, Sister Parish.

Rhoads got so sick in the New Year we almost had to take him to the hospital for rehydration, but he cuddled against us feverishly and from time to time
asked for his *ba-ba*. When he had finished sipping it, he handed it back to me
and flopped his head down on a pillow about to fall fast asleep, only to rouse
himself to enquire in a sickly but enchantingly sweet high voice, "Dad?"

"Yes Rhoadise?"

"Love you."

And so to sleep. Dearest baby boy, I love you too.

*Clear brilliant dawn*
*Time to pick up and travel on*
*But don't forget the roseate sky*
*That lifted hearts and shook a sigh*
*Loose upon the grassy lawn*

Pierce still gets worried that I am away and wonders when I won't "have
to go to Florida" anymore. Rhoads insists, when sick, on sleeping in our bed
and cuddling in the crook of my arm, assuring the latest in a long series of
recent neck cricks and sore backs. That is, until I rise in the pre-dawn black,
shower and shave and prepare to depart only to find him happily placed on
top of my suitcase so I cannot finish packing. Our last baby and equally as
precious as Pierce was. There's a certain poignance at the thought that each
giggle, game, diaper change, dressing, snuggle and kiss will be the last with
a baby until these lads produce their own, assuming they so choose, and we
are so blessed as to be around.

Lanie and I saw *Ransom*, a well-done kidnapping thriller with Mel Gibson
and Rene Russo and afterwards had a delicious chicken masala, vegetable
pilau and nan supper at Dawat, followed by a sweet night in town, which
our marriage could only profit from more of to remind us of our underlying
happiness and compatibility, a fact obscured by present stresses of work and
travel and the very real, never absent demands of small child rearing.

Dream: The magic train that carried all my hopes and dreams pulled into the station. It was darker than black and try as I might I could see no doors or windows, and there was no way at all to clamber on.

## 1997

The Sunday night routine, trying to think ahead as one enjoys the lingering fire and cherubic presences, even as one climbs into bed, comforted by the presence of his drowsing wife, even as he tries to sleep, casting his mind ahead to the week bearing down, sleep not coming, because so much crowds the room. Rising at one to check the baby and at two to check Pierce, and at three to check the strange noise in the kitchen and at four to rouse . . . too early of course, so falling back, nuzzled against Lanie, saying a prayer for us all, rising at five to shower and shave, load the pc and cell phone into the bag, kiss Lanie, kiss Pierce, be assured that a slumbering Rhoads, head tight against the crib rails, is still breathing, descending to the kitchen for a sip of juice, seeing the taximan drive up in into the snowy lane, and setting forth, in darkness, once again.

2/15: After a sweet Valentine's. The sheer joy in Pierce's voice as he burst into my study and said, "DAD, DAD! Guess what? They're some new kids in the neighborhood." The Madsen's had arrived. Moved into Donna Johnston's house, (the Ferris house it was called when I was a boy) and life got noisier, but much better for the kids on the IOW.

3/8: Wonderful older Irish cousins Joe and Dymps Carton are here in New York on holiday and came to the house for Mexican dinner. Pierce, a bespectacled six, sings "McNamara's Band" from International Day. "Whoever taught you that, Pierce?"

"My kindergarten teacher, Mrs. Rosenberg."

Joe roars with laughter, former rugby star that he is, and Dymps the baby of the Wrenns (all Gaelic names—Geralda, Columba, Fidelma, Eithne, Una and Dympna), consummately cheerful.

3/10: Purple ground cover is up. Treddy was cheerful in the hospital when I saw him, but his legs are finger thin and he looks frail. Could he stand up to radiation? He wants to get well, which is good, but after so much internal bleeding another severe setback may pin him to the mat. I still see him hitting passing shots down the alley, reverse corners in the squash doubles court, swimming from the Dall's dock and making everyone feel a little bit cheerier, and I don't want him to go.

And I turned 45, feeling lucky to be alive at all, lucky to have Lanie, Pierce and Rhoads, lucky to be working and ready to soldier on, as long as it takes.

3/16: The Hebrew Academy of Long Beach has bought a nearby house under false pretenses and is now bidding on its neighbor, hoping to construct a boy's yeshiva for 600 students in violation of all village codes. The parking lots and buses would destroy the wildlife here at the water's edge. A fight is shaping up, and our former mayor Penny Coe has vowed to lie beneath the first tractor that tries to start construction, her oxygen tank in hand.

3/27: Tony Coe is dead at 71 of unattended colon cancer that went to his liver while we all worried about Penny. I loved him for his politically incorrect ur-WASP pronouncements in a deep bass-baritone and love of good books. Early on he had sold books for Farrar Strauss & Giroux until he got a job at Chase Manhattan and told Roger Strauss he was leaving. "But why, Tony?"

"Because you're about to fire me."

"How did you know?"

Mourned by the Holland Lodge, Ducks Unlimited and Groton School. "An insufferable ass," Blair Gammon called him with real relish. But Tony was more than that and a good friend to me.

Rhoads has chicken pox and scratches. Sitting in his crib and playing with his furry monkey he sees me, picks it up and throws it at me. After I bathe and dry him, he looks at himself in the mirror, sees his spots and yelps in dismay. An early sign of vanity!

In New York for a day, underwhelmed by the late Pollocks at MOMA but the park afire with dogwood, magnolia and tulips as I entered the Writers' Walk. Lanie and I walked here seven years ago, and the 12th Street Stompers were playing their rambunctious Dixieland jazz at the head of the walk. "Hire us for a party," one said as I threw a dollar into the hat. "If she'll marry me I will," I answered. Five months later I did, in Peggy McEvoy's Turtle Bay garden, and it was a great night.

The muskrats have dehibernated and one was shmoosed by a car on the Causeway.

Muskrat live in dens in banks, the entrance holes of which are under water. Somewhere a small air hole leads into the den. In winter they build a mound-like house of cattails in a pond, that entrance too being under water. They love carrots and apples and will raid garden patches. Seen swimming quietly in pond or Crooked Creek, its flattish tail stretched out behind and sculling gently. When it sees me looking it up-ends and swims to safety under water.

Raccoon are also plentiful now that the craze for coats of same is 80 years past (Bill MacMillen had the last one I saw and enjoyed wearing it to Giants games). They live in hollowed out tree trunks and go through "washing" even when not near water. The possum, on the other hand, is the only marsupial in North America, dense, primitive and stupid, incapable of responding to love, care or training. We have them both heareabouts.

At the yacht club dredging began. A plane sky wrote at 20,000 feet. Red-breasted blackbirds, bluebirds and cardinals abounded. The birdsongs at 4 a.m. are symphony enough, especially when Rhoadsie's mophead pressed into one's side is the first sensation of the new day, and Lanie's foot resting lightly on mine is the second.

On my last day at home before another spell in Orlando I drove to the hospital to see Treddy again. He was being fed through an IV, discharging fluid from an open wound into one bottle and waste from another. There is a fistula in the colon that they hope will heal of its own accord but may require additional surgery. In the hour I was there he fielded half a dozen call from school and Yale friends, fellow Jesters and even old campers he counseled (e.g. Paul Lambert, Whitney Tower, Schuyler Chapin). Afterwards I took advantage of the beautiful day to play my usual horrible golf. As I walked off the course Dario, the country club's ever exuberant Maitre d', challenged me to sweaty squash.

4/26: Back from Florida again and my first club board meeting in eight months. I enjoyed the company of Bob Hart, vigorous in his 80th year, John Walsh, an effervescent Boston lawyer and the longtime secretary, Uncle Tim Carpenter (not my uncle but we have always addressed him so), Fred Heath, the baby of his fantastically athletic clan, Brian Mullen, Fiske Warren, everyone's orthopedist, Ann Thornton, an oasis of southern gentility and good decorating ideas, and John Conway, "just a boy from Lowell trying to get along," but willing to get into red-faced shouting matches when he suspects money is being wasted. That makes serving on a non-profit board more amusing than it otherwise would be.

It was Jack Bierwirth's last meeting, and he stayed for dinner, reminiscing on how his father first came out here from Brooklyn to shoot snipe with Newbold Herrick and his brother, how the Five Corners was the only point of dry land in the marsh in those days, and the village itself was the first really solid ground. There were no houses on Atlantic Beach or Long Beach at all until 1924. At home I smoked the last of Eric Stephenson's fine Cubans and walked under a full moon before coming back inside in time to hear Lanie finish a bedtime story to the boys, who smiled and wanted to wrestle with me. At six in the morning it was beautiful again, and I started south into the tornadoes. We flew the last 200 miles into Orlando at 800 feet, and the sky was punctuated with lightning strikes.

May: The Isle of Wight is the kind of place where songbirds sing before dawn, kids still walk and ride bikes freely on the lanes, find secret hiding places in the marsh, and form clubs in tree houses. It's the kind of place where houses hang lopsided, and 50-year-old hollies bend into the wind. Rhoads' second birthday is a huge pleasure after a rough winter. Healthy again, he spouts gibberish cheerfully but says, "I like it!" and "Thank you!" with great distinction. Pierce told a story about ghosts. I planted columbine, wild purple blossoms recalling our Colorado summers, a hardy perennial. Lanie's pansies are a delight in the courtyard. I felt I should jog but was much too tired.

At five thirty the next morning I looked out onto the field and saw two rabbits at play, charging each other and jumping into the air. The bees are out, and the smell of lilac is everywhere along the fence line. Rhoads belly flops on the top rail and topples over onto the other side, hitting his head on the ground. But he doesn't cry or complain. He is happy to be outside, running and falling, happy to be alive.

I went to visit Treddy today. His color is fading and face covered with yellow scales. He is sitting up but has less strength. If he can withstand surgery he has a chance, if the lymphoma has not spread.

"London Assurance" with Brian Bedford was a great drawing room farce. And the Byzantium exhibition at the Met is simple, sublime, devotional. Afterwards Lanie and I had a quiet dinner (could a single restaurant here hold more talent than all of Orlando?) and a good night amidst the hustle and bustle of the busy world.

6/2: Sunday I woke at 3 and worked till dawn. The night before we had had 200 to drinks on the lawn, the last part of our Lawrence re-entry. Kiddies played and the gnats swarmed. Ed Yodowitz, the Henrys, Dr. Maisel, Joe and Ginny Nerich, the Friedmans and Rosenbergs, and all the neighbors of course. I introduced young Pierce's kindergarten teacher, Mrs. Rosenberg, to Helen Corroon who was my brother Pierce's pre-school teacher, and Helen helpfully recalled, "Yes, and Pierce went to the bathroom on my foot."

The next morning Peggy Finch called to say, "We had to park all the way down the Causeway and as we walked back to the car I turned to Steve and said, 'It's like the old days again.'" Sweet of her, one of mother's oldest friends, in her antique way.

At Pierce's Moving Up day his class sang lustily, "I Won't Grow Up." Utter greeness of the green June as red and white peonies bloom. Sea birds mixing with songbirds in the blue sky, sun rays burning the skin even through heavy clouds.

As I jogged back from the ocean up the beach today, I saw my two boys hurtling toward me. They had seen my trousers hanging in the bath house and insisted on running to find me over Bibi's objections. Bliss, to walk sweatily with them in my arms. When I left for the airport later Pierce cried, and Arthur Schriever, dean of the Cedarhurst taxi drivers, said, "He don't want you to go." No. Pierce now has a clutch of freckles on the end of his nose, as cute as Lanie's.

Late June: First weekend of summer. When I got here from Orlando around seven Friday the kids were playing in the yard with the Passeggio's cocker spaniel puppy, Sally. The next night was Katrina Burger's beautiful wedding at the beach to Kim Brooker. John Eastman told me, "The last time I was out here was 20 years ago playing tennis with Elton John." 100 Iranian cousins of Mina's arrived by bus. Great fun. Mrs. MacMillen declined to dance with me on account of age but later said, "You're a very good dancer. Unlike your father. He just walked around. Terrible!"

July: The tension and possible catastrophe over America's Health Network's acquisition by Columbia Healthcare is building. Belo bought Providence Journal for the television stations and decided it did not want to continue funding a start-up cable television network. Belo and Columbia are engaging in last minute legal maneuvers, as our available working capital drains away. The strain is taking its toll on staff and management.

I was hurt by Lanie's non-responsive, close-to-rude phone manner last night. Maybe at 9 p.m. it was too late to call, but I was just leaving work. Rhoads was crying, and her father's illness must weigh heavily. Still, it was unpleasant, and I woke at 1 a.m. and brooded. Which, I guess, is the price of marriage and its many joys. A busy life, and one hopes for better times.

The summer wall of heat blasts one's face. Rhoads and I spied a frog in the garden as we walked the other night. He sat on my shoulders absolutely alert, taking in the night and all of its shadowed nuances, all the aromas of the late spring—wisteria, clematis, wild rose, rising and mingling in the night-time sky.

Later that night came the first storm of summer, the sky turning yellow, and peals of thunder followed by lightning flashes, rising winds, and, finally, after funereal stillness that felt like hours but was probably only fifteen minutes, the shoals of rain came pouring in, dumping water everywhere, and the parched earth lapped it in. Early the next morning renewed bird calls signaled that the storm had passed.

And we heard that Lee Sauder's cancer had entered into his spleen.

At the beach barbeque in the summer sunset, Rhoads and Pierce played volleyball. Rhoads is promiscuous with his kisses towards Harper Robinson, demonstrating good taste! A double rainbow appears in the night sky and augurs an auspicious summer.

Mid-July: Days in Colorado and in Dallas to spend time with Lee Sauder. His appearance is shrunken but his voice is still strong. He loves seeing the children and vice versa. The boys and I spend hours in the pool. Lanie and her siblings are putting differences behind to attend the sick.

Back to Orlando details of the Columbia deal drag on, and one worries even as he has to reassure 110 programming and production personnel looking for any sign of hope. We are all suffering system overload, our hard drives dead, operating systems moved to trash.

7/23: Belo was to have signed yesterday; Columbia today. Columbia's press grows ever worse, and rumors of a federal investigation and lawsuits abound. Last night arrangements were made to wire our funds today. But this morning 700 FBI agents surrounded their Columbia HCA headquarters in Nashville with search warrants, and today the board has halted all transactions. Disaster! We are out of cash.

Inevitable finger pointing and enough blame to go around for all. Perfectionism, Programming, Distribution. Advertising. Merchandising. Etc. Joe Maddox stoically tells Web to go home to be with Alison. Rick Scott resigns from Columbia, "the ultimate proof of his commitment to it." Newspeak.

7/27: On Long Island, a surprise 70th birthday party for Sheila McCarthy, a dear friend of mother's, who has survived a scare with breast cancer. When she saw the crowded casino room at the beach club and realized what was up, she burst into tears, as did Winnie who had come on from San Francisco to organize the party. Then she made her way through the room greeting everyone one personally.

Sandy Whitman pointed to his beer and explained, "This is all I drink now, thanks to my doctor and to Sylvia. He asked me how much I drank, and I said about seven ounces a day. He looked like he would faint so then he asked if there was ever a time when I didn't drink, and I suppose I must have hesitated, because before I could answer Sylvia piped up and said, 'Yes, there was one Sunday in Nova Scotia when all the liquor stores were closed, and the only bottle we had at the motel slid off the bureau and broke into smithereens when it hit the floor,' and I said, 'Thanks, Big Mouth.' The doctor restricted me to beer from then on."

Afterwards I sat on the bar deck with Nick Hayes and Nonie Watters, on a foggy night that could not conceal the surf beating down below on the shoreline and spun tales from 40 and 50 years before as the wind rushed in atop the angry sea and coated us with a thin covering of salt, and the ebbing moon filtered faintly down. Unlike Lot's wife we were able to rise and walk away after glancing backwards. The place was shuttered and silent by then.

At AHN each of the 215 employees has their story. Mike Brodsky is about to be married, Cara Birritieri just moved from Boston, Derek Dunne was diagnosed with cancer. No one knows what to do. A far cry from the excitement of the day we launched. An idea, a dream, a plan, and ultimately a reality, now shipwrecked, but capable of rising again.

August: I picked up Lanie and the monsters at the airport returning from Colorado. Good to have them messily back in the house again. The next day I lost to 22-year-old Jack Oliver 7–5 in the third set in the singles semis. After two and a half hours in the heat I didn't have much push left in my legs at the end. He is 20 years younger and hardened by summers on the European satellite tour, and won the tournament the next day, deservedly.

Next morning the melancholy settles in and asks what the next step is. I don't know. AHN could all end here. It's best to plan for the worst. Four years of hard work. I haven't felt this pressure on the brain or sinking sensation in the gut for years.

Reeds fall over the Sage Pond fence, sea birds skirt the overhead sky. Raspberries begin to form in their bushes. The hollies show purple flowers, and the grass grows patchy from the heat. But then the rains came, following thunderbolts and lightning flashes and a sky so dark it was impossible to see. And after a night of it no blade was unglistened or bush undrenched. The air began to cool, the jelly fish grew, the rush of summer easing as the sun begins to fade. Pierce won his first open swimming race! He kept his head down and stayed at it; he looked like a worm in the water. I walked and ran all the way to the end of Atlantic Beach, where the nesting ground of tern and piping plovers was teeming with birds, and on the beach were dozens of horseshoe crab shells.

"Ola means hello," was the Sesame Street song Rhoads sang and danced to this morning. Next, we did yodeling, which was so satisfying he insisted on ten encores. A cricket chirped from inside the house, and birds flutter from branch to branch of the cherry trees, eating the berries. Bibi and I shared a pear from our tree out back, and it wasn't bad. I plugged my new printer into what I thought was the right port on the back of the computer, and black smoke began to rise. On August 31st, Princess Diana died in a car crash in the Pont de l'Alma road tunnel in Paris, as her driver tried to outrun paparazzi. My brother Schuyler won the golf championship for the fourth time, in four different decades, coming back from six down.

9/5: Victor Frankl dead at 93. *Man's Search for Meaning* is a great book and repudiation of Freud's concern with the baser drives as opposed to the more exalted—man as a creature of consciences and not merely a bundle of appetites. "We cannot pursue happiness; it ensues when we accept life on its own terms."

Pierce's first Yankees game. He bought everything in sight and put his pink cotton candy into the lady with the beehive hair-do beneath us (a palpable improvement, though she didn't think so). He was in Heaven, and after fourteen trips to the head the Yankees won.

Mother Teresa is dead at 87. "To me the countries that have legalized the killing of children are the poorest." A fool for Christ whose example will be with us always.

And Princess Diana buried, with one of Mother T's rosaries.

In a beautiful cool September dawn and Pierce and I walked to the pond for the first school bus of the year. He is starting first grade. Lanie and Rhoads came out to join us. Happy to be together.

9/9: Nice night in New York with Lanie after trying to resuscitate AHN. A pop at PJ Clarke's, then dinner at Zarela's, where we sat at the same table as on our first date in January of 1990. Back on 55th Street we made love with something like the same enthusiasm of eight years ago. And again in the dawn. Could it be a trend?

Treddy Ketcham returned to the Rockaway Hunt Club, after a successful operation and extensive physical rehabilitation, looking gaunt but was granted a standing ovation as he accepted an award from the Village of Lawrence on its Centennial. Next morning Lanie rose noisily at 5:30 to shower. "Why are you doing that?" "Because I thought it was 6:30." I asked her to note the heroic charity with which I received said announcement, but she provided no assurances. Her father is fading, alas.

I played in the USTA National 35s Grass Championships and got to the quarters of the consolation. Pete Bostwick and I played in the doubles, a gimpy 62-year-old, but ever so graceful and coordinated. I had played with his Dad, the great amateur steeplechase jockey (we used to lob him mercilessly!) as a child in Saratoga, and Pete III and I had won our member-guest one year, but this was the first time to play with him.

Later I sat on the Yacht Club deck and watched the high tide swell. Strange birds were eating the fiddler crabs. Rhoads found a dead crow on the road last night and what looks like a rabbit skeleton lies in the field, possibly a victim of one of Tyler Mullally's cats. Fiddler crabs appear in the ditch by Steve Madsen's driveway.

My colleague Jim Higgins is facing the AHN crisis with wonderful black humor. He calls bridge loan financier Howard Millstein a pig who likes to brag about how he "fucked" someone with lawsuits. Rick Scott, who may invest in AHN privately now, is "radioactive" in Higgins view. On a salty-aired September night, Rhoads stayed up late to watch "Free Willy" again and ran upstairs crying, "Dad, Willy's free!" Then he snuggled in my arms and snuffled all night long. And I dreamed: On a plane with brother Peter, Jake Carpenter, George Gilder and others. Shallow take-off in the rain. Can't make it. Somehow, I bail out on a hillside and look up to see the plane crashing—Joe Maddox at the helm! On my first step out of the door the next morning a yellow warbler stares at me from the cedar. Joyous start to the day.

Terry Blanchard's 60th at the Union Club. Good to see Kate Whitney again after so many years, and many others. Enjoyed *The Peacemaker* and *L.A. Confidential*. Wind blew in from the west and rocked the house all night long. When I jogged in the morning, many oak and maple leaves were down. Nick Benvin was limping to work from Main Street to the Club, nearly 50 years on the job, paper tucked under his arm, John Conway was walking his lab, Charlie, John Passaggio with Sally, John Michael Donovan waiting for the bus. Houses whose owners I knew so well and are so long gone— Mopsy Ijam's "Lauderdale," the Albert Hart's "Edencroft," the Herricks, Owens, General Wickersham's, Otis Chapman's (now Peter and Heather

Boneparth's), the senior Bierwirth's, Mrs. Kniffin's. The sun rose beautifully over the marsh.

9/25: Johnnie Marie called around 2 p.m. on Sunday, her voice cracked, and I knew before she started that Lee had died. He came back from the hospital Thursday and had slept most of the time. She went to lunch with Will and Suzanne, and when they returned, he was gone. Lee came out of Madison, Kansas, played basketball, got his degree in geology, was a pilot in the Pacific in the war and went on down to Texas to work for Texaco, often prospecting on horseback in those early years. He wooed and married Johnnie and did well.

Lee was always kindly to me, and I will miss hearing the sense of wonder in his voice as he discussed rock formations. He delighted in Pierce and Rhoads. Lanie, of course, has her own POV, which must be respected. I'm sorry to see him go.

The funeral was sweet and impressive. Wichita Falls turned out. Johnnie's friends—Lulu Sidell, Mrs. Huff and Mrs. McMahon, among others—wonderfully rising to the occasion. The house filled with food, Sauders, Pattersons and Waggoners. Pierce swam, met his cousins and watched the Yankees. He said he wanted to see the "ceremony." a word he had learned recently when his class had an outdoor service for a deceased frog. It was a hot spell for late September and the peak of the Monarch butterfly migration. They flitted through the mesquite, and Father Payne said they reminded him we were all just passing through. Johnnie said she'd seen one flying solo that reminded her of Lee.

A wonderful line written by an irritated Evelyn Waugh to his dear friend Nancy Mitford: "We are all very lower class to God, and our cleverness and secondhand scholarship bore him hideously."

*The Ice Storm* an interesting though chilly take on the suburbs in the 1970s.

The turn to fall. Dark until seven in the morning. Last Saturday Bill MacMillen and I went racing and the clouds hung over the backstretch of Belmont Park in a perfection of pale purple and rust-colored rose. We slept with both boys in our bed last night. Pierce got roller blades yesterday, and the Jets and Giants won. Darkness fell. I fought on, although working for AHN is like breathing in a vacuum until the deal gets done.

Mr. Dachowitz, who bought "Lauderdale" after Mopsy Ijams died and renamed it "The Castle," was busted on numerous scams this week, involving collecting insurance on his fictional brother's death in Israel of AIDS. Held on $100,000 bail. Why wasn't he exposed as a fake rabbi sooner?

*Boogie Nights* is a powerful movie. Porno as metaphor for showbiz or for life itself. In one sense it's a business case: How entrepreneurs adapted to the home video revolution of the early '80s. But It's also a dark meditation on our fallen state.

10/25: First day of new darkness and the familiar mania linked with despair descending. Manage it . . . be patient . . . go at your own pace. A cup of hot tea, a homemade BLT, the cattails changing color and a hitherto unnoticed berry growing on the vine beside the pond give one pleasant pause as the rush to oblivion gathers steam.

Treddy is back presiding as president of the RHC, ten minutes late for the board meeting, thin but chipper, and all are thrilled to see him recovering.

10/31: Jack o' Lantern lit, scallop-shaped clouds fade to night, and we walk the lanes, Pierce an alligator and Rhoads a shark, trick-or-treating. PP cries when I go out to dinner, waits for me to come back and joins us in bed. Rhoads wakes and wants his baba. Pierce slumbers against him. "Piercie bad boy," Rhoads says emphatically. "Why?" I ask. "Cuz," he answers with his first known use of conjunction, "he be bodderin' me." Ebonics! In the morning Rhoads cries when I go downstairs, and I take him with me and put him in front of one of the few videos that he hasn't broken. He watches enthralled, the cab comes early, at 5:40, and I sneak out of the house for the airport, a brisk wind blowing, and beautiful sun rise in the offing in the reddening eastern sky.

The world all gone golden and hot red. When I went away to school and college, I regretted not spending September here. As a bachelor in NYC, I regretted missing so much of October. Now I am grateful to be here in the mellow yellow late burst of flame and slow demise of color called November.

11/4: Back from Orlando, I bathe and play with Rhoads, his angelic features and golden curls straight out of a Gainsborough. Then I cook a curried chicken with peas. After I put Rhoads down in his crib, I talk to Pierce about baseball, smoke a cigar on the Novemberly but still comfortable porch, speak to Treddy on the phone, and then put Pierce on the line to get Lanie's sweet goodnight message from the Jung meeting she is attending on the west coast. I take him upstairs where he reads his baseball book to me and cuddles. It's 9 p.m. I wake at 12, Pierce pressing against me. Rhoads stirs, jumps from his crib and runs in little, short steps to our room. "Hi Dad," he cries and hangs limp against me. The two kick and curl and squirm against me all night long, and I wonder at our blessings, remembering with no little awe the many years I thought I'd never have children and then those few that only one seemed likely. And the dawn was more glorious than any before.

11/11: When we woke up yesterday Rhoads flashed his merriest smile and asked, "Are you a donkey named Eeyore?" So we did a couple of minutes of Pooh characters. Rhoads Walker denied that he was Christopher Robin, tentatively accepted Winnie but then reasserted that his name was "*Whoadsie Mawayuh.*" His diction is clearer and sentence structure more complex. He and Pierce were running in a circle around the house and then climbing the sofa and jumping with a grunt to the cushions they had assembled on the floor for the purpose. The house is a war zone: Will it ever change?

Two years since we moved here! A blessed break out. Where did we ever get the nerve?

The Rick Scott/David Vandewater era begins at AHN. "I don't think we'll ever have a funding problem again," Web tells me, exhilarated and exhausted, over the phone. We'll see. To Orlando for a few days for a management retreat. What we need is a management *attack*.

11/15: The tides have been swelling, running up Stable Lane ten feet farther than I have ever seen them before. Water is flooding the Brooks' garden and making the Madsen's old shingle style wooden summer house seem more a proud tower than ever before. Yesterday the water was so high the road was impassable for the school bus, and I took Pierce in the jeep to the pond to meet it.

First freezing weather, cold seeping into my hands, yet the geraniums are still in bloom, and the sun shines golden on the leaves. Last night Bob and Marian Hart celebrated 50 years of marriage, and Cloe Winterbotham came on from Chicago, as did Court and Polly Dixon from Old Lyme. Good to have them back. Courty straight out of a Howard Hawks movie in his pressed lounge suit at breakfast. Addresses old friends as "You old poop!" and asks me if I have a "little black book" to write his number in. "He was the best-looking guy down here in the '30s," Norcross (Skippy) Tilney used to say, "and he knew it!" Very much the Big Man on Yale Campus, and as a former Whiffenpoof still ready to break into song. On his house: "My father bought it in 1892. I can't stand to go by it. I gather it's now called 'Lawrence Court.' Gawd!"

"What was it called previously?"

"It wasn't called anything. It was simply a house in which lived a family named Dixon."

Mother never forgave him for his affair with Jean Drisler, revealed to her by Myra, our cook, "Missus, I've just heard the most horribilist thing." Hot stuff for the Fifties but life went on, somehow. When a year or two later Courts asked, "Can't we all be friends?" Mom gritted her teeth and later called him an ass. But that was a long time ago, and I was happy to see them both.

11/20: Brother Will (Winston) is up for Thanksgiving and comes to The Brook for a lunch with Kevin. The first person we ran into is Henry Kissinger, whom Will had seen two weeks previously at the Baker Institute at Rice in Houston. Will is wonderful company, and I enjoy his innate, strong silent virtue. Afterward we go to Davidoff's and smoke a good cigar.

On Thanksgiving morning, I delivered the papers early in the morning to my in-laws staying at the Hunt Club, had a nice chat and headed back home. An ambulance flashed by at full tilt. O God, I thought, is it Treddy? And followed it. Just off the fringe of the fourth green a large man was lying still, surrounded by medics administering CPR. They shocked him several times but there was nothing to be done. He was dead by the time he hit the ground. It was Rich Walker's father-in-law.

Thanksgiving with the Sauders a sweet time on Long Island. Bill and Ba MacMillen had us to drinks and then we had a long lunch at RHC thereafter. The family seems to be coping well, and Johnnie Marie is taking an active role in Lee's estate. John and Cheryl were here for the first time, as were Jay and Gracie, which delighted Pierce. The Mad Woman in the Attic made an appearance when Lanie bolted from the house before her family arrived for turkey sandwiches that evening and took a three-hour walk. The others repeatedly wondered where she was, and there was little I could say.

"Suzanne is just undone by family," Will mused.


11/29: Two heat seekers on either side of me, tossing, turning, grinding their teeth. Bigger boys now. Angels by night and terrors by day. In the dawn come sounds of guns popping out on the marsh. Last night Rhoads tumbled around me as I read the Atlantis CRTC license application for our health channel co-venture in Canada. Riveting. *Holiday Inn* was on in the background and Bing Crosby sung, "Be careful, it's my heart." That was the one song my Dad ever asked an orchestra to play, the beaten down trio at the Shamrock Cliffs in Newport, when we stayed there with cousin Stuart late in October of 1965 looking at schools. I had never heard it since.

To Orlando and then Mexico City searching for a possible Latin American health network deal. Mexico City was even more congested that I remembered it from 25 years ago, and the smog is awful. Televisa's studios were wondrous little worlds. At a meeting of 12 around a large table at least a dozen different cell phone conversations were going on.

Rhoads beams at the Christmas Carols, standing on a chair and mouthing words, screaming out, "Daddy" in delight as I help out in the chorus, wading into the crowd of older children to hit up Santa and petting the reindeer most affectionately.

On Xmas Eve Rhoads and I made an early exit from church after he growled three times in the pew, almost giving the elderly lady in front of us a heart attack.

Christmas Eve drinks were at the MacMillens again. "It's your mother's party," Mac says, "We just happen to be giving it these last few years." A revived Treddy and Mac joust verbally as of old.

Rhoads and Pierce went to bed after PP left out cookies and a present for Santa. Christmas morning Pierce came down groggy and blinking, and when he saw cookies left exclaimed, "He saved me some. And he took my present back to the North Pole!"

And a festive feast at Sky and Dean's.

*Chapter 3*

# Looking Back at the Sixties

At year's end, one takes stock. I never expected to live in Lawrence again. After boarding school, I went to college in Baltimore, did graduate work in England, joined the Peace Corps in Thailand and for several years directed health care and agricultural development projects in Burundi, central Africa. It was all so very far from my childhood on Long Island I have to force myself to remember what it was really like here in the 1950s and 1960s.

The 1960s started out slowly and serenely, then gathered steam and ended in a frenzy of anger and regret. Those who remember the decade fondly grope for words like "intense" to praise it. But for many like me the overriding recollection is one of confusion.

I was seven when they started and eighteen when they ended, traversing a time from the second grade to the cusp of college.

The 1960s accelerated from something close to stasis to the speed of a particle collider.

Our parents' generation had come back from World War II not wanting to talk about it, going to work and quietly getting on with their lives. Nothing much happened in the 1950s compared to the War. By comparison to what they had seen and done, that was fine by them.

My father had joined the Squadron A Cavalry fresh out of Yale and was due to be discharged three days after Pearl Harbor on December 7th, 1941. After the sneak attack, he immediately volunteered for the Air Force and learned how to fly in Texas before shipping out for the Pacific, where, based on the tiny atoll of Attu at the end of the Aleutian chain, he lost several colleagues who smacked their planes into the steep mountain side that loomed menacingly at the end of the short air strip. My mother thought he may have had a nervous breakdown there, because he was sent to the mainland of Alaska for a month of R&R. For decades after his sleep was bedeviled by a nightmare in which the island was socked in as he was trying to land, and Dad repeatedly cried out, "I can't see!"

My brothers and I went to the Lawrence School on the South Shore of Long Island, one of the country day schools founded by B. Lord Buckley, the educational entrepreneur, along with Buckley, Buckley Country Day, and Greenvale.

In the fall of 1960, entering the third grade and ascending from the "Primary" to the "Junior" department, we donned coats, neckties and exquisitely uncomfortable Oxford shoes, which at least in my case were all more or less permanently askew. We played our first six-man football game against East Woods and lost 40–0. When in the rematch we narrowed the margin to 20–0, our Headmaster, Mr. Barber, hailed it in assembly as "a moral victory."

*Enthusiasm* might have been Mr. Barber's middle name. His name was Anthony Victor Barber, and he wore a gold tie clasp with the initials "AVB." If one asked him what that stood for, he would look somewhat pained and then confess, "A Very Bad Boy." He stood in the front hallway of the Hewlett Bay Park campus every morning and firmly shook the hand of every student who entered, looked them straight in the eye, addressed them by name, and expected them do the same in return. Morning assemblies included band presentations of variable tunefulness, the Pledge of Allegiance, readings from Scripture, the Lord's Prayer, a hymn or two ("One World Built on a Firm Foundation," "No Man is an Island," and the Navy Hymn were all perennials), capped by congratulations on what had been accomplished and an exhortation to do even better, always in Mr. Barber's booming voice.

He retired to Tuxedo Park in 1963, when my class was finishing fifth grade, and since I was living out of the country for some years after college, I had no contact with him for well over a decade. One day in the early 1980s I ducked out of the Time-Life building on Sixth Avenue and raced over to the Racquet Club for a noontime squash game. As I was changing in one of the dressing room cubicles a voice rang out, "Good morning."

"Good morning," I muttered, rushing to my court.

"I SAID 'GOOD MORNING' MR. MacGUIRE."

Startled, I looked up. He was dressed in immaculate white flannels, having finished his morning court tennis doubles match. He was well into his 80s by then but still vigorous. I sputtered my apologies for not recognizing his voice at once, and he let me off with a relatively gentle needle: "Didn't I hear that you spent a year or two at Cambridge after finishing Hopkins?"

"Yes sir, Mr. Barber."

"Not bad," he allowed with a sly smile. Tony was proud of being an Oxford man.

1960 was the year the Mau Mau rising ended in Kenya and no fewer than seventeen African countries gained their independence. Construction on the

Aswan High Dam began in Egypt. The payola scandal erupted over radio disc jockeys accepting money in return for playing particular records. In March of that year Lucille Ball filed for divorce from Desi Arnaz after 19 years of marriage, ending not only the Lucy franchise but our fond hopes they would buy an east coast estate in nearby Woodmere called Foxhall. Instead, it was developed with 30 houses. There were 179 million Americans. "Ben-Hur" won the Oscar for Best Picture. In May of that year, Gary Powers' U-2 spy plane was shot down, "The Fantasticks" began its 42-year run at the Sullivan Street Playhouse, the FDA approved an oral contraceptive, Mossad agents abducted Adolf Eichmann in Buenos Aires, returning him to Israel for trial, and Sputnik was launched into orbit by the Soviet Union. Domino's Pizza was founded, and Harper Lee published "To Kill a Mockingbird."

In July of 1960 Ceylon elected Mrs. Sirimavo Bandaranaike as Prime Minister, the world's first woman elected head of government. Rafer Johnson starred in the decathlon in the summer Olympics in Rome, and Cassius Clay won the gold medal in the light heavyweight boxing division. In September, Hurricane Donna lashed the Eastern seaboard and killed 50 people.

That fall, Nikita Khrushchev pounded his shoe on a table at the U.N. to protest discussion of Soviet policies in eastern Europe. "The Flintstones" premiered on ABC ("Yabba dabba dabba dabba doo!"), and Richard Nixon and John F. Kennedy appeared in the first televised presidential debate. My parents watched it in a store window on Madison Avenue after leaving an A. A. meeting in New York.

The great tragedy of the year in my eight-year-old world view was the Pirate's defeat of the Yankees in the seventh game of the World Series, despite being heavily outscored over the seven games. Kennedy defeated Nixon in a close election, and "Peter Pan" and "The Wizard of Oz" returned to TV.

If I have only middling memories of early teachers (kindergarten was Miss Hatcher, known as "The Hatchet"; second grade was a Dutch woman with a moustache named Miss Van Dort; and third grade a genteel Scots widow named Mrs. Thompson, who always appeared on the verge of fainting thanks to the brutish behavior with which she was confronted), there was no ambiguity of feeling between Miss Anna Smith, our fourth grade teacher, and me. She disliked me from the start, and the sentiment was mutual.

Miss Smith was an elderly, craggy-faced, Ulster woman, who in those pre-politically correct days minced no words in her dislike of Catholics (I would estimate that there were twenty or so in the student body in those days; the number of Jewish students was about ten, and that was the Rainbow of diversity, such as it was), and I was occasionally late to school on account of some-times serving as an altar boy at early Mass at St. Joachim's in Cedarhurst.

She shrewdly sized me up as a slacker, detaining me from several sporting event so as to redo my work. Miss Smith was an idiosyncratic instructor in the standard curriculum but an ardent advocate of nudism in the home, of bra-less blouses in the workplace, and her annual trip to the bare-bosomed statuary of the Egyptian Wing of the Metropolitan Museum of Art was an occasion of great glee to her students.

And yet Miss Smith principally lives on in my memory for the glorious incident that occurred on the afternoon of Hallowe'en in 1961. As she turned in her chair to look in a mirror that stood on a bookshelf nearby so that she could apply rouge and lipstick, a breeze rose through an open window, the mirror tottered and fell with a resounding smash, and a truly gratifying spread of shattered shards of glass scattered around the floor. As decorum yielded to a tsunami of hysteria on the students' side of the classroom, Miss Smith gamely faced us, smiled and said, "Seven years of bad luck."

1961 was the year Dwight Eisenhower warned against the military-industrial complex in his farewell speech, JFK electrified the nation in his Inaugural: "Ask not what your country can do for you, but what you can do for your country." President Kennedy established the Peace Corps that April. In the same month the Russian Yuri Gagarin orbited the earth once, becoming the first human in space. Later in April the Bay of Pigs invasion failed miserably.

In May Alan Shepard became the first American in space in the Mercury program. In June Rudolf Nureyev defected from Russia while in Paris with the Kirov Ballet. On another cultural note, Six Flags opened in Texas the next month. In early October Roger Maris broke Babe Ruth's home run record with his 61st, my hero Mickey Mantle trailing with 54 after an injury-plagued season.

Baseball was my first athletic obsession, and I spent endless hours recreating Yankee games by throwing a tennis ball against the brick façade of our house at 50 Cedarhurst Avenue. The batting order at that time was Bobby Richardson, second base, leading off; then Tony Kubek, shortstop; then Maris. Mickey Mantle was the cleanup hitter, followed by Yogi Berra or, later, Elston Howard. First basemen Moose Skowren batted sixth, left fielder Hector Lopez seventh, Golden gloved third baseman Clete Boyer eighth and the pitcher ninth, although, since he was so good at opposite field doubles, when Whitey Ford was on the mound that could be quite exciting.

I was the fifth of the six boys in our family, and all the rest were right-handed, so, I learned to play the way they did, but I did teach myself to switch hit in an homage to my hero. Like the Mick, I had more power from the left-handed side but a higher batting average from the right. That is, until I encountered my first curve ball.

My games of throwing the tennis balls up against the side of the house (lower for grounders and line drives, higher up against the third floor for extra bases and home runs) were rudely interrupted by mother when she heard the ball connecting with a window pane or by Dad, if he was home, who did not appreciate being awakened from the nap he liked to take in his dressing room.

Then I would retreat to the radio or black and white TV. We got 7 channels: 2 (WCBS), 4 (WNBC), 5 (WNEW), 7 (WABC), 9 (WOR), 11 (WPIX)—the Yankees channel, and finally Channel 13, the educational broadcasting network. I listened to Mel Allen ("Hello there, everybody!"), Red Barber ("Sittin' in the catbird seat," or "They're tearin' up the pea patch.") and the Scooter, retired shortstop Phil Rizzuto ("Holy Cow!") narrate the play-by-play with their signature expressions. The Scooter also made rueful commentary on current events, such as when the announcement of Pope John XXIII's death came on the air during a game: "Gee, that puts something of a damper even on a Yankee's win." *The Mickey Mouse Club, Davy Crockett, The Swamp Fox, Red Skelton, and The Million Dollar Movie* were all highly rated programs in our house as well.

Summers were idyllic. We played baseball in the backyard or on the golf course, and I began a life-long love affair with tennis. Golf was a more frustrating pursuit, but the beauty of the seven water holes on the Hunt Club links with its gentle breezes and teeming bird life was a constant source of beauty and peace. At night the fireflies would light up our backyards as we played ball in the waning light, and as summer lengthened the sound of the cicadas rose.

Then there was the ocean ten minutes away, the beautiful white sands and dunes of Atlantic Beach. Most days we got there on the bus driven by Otis, a gentle giant in his dark glasses and driver's cap, who plied a route from the Lawrence School down Ocean Avenue and ultimately across the Atlantic Beach Bridge. We took swimming and diving lessons from 1956 Olympic and longtime Williams coach Bob Muir—a great, wise and gentle man. As we got older, we would body surf and cruise to the other beach clubs nearby, or sometimes crawl under the boardwalk to beneath the Ladies Sunroom where naked sunbathing was rumored to occur; but the spaces between the slats in the boardwalk were too narrow to get a good look.

Later we would cross Reynolds Channel in Bobby Hart's Boston Whaler, drinking beers at night and skinny dipping, or waterskiing under the moonlight into the narrows of Crooked Creek.

We lived in a three story, vaguely Georgian brick house with more than enough bedrooms to sleep six boys, my parents, Mary O'Connell, the cook, and Nanny, the tiny but indomitable Theresa Gately, who in time, after Mary married, would take over the housekeeping and cooking as well. Since my eldest brothers were nine and ten years older, they were already away in boarding school and college by the time I remember much, more like uncles than brothers. In those pre-Google days, my principal utility to them was as a reference resource to settle sports trivia disputes they entered into in one or another of the village taverns. They would put a dime into the pay phone by the bar, dial CE 9-6877 and ask Theresa to wake me so they could settle the bet they had made. "What did Joe DiMaggio bat in 1941?" When Mother heard about it, she was not amused.

The house had a large front hall, a formal dining room, pantry, kitchen and laundry room, a beautifully furnished but seldom used living room, and behind that a sunroom where we boys mostly congregated to rough house or watch TV. Over a blueberry pancake breakfast after church on Sunday mornings, we would fight over the *Daily News* or *Herald Tri*bune "Funnies" (the comics sections) and the sports pages. On week-night evenings Dad would bring the evening papers as well—the *Journal-American, The World Telegram,* and *The Post.*

Our parents were readers and tended to stay by the fire in the little den beside the dining room. Occasionally, however, Mom and Dad would invade the TV porch to watch Kelso run on a Saturday or the Giants play on Sunday afternoons. On Sunday night, we would often eat burgers on a tray there as we watched "Bonanza" or Dad's Eli classmate, Efrem Zimbalist Jr., on "The FBI."

In the fifth grade our class was graced by an extraordinary English teacher. Derek Sutton had read history and been a chorister at Kings College, Cambridge. He had the ability to infuse his students with the excitement of learning—most especially the high points of English history—and the necessity to express oneself clearly and precisely in speech and writing. He arranged pen pals for us in the UK. He also had a fine tenor voice and gave several exhilarating concerts to the school. At year's end he gave us farewell gifts. Fred Alexandre received "The Moonstone" by Wilkie Collins. Mr. Sutton gave me "The Mayor of Casterbridge." Because he had given it to me, I struggled terrifically to read it that summer, and out of that experience began a love affair with Hardy 's fiction and poetry that endures to this day. Derek returned to London and eventually became the headmaster of the St. Paul's Cathedral Choir School, in which connection he was televised worldwide supervising his charges during the Royal Wedding of Charles and Diana in 1981. He retired to his native York, still assisting at the Minster, and, with a group of fellow senior choristers, singing Sunday services at outlying parishes throughout Yorkshire. Upon his death he was accorded the honor of being buried in the precincts of York Minster, beneath his favorite stain glass window.

In that year, 1962, two of the highwire Flying Wallendas were killed when their seven-person pyramid collapsed during a performance in Detroit. We watched on a miniscule TV in the assembly hall on February 20th as John Glenn orbited the Earth three times and crashed safely in the ocean after. Wilt Chamberlain scored 100 points in an NBA game. The film of "West Side Story" won the Oscar for Best Picture. Rwanda and Burundi gained Independence. Rachel Carson's "Silent Spring" was published.

A recent Oscar season's award nominee, *My Week with Marilyn*, was a charming movie based on a memoir by Colin Clark (younger son of Sir Kenneth Clark of *Civilization* fame), and beautifully acted by Kenneth Branagh as Sir Laurence Olivier and Michelle Williams as the eponymous starlet. It brought back memories of seeing *Some Like It Hot* at the Central Theatre in Cedarhurst one Saturday matinee, our sainted Irish Nanny being "in the roars of laughter" at the cross-dressing antics of Tony Curtis and Jack Lemmon, and my younger brother and I laughing along with her. Mother was not quite so amused as we at Nanny's choice of films for a seven- and four-year-old (apparently *Old Yeller* or a Jerry Lewis comedy like *Hole in the Head* would have been more "appropriate"), but no lasting harm was done. I still think Billy Wilder's masterpiece is the funniest movie ever made, and I was in love with Marilyn (aka "Sugar Kowalchuk") ever after.

I mention this because the summer of 1962 was my first, blissful experience of sleepaway camp (Nanny did not accompany me but thoughtfully sent up shoeboxes of brownies and chocolate chip cookies every fortnight). Camp Monadnock was outside of Jaffrey Center, New Hampshire, just across Thorndike Pond from Mount Monadnock, at 3,165 feet the most prominent New England peak south of the White Mountains and east of the Berkshires. The word means "mountain that stands alone," and the physical setting was spectacular. At chapel in a stand of pristine birches we would sing:

*"Here at the foot of Monadnock,*
*Towering over the plain;*
*Here at the edge of the waters,*
*Sing we our glad refrain."*

There was swimming, canoeing, sailing, archery, a rifle range, and nature program. The July 4th counselors' softball game was between Yale and Harvard, and there were almost enough guys from those two colleges on staff to field a complete team (some assistance from Amherst and Williams usually did the trick). We saluted the flag at dawn and sundown, played ping pong on the porch and thumper at the dinner table, sang beer jingles (but drank only "bug juice," a low rent Kool Aid), sucked on Sugar Daddys, rowed to our tent's private campsite on the lake for cookouts once a week, told scary stories around the campfire, contested Indian and Naval War Games, read Edgar Allen Poe by a blazing fire in the Lodge on rainy mornings, and ended the seven week season with a Treasure Hunt that began with the annual appearance of Phineas T. Spalding, a pirate who had lived underneath the Pond for the last two hundred years. Future Pulitzer Prize winning cartoonist Jeff MacNelly was an assistant counselor who drew brilliant posters for the Saturday night movie. The season ended with campers' and counselors' Follies that were almost as hilarious as *Some Like It Hot*. As the buses started up to take us back to Boston or New York on closing day, the counselors would sing to the tune of "Bye Bye Baby,"

*"Bye bye kiddies,*
*Just remember you're our kiddies,*
*When you go back to School, . . . "*

And we did, often with a catch in our throat.

The absolute highlight of the camp calendar, however, was the Long Camping Trip fortnight (or "LCTs"), when myriad groups went forth to climb or canoe around New England. My first year our gang walked the Long Trail until it crested at Stowe, on top of Mount Mansfield, more than a thousand feet higher than Mount Monadnock, and a good test for a 10-year-old after walking up and down several other peaks on along the four-day trip. It was a Sunday morning when we walked off the mountain, and our counselors let us go into the general store at the bottom to store up on Hershey Bars and M&Ms for the long ride back to camp. I was also interested in checking out how Mickey Mantle and Roger Maris were doing for the Yankees and invested in a Sunday *Herald Tribune*. The headline was huge: *MARILYN MONROE IS DEAD AT 36*.

First love is often painful, they tell us, but all I can say is that it had been a great three years; and I am grateful to Colin Clark's movie for reminding me so happily of my own affair with Marilyn.

In October of 1962 James Meredith registered at the University of Mississippi, accompanied by Federal marshals. The first Bond film, *Dr. No*, was released in October. The Cuban Missile Crisis began on October 14th and was not defused until the Soviets began dismantling their missiles in early November. The 1962–1963 newspaper strike began in New York City and lasted for 114 days. It was painful since there was so little sports on TV, comparatively speaking, in those days. Eventually a strike-breaking paper was put out with much reduced copy, and we had to make to do with that and the weekly magazines like *Time, Life* and *Sports Illustrated*.

Leonardo da Vinci's Mona Lisa was exhibited in the US for the first time at the National Gallery in January of 1963. Patsy Cline was killed in a plane crash in March. *Lawrence of Arabia* was shown on a giant screen on Broadway and won the Oscar for Best Picture. It went on forever, and the myth of there being surreptitious Coca Cola ads built into the desert scenes was highly credible to my best friend, Lars Potter, and me. On August 28, 1963, Martin Luther King delivered his "I Have a Dream" speech on the steps of the Lincoln Memorial to a crowd of over 250,000 people.

One Friday afternoon that November we walked home from a touch football game on the golf course (school let out at noon on Fridays so we could have our doctors' and dental appointments) and learned that President Kennedy had been shot. John Jankosky, my mother's contractor, was redoing the television room, his transistor radio blaring, when I came in. He was a large, florid man, bent over with grief, choking back tears.

(Today few remember that Aldous Huxley and C.S. Lewis died the same day.)

Two days later we were sitting at John Carr's house watching the television with his father, Rufus, when Lee Harvey Oswald was led from prison and Jack Ruby, a night club owner with reputed mob ties, jumped out from the crowd and shot him.

But the year ended more happily as The Beatles released "I Want to Hold Your Hand," and "I Saw Her Standing There," on the day after Christmas, and Beatlemania became global.

There were other fine teachers at the School as we were promoted to the Senior Department. DeeDee Baker came out of retirement to teach us Latin with exemplary clarity in our seventh-grade year. Her reading of "A Christmas Carol" to the class was unforgettable. I also never forgot her telling us she believed that pet dogs and cats had souls, although years later, in her second career as a priest of the Episcopal Church, she told me she did not remember that. Mr. Wilson made us memorize all of New York State's 60-something counties and innumerable dates in the Revolutionary and Civil Wars. Miss Littlefield taught music for over 20 years and produced one or another of the Gilbert and Sullivan operettas each spring. When the class got carried away, she would lay her head on the piano keyboard and hit high C until order was restored, but her good humor never gave out completely, and she took a train into town every week to attend church services and teach Sunday school.

Mr. Clark guided us through the mysteries of early algebra, often exclaiming, "Don't just stand there like mashed potatoes and beefsteak." He never quite could make an experiment work in the often-smoke-filled science lab, confounded us with his "mystery ball" on the mound and, in his frequent visits to their apartment in the converted campus garage, was a daily example of utter devotion to his invalid wife.

In 1964 Barry Goldwater won the Republican nomination for president, beating out Senator Margaret Chase Smith, the first woman to run for president, Nelson Rockefeller and Pennsylvania Governor William Scranton.

Surgeon General Luther Terry reported that smoking *may* be hazardous to health. *Meet the Beatles* was released in January. The next month the Fab Four arrived in America and appeared on the Ed Sullivan show, seen by 73 million viewers. *Hello Dolly* opened on Broadway. Cassius Clay beat Sonny Liston in Miami to become heavyweight champion. The first Mustang rolled off the line at the Ford Motor Company. Richard Burton and Elizabeth Taylor married for the first time. Merv Griffin's *Jeopardy* debuted on NBC. The Polo Grounds, hallowed temple of the baseball and football Giants and later the Mets and Titans (the original name of the Jets), was demolished. Sidney Poitier was the first African American to win the Oscar for best actor in *Lilies of the Field*. The World's Fair opened in New York.

There were several other colorful figures at the Lawrence School. Frank Behne, the gravel-voiced superintendent, taught shop as he chain-smoked in the basement and regaled us with stories of General Pershing's expedition into Mexico in search of Pancho Villa. Fred and Nora Martens ran the kitchen and stoically produced meals that after the privations of boarding school and college one remembers as having been pretty good, none more so than the treat of outdoor cookouts on fair fall and spring days, when the smell of hamburgers on the grill would waft through open classroom windows and end all hope of concentrating on the subject at hand. They were assisted by a fellow German named Emmie, who spoke almost no English, and when asked what was for lunch would always answer exuberantly, "Pumpkin Pie!" a dish that was never served. Emmie had lost her husband in World War II and set a place for him at dinner every night in her rented room.

Our food at home, by contrast, was delicious and beautifully served as mother presided over her table with bell in hand. Roast chicken, lamb, pot roast and a variety of fish on Fridays, including soul amandine, baked clams, and cream of tuna with sliced hard-boiled eggs peering out of it like fisheyes. For special occasions there might be squab or crown roast. Nanny's and Mary's popovers (or, occasionally, pop*unders*) were highly anticipated as were the cakes, pies, ice creams and souffles they so lovingly prepared.

Mother was gregarious and devoted to family. Both of her sisters had moved to Lawrence after the War, so we had sixteen first cousins close by. My father suffered from bi-polar disorder. When depressed, he slept for sixteen hours a day and sometimes could not even bear to get out of his pajamas to dress for dinner. On one of his highs, on the other hand, he would be up at five, into his Wall Street firm early and, after lunch at the Squadron A Cavalry Club in the Biltmore Hotel, to his family real estate office in the Lincoln Building. He would plan trips, attend multiple AA meetings, bringing his comrades from there home for weekends, and filling the house with chatter and laughter. He was handsome, athletic, charismatic and funny; but even in those very good times I remember noticing the plumes of cigarette smoke rising from both ends of the dining table. Mother smoked three packs of Marlboros a day and Dad four packs of the non-filtered Chesterfields. As the years went on their coughing worsened.

So long as Dad was well the house was wide open. Family and friends were always welcome to drop in for a drink or dinner, or to stay the night over. In summer, we for the most part lived on the airy screen porch in the back of the house, looking out over the terrace, back lawn and large apple tree at the back of the property. I can still remember the taste of the slightly warming milk Mary would put out in a silver pitcher half an hour before dinner was served.

Our bedrooms had fans in the summer (although eventually Mom and Dad acquired an air conditioner). There were frogs, garter snakes, and lots of rabbits in the field adjacent to our house. Behind us was an abandoned stable where you could still find a horseshoe or two. The attics on the third floor were filled with curiosities, and one had a hidden room where I set up a private club.

I can remember the cry of the crickets, the many birds, the smell of mint growing in the laundry pen beside the garage, the acrid smell of the vinegar Nanny applied to her County Roscommon skin to ward of the burn of the beach sun, the taste of her bacon sandwiches as we ate them on the sand, the musty air of the attics, the flowers blooming in the garden Mother tended, the silver and furniture polish, the honey suckle vines blooming in the heat of summer, the beetles beneath the curb stones in the driveway, and the two new cherry trees blooming in the front yard.

I can remember the wind blowing across the 7th fairway as Dad redeemed an ill-considered January promise to take me camping on the golf course one June evening. With great hilarity Mother helped us load up the station wagon and escorted us to the tent-pitching site. Under the moonlight I asked if he liked sleeping outside, and he told me with complete conviction he would rather sleep like this than anywhere else. In the morning I declined his offer to go to the country club for a "really good" breakfast and enjoyed putting my slice of bread on a stick to toast above the fire. When we got home, I followed my father up the stairs and into the master bedroom where he plunked himself down beside Mother eating breakfast in bed off her tray and groaned, "God, this is the most comfortable thing I have ever felt in my life."

Lawrence School's smaller size made competing against Buckley and Greenvale in football, basketball and baseball ever challenging, but we held our own. We looked forward to sports all day. I am angered when I read of large doses of Ritalin being prescribed for "hyperactive" boys in schools—especially inner-city schools—today. A far better medicine would be ninety minutes of strenuous exercise under the guidance of a competent coach from whom young men could learn the value of working together as a team for a goal greater than oneself. *Mens sana in corpore sano.*

We were all athletes: Dad a fine horseman, tennis letter winner at Yale and several time Club champion; Mom a good golfer; Phil nationally ranked in squash and a leading tennis player as well; Schuyler a triple threat in football, hockey and baseball, who went on to be called "the poor man's Roger Staubach" in the Washington *Post* when he quarterbacked the Georgetown team back into competitive football; Kevin a fine squash and racquets champion; Pierce in many ways the best coordinated, a squash and skiing wonder; and Peter a squash champion and court tennis player. But in those days, it was most often touch football on the side lawn and hitting pop flies up into the darkening summer sky, water polo at the beach, and tennis in the sunset's lingering light.

Realizing my younger brother Peter would eventually be left alone at home, my father brought a wonderful flat-coated retriever named Paget for him to keep company with, and Peter sweetly shared the joy of dog ownership and many adventures and misadventures with me.

LBJ proclaimed "The Great Society" early in 1965. Shortly thereafter, Sir Winston Churchill died at 91, and his State Funeral exceeded all others in pomp and ceremony. Henry Luce chartered an airplane and outfitted it with dark rooms so that his *Life* photographers would have the scoop on other magazines.

In March *The Sound of Music* premiered at the Rivoli Theatre. 5 days later, on March 7th, some 200 Alabama state troopers attacked 525 civil rights demonstrators in Selma as they marched to the state capital in Montgomery. In late March funeral services were held for Violet Liuzzo, who was shot dead by 4 Klansmen as she drove marchers back to Klansmen after the civil rights march.

On May 9th Vladimir Horowitz returned to the stage after a 12-year absence to perform a triumphant concert at Carnegie Hall. In July Bob Dylan "went electric" at the Newport Folk Festival. The Beatles "HELP" premiered in theatres. In August, the Watts riots began in LA. Casey Stengel announced his retirement from the Amazin' Mets after 55 years in baseball.

Pope Paul VI visited the US. (In John Guare's play "House of Blue Leaves" groupies wear their "Paul" buttons from The Beatles recent trip). In October the Saarinen "Gateway Arch" was completed in St. Louis.

In November John Lindsay was elected Mayor of New York, over the insouciant Conservative, William. F. Buckley Jr., and Democrat Abraham Beame.

But before Fun City could begin, on November 9th the Northeast Blackout cut power for over 13 hours. We lit candles at home, tickled our overnight guests Jake and Carolyn Carpenter, and relished the reprieve from homework.

In December *A Charlie Brown Christmas* aired for the first time. In January of 1966, Mike Quill and the Transit Workers Union went on strike and Fun City was not so fun for "Mr. Linley" thereafter. Nat King Cole died in February.

The times were changing. In April *Time* magazine asked on its black cover: "Is God Dead?" As our TV tastes became more sophisticated, we tuned to "Shindig," "Hullaballoo" and "The Man from U.N.C.L.E.," all the more so when the daughter of Mom's best friend, model Katherine Carpenter, married David McCallum, who played the long-haired Ilya Kuryakin in the series.

In June of 1966, our class graduation coincided with the 75th Anniversary of the founding of the Lawrence School, and we were invited to join the large luncheon that followed Commencement Exercises on the circle lawn in front of the school. Mr. Barber returned for the occasion, and prominent alumni reminisced on their respective eras at the School. *Life* Magazine columnist Loudon Wainwright, also an alumnus, gave the keynote address, at one point remarking he believed he could still find the gap in the hedge where he had used to steer his bicycle onto the school grounds early in the morning.

I was glad to be moving on. The truth was that I was bored to death the last several years at the school and had asked to be sent away in the eighth grade. My father talked me out of it, counseling I might enjoy being a big fish in a small pond rather than being back on the bottom rung of the ladder. He spoke from experience, having been sent off to the then still new Portsmouth Priory in the seventh grade in the early 1930s. So I stayed, enjoyed my family and friends, editing the school newspaper, playing sports, early mornings by the fire reading the paper with my Dad, walking Paget to the village after school to buy baseball cards, and the first horribly awkward parties with girls, where virginal kisses playing Spin the Bottle tended to taste of potato chips and M&Ms. I read and wrote a favorable review of *The Green Berets* that year, and, not long after, Katherine Carpenter's brother George, my old camp counselor, left Yale suddenly, signed up with the Marines and was shipped off to Viet Nam.

I remember the joy of riding bikes to school, pedaling through the back lanes of Lawrence, Cedarhurst, Woodsburgh, Woodmere, and Hewlett Bay Park, chattering and laughing with one's companions, while smelling the fallen leaves in fall or the intermingled fragrances of lilac, azalea, blossoming fruit trees and freshly mown grass in spring. But the actual days in class became endless. I was sure something more exciting lay beyond the perimeter or our little world, and if boarding school was the way to get there, my feeling was: Bring it on.

# Chapter 4

# High Hopes, Steep Struggles

### 1998

Like a sea slug, a beached whale, a beaten eight, a bruised fruit, a jeep stuck in mud, Elmer Fudd . . . blabbering. The January thaw happened the week after New Year's this year and continued into the following week. Rather odd for it to come on so early, but we'll regroup and doubtless suffer winter's onslaught later.

1/6: A big day for Pierce. His tooth loosened Sunday night, was noticeably askew at breakfast yesterday, and fell out as his class lined up to enter school. As of 3:59 a.m. this morning it was safely under his pillow, his smile now a jack-o-lantern. At bedtime he was both proud of his achievement and tender toward his loss of a shard of self. "Toothy," he apostrophized.

Greetings from friends all over. Susanna Porter figures in a Bill Buford piece in the *New Yorker*. Gone from us—Rufus Carr Sr., father of my childhood friends and blind in recent years, Brendan Gill, 83, a lover of New York, good architecture, Norfolk CT and the *New Yorker*. His stint at the theatre desk was outstanding and his book the best written on the magazine to date. I miss his intelligent eyes, insouciant irony and ingrained courtesy. Plus which he was fun!

As I write this at 3:30 a.m. there is a thumping of feet on the floor above and a voice crying out, "Mommy, mommy, the tooth fairy came. He left me a dollar."

One of the most powerful full moons ever lighting the early morning sky.

The snow geese pass through noisily close to dawn. The ugly stork-like Great Blue Heron waits patiently by the ditch at the end of the Causeway for the fiddler crabs to surge up with the tide. Most of the duck have been shot this season, and my boys sleep upstairs, growing handsome and strong.

Presently they enjoy playing a game called, "Nananananananaa," in which I chase them around, Rhoads usually too paralyzed with giggles to move at all. Snow starts to fall. The sky is a wintry yellow grey.

1/21: The America's Health Network recovery continues. I am now in charge of business development which includes foreign deals, books, radio, Internet, and, most of all, finding ANY additional source of revenue. Rick Scott is smart and tough-minded. Hard to find an overarching ethos there. He seems enamored of the Internet only in terms of potential valuations, and I doubt that is a good reason to build a business long term. "I'm prepared to spend 100 percent of my time on this," he says.

Programmer of the Month: After the four o'clock news on WQEW Radio ("A station of the New York Times") this afternoon headlined with President Clinton's denial of an improper relationship with an intern, Jonathan Schwartz led off the next half hour, without any comment whatsoever, with Barbra Streisand singing, *"He Touched Me."*

Sunday. Sun streaming in and high winds after days of overcast and rain. Jacqueline Dupre is playing the Elgar concerto, tripping across a light-hearted phrase before sinking back into gloom. I saw her perform it beautifully in Baltimore in 1971. She was still healthy then.

The wind roars up. The sunlight heightens a desert pink in the eastern sky. Cormorants keep their vigil on the telephone pole. An old rabbit scuffles across the lawn back to the reeds. Of all my Sundays here by the shore is much the best, surrounded by two sons, the sun and the winter wind.

At Nancy Hart's christening party last night Father Rahilly recounted a recent meeting with Cedarhurst village officials in which a Zionist board member refused to call him Father even while addressing others as "rabbi." Rahilly said he had never lived in a place where he felt discriminated against before, and, if it continued, he would have no choice but to denounce anti-Christian bigotry from the pulpit. "I consider you a worthy adversary," said the man, meaning it as a compliment. "I'm not your adversary," Father Paul replied, "I'm your brother." Good for him.

2/16: Tuesday night it snowed if only in short and somewhat dainty sprinkles. Then the air warmed and fog blew in. Before long visibility had ended, and as light seeped up the dusting of snow on the ground that had glowed in the moonlight was gone. That night the rain poured, rattling the windows, though all was calm.

Pierce got a two-wheeler for his seventh birthday. He broke the chain guard within seconds but was riding well within an hour. By the end of the day, he could mount and dismount. I remember Mother helping me unscrew my training wheels and riding across the back lawn under the old apple tree out back of 50 Cedarhurst Avenue until she said I could take off down the road. Happily, the Isle of Wight is still a place where kids can do that.

Lots of destruction around the house this week as a leaky ceiling was opened by Paul Jankosky so Bernie Pastor could test the pipes, and then Paul caulked and grouted for a day in the bathroom. He found a dripping pipe and fixed that too.

2/20, The Seals and the Swans: I woke at four last Saturday, daylight dawning earlier as we come deep into February. As the sky brightened and a rose ring circled the horizon, I climbed into my gardening clothes and beat a path toward the shore. The vines and trees that bloom in summer are bare of course, the reeds trampled down by ice and cold. The old moon lingered in the sky, pale and powerless. Tony Mortimer is building a new "media room" to keep his pretty daughter Bree home from the Yacht Club. Other cottages are shuttered for winter. Gaggles of geese honk in their flight. This is a time of year when we see osprey and cormorant, I think, as I turn to the sandy Little Beach, where a bulldozer is shifting the sludgy sand drained from last year's dredging. At the edge of Reynold's Channel, a swath of plump swans has migrated from the northern shore for a morning browse in the relatively mild winter breeze. They fill the eye with their whiteness, gliding, flapping furiously to get under way without ever really rising to get off the water's surface. Following one's not-quite-flight I see something out of the corner of my eye that looks not right: Two brown forms on the dingy dock. Three and a half or four feet long they are, and one cranes its neck around as I approach. A pair of harbor seals! What are they doing here? Fishing for flounder? Most human of animals and subject of so many legends along the Celtic fringe of Scotland and Ireland. One seal keeps looking back while the other flops happily on the dock. I weigh moving back or coming forward but am mesmerized and stand still. Then one nudges the other and they flop forward to the dock's edge, slipping swiftly into the silent sea. I scan the water for twenty minutes to see where they'll surface next; but so far as I can tell they never do.

2/26: Five planes in five days, and I threw out my back, which was improved by chiropractor Lorraine Whyte Heath, whose grandmother, Delia, brought Nanny from Ireland to us. Lulu does some good, but in my follow up stretches I pop my hamstring! Then the boss calls to suggest tennis at 6 a.m., so I wake at four to drive to Tennis Port on the East River in Queens and stir the sleeping Mexican guards to open up before Web Golinkin arrives from the Waldorf in a cab. In a meeting last week reviewing financial results David Vandewater leaned back and drawled, "Well, the only possible explanation for these numbers is that you lied to us or were seriously misinformed."

Of course, when Web and Joe wrote a budget last August their first urge was to save the company, and the ratings assumption was twice what we were then at. But maybe there's a budget, however austere, in the making.

3/4: 46 years old this sunny day in New York City. Last night Lanie gave me a beautiful dinner with Sally and Kevin at Gramercy Tavern. Poached oysters and lamb. Mercurey and a blended red from Arroyo Grande. Happy times and innumerable blessings. We've pushed on, and despite challenges I've never lapsed. With as sweet a girl as Lanie cuddled up beside me this morning, I hope I never do. But then of course in the same minute there's the fish wife who accused me of drinking too much last night:

"It was my birthday!"
"Still."
"Can I help it if I was over served?"
"You did all the ordering."
She has a point.


3/8: I spied the first blooming daffs in June Finlayson's yard today. "They're from the Queen Mother's garden," she said in her proper Kiwi voice. Al the barber goes there to cut housebound Al Finlayson's hair, as he did with Carlie Timpson, Whitney Dall and others. Contractors at several houses are scurrying to be ready by summer, but I am more attracted to the changing cast of characters on the pond, the white-breasted duck, the ibis that flew down Stable Lane and landed on Susie Gatehouse's lawn, and the cock pheasant peeking around the Madsen's fence. This is the end of the five months of the year when we hunker down as if in a country cottage and stoke the fires. The cacti bloom in winter and Mother's jade plants bear up on the sun porch, but it's better as the grass greens, the light lengthens, and the great cycle starts anew.

Rhoads was adorable last night when Pierce began to read his new bear story. Eager for attention, he said, "I can read . . . once 'pon a time, there were three little pigs . . . and . . . "

Dreams: Driving with Dick Aldrich onto a foggy bridge, Rusty and Pierce climbing all over me in the driver's seat. Dennis Carroll, the school headmaster, screaming violently, which would be healthy for him who too often has a pained expression in the face of some hectoring parent as he softly says, "I hear you."

In real life Pierce wets the bed and writes in black ink on the sheets. Rhoads tarries in toilet training, and a late cold snap arrests the too soon Spring. We played hide and seek in the sand dunes yesterday after a picnic, and then Pierce and I had a rousing game of street hockey on Stable Lane, Seton Ijam's car being one goal and Suzy Gatehouse's driveway another.

Jon Krakauer's *Into Thin Air* was as disturbing as it is gripping. It brought back many memories of Kilimanjaro. I was alarmed at the lack of coordination and discipline at the top, the failure to fix line, flouting of pre-determined turnback times and a clear conflict between ethical obligations and monetary incentives. Respect the mountain! Or pay a terrible price.

Back from consumer focus group testing in Cleveland, a city quarried from some of the darkest stone I have seen. Reading T. Corghesson Boyles' *Lands End*, a wonderful account of life in the Hudson Valley among a relatively fixed gene pool for over three centuries. The portrait of the Last Patroon was hilarious.

With spring came the snow and we sledded on the fifth hole, the boys in their snow suits. Then a satisfying sneak snowball attack on Uncle Schuyler. Ensemble Wein-Berlin played superbly in a program of Beethoven, Hindemith, Ligeti and Enescu at the Chamber Music Society.

3/30: As buds bloom I remember 50 Cedarhurst Avenue, the abandoned stable in the empty lot across the street, beetles under the rocks bordering the gravel driveway, termites, and the hamster Peter won at the Easter Egg Hunt which mysteriously escaped (Mother!).

Last night at dinner Bill MacMillen remembered Grandmother MacGuire pouring liquor into her coffee at breakfast at the Little Club in Saratoga. A pleasant night that began badly when Lanie accused me of having thrown out her olive bread (she had hid it on a top shelf we seldom use). How many times has she done that?

4/20: Worst dream in the world . . . Pierce, Rhoads and I are on a bridge. I have to get out of the car. Rhoads squirms loose from my hand and slips through the opening between railings and chicken wire. My own life felt ended, and I was ever so grateful when I woke to find him sleeping upside down, head cuddled against my knee. He's almost three years old now, cutest of curly blonde-haired children. He loves batting baseballs and sword play. "Knock knock," he said to Lanie on the back of her bicycle the other day. When she asked who was there, he growled, "THE WOLF!"

The poet Octavio Paz is dead. Our good friend and neighbor Bill Miller's 75th at the Union Club was a happy event. Fiske Warren is leaving private practice rather than paying $400K in liability insurance. "I'd have to do eight arthroscopies a week to break even. It's possible, but the pressure to operate on patients who might not need it makes me uncomfortable."

I am inexpressibly depressed as others around me complain of the same thing with far more reason. AHN is mired. I seldom feel this way in the sunny months and don't like it. Around us the fruit trees bloom, the hedges green up, and here we are, flummoxed by foolishness and doomed to fail, but not without fighting forward to the very end.

Damp spring, Nor'easters in May, tides running above the bulkheads, the birds atwitter, the chestnut sprig has yet to bud. Already the lilac bushes have overhung the fence and shifted a rail with their fragrant weight. The marsh is so flooded it looks like a lake we could water ski across towards the sunset had we only seen one in the last 12 days. The children are snoring upstairs. It's Mother's Day, and Lanie, most beautiful of 45-year-old Mums, is off to church.

Rhoads wakes. "Dada, you play squash and tennis?"

"Yes."

"And hit the ball so far?"

"Try to."

"Who you play with?"

"Steve and Dario . . ."

"And Treddy . . ."

"Well, he's retired, but he was national champion . . ."

"And they gave him a cookie?"

"No, a trophy, a big silver cup."

"But then they gave him a cookie too, right?"

"Right."


5/17: The world is a more dangerous place as India explodes three nuclear bombs, Pakistan to respond shortly. Netanyahu and the Palestinians harden lines, Frank Sinatra is dead at 82. I struggled back from Mexico City to take Lanie to a benefit for Fountain House organized by Anette Goelet that I enjoyed hugely, but Lanie came only reluctantly. "1776" was an unexpected joy.

Pierce's first night in the new bunk bed. Rhoads climbed all over. This morning he came down sleepily talking about a dinosaur in the pool and how he had escaped. "So it was a nice dream."

5/18: Pierce's first sleepover, at Casey's. He was bursting with pride and joy when he called me in the morning. When he came back, he hugged his brother. "It's all right, Rhoads. I'm here now."

Robert Duvall in a bravura performance in *The Apostle*. He reminds me of Rick Scott in his deluded certitude.

5/29: Gary McBride, GEMS CEO: "When we started we were the 5th pan-Latin American network. Now there are 117." *Last Days of Disco,* Whit Stillman's lively elegy to Studio 54: Evocations of a life in NYC, herpes and coke included, quite winning. Glad I was in Burundi and wasn't here to share in the fun.

The birds begin singing not much past 4 a.m. Pierce is a little boy now in his rooster red collared shirt and checked shorts. He fell in love with reading this year. There's new growth on our white pines, the wind rustling through them.

Gordon Forbes marvelous memoir, *A Handful of Summers*, was given me by our new head racquets pro, Steve Bromley. It's the best tennis book I have ever read:

"I returned to South Africa and discovered to my surprise I had become a reasonable tennis player. Moreover, I firmly believed I would become much better. . . . the best player in the world, perhaps. I did become better but never the best in the world, nor Wimbledon champion, and now, looking back, the reasons seem quite plain. I did not at any stage commit myself strongly enough to becoming Wimbledon champion; and I hopelessly underestimated the dedication and patience required to achieve perfection; didn't think it was special enough; fondly believed that some preposterously benign tennis gods would help me out with let cords or fluky shots when I was in dire need of them. They didn't of course. They very seldom do. The only people upon whom they bestow fluky shots at very critical moments are those who have either irrevocably dedicated their hearts to those moments, or else, on rare occasions only, to those who have approached the moment with such honest courage and daring and valour, that in reluctant admiration they have awarded them the benefit of the doubt."

Forbes recounts asking a grounds man at Wimbledon to ignore the members only rule and let him, newly arrived in London on a ship from South Africa, see Centre Court. Later he describes how he lost serve in the first game of his first match on Centre Court because he was overcome with tears at being there and could not see the ball. I know the feeling.

At the Ranch for Johnnie Marie's 70th. I was minding my own business in the main ranch house when the door bursts open. "Bless the Lord! Ain't it good to see you again! Now give me a hug." Suddenly a 250 lbs. Caroline, Baptist minister and Johnnie's housekeeper, is bearing down on me, and there is no retreat. She is here to fry the chicken, steam the greens, cut the watermelon and generally keep spirits high.

"Jamie, you know Lanie and I was in school together?"
Lanie is dubious on this point.

Last night Pierce came running from playing ball and squealed, "There's an animal out there. I think it's a pig." His first armadillo.

The dear Pattersons trickle in. Dr. Tom, is recently retired and has moved to assisted living. Dot, 88 and ailing, arrives from Weatherford. Don is 95 and housebound there, a cousin of Mary Martin's. Pierce was thrilled to meet his third cousins. Rhoads focuses on stomping a cricket. Caroline produces mountains of chicken, greens and black-eyed peas. Johnnie is assisted by Rhoads in blowing the unquenchable candles on her birthday cake. After hours of communion, Tom walks Dot to her car, arm in arm, the sweetness of the Pattersons united in mind and spirit, and Lanie speculates it might be the last time we see her.

6/16: AHN's Live Birth webcast on the Internet attracts much attention from the major media, and two weeks later the *National Enquirer* helpfully reports that the mother is a deadbeat with two arrest warrants outstanding for bouncing checks. The joys.

6/25: Van Vechten Burger is dead at 96. Van and Dodie, two of mother's dearest friends, benevolent aunt and uncle figures to her really, the house a sanctuary of order and graciousness although sometimes a straitjacket for Van Jr. There was always a jollity about them in my memory. They felt duty bound to do things with the grandchildren and their friends, but I always felt they enjoyed us too. Dodie had a hearty laugh; Mr. B. was always a bit more serious, making fine distinctions, though not without humor himself. Of an old New Amsterdam Dutch family, father a boom or bust mining engineer. His world view was shaped by two world wars and the great Depression. His father died when he was 16; the family struggled to get him through Yale. He went to Wall Street in November of 1929. A colleague told him the boss wanted to see him. "I think he wants to make you office manager." Fired him instead. Mr. Burger never complained about such Chaplinesque reversals ("You've got to play the cards you're dealt.") and slowly climbed to the top. He didn't seek credit for all the good that he did either. But he was capable of the terse comment on Dodie's Farmington classmates who married Italian aristocracy: "Counts no-account." His father-in-law Evans bought his seat on the Exchange. In due course they were able to build their country place and called it High Time, a lovely double-entendre. "His philosophy of life was simple," said young Van at the funeral, "Do the best you can, and try to leave the world a little better than you found it. He sure did that."

Rhoads, after a year of laggardly interest in toilet training, called out triumphantly on the phone last night, "DAD! I did a pee pee upstairs and a BM downstairs."

Kathy Rasenberger gets a call from headhunter to take Web's job. Nice work, Rick.

Tennis on a blowy evening. A locust lies upside down, legs thrashing in the kind of futility one associates with launching a cable TV network. PP takes *Goosebumps* to bed at night. When I check at 11 p.m. he's fast asleep, still bespectacled. A marvelous storm at 5 a.m.

7/13: Lanie's and my 8th anniversary. Quite a long time, really, for "two of the most complex people I know" (Chappy Morris). Let's steer a steady course onward. At dinner we talked about the continuing health care crisis, the failure of the HMOs, and the challenge to the politicians. The kids were asleep when we got home, and the evening ended tenderly.

Our new tennis pro Steve Bromley exhorts the Ladies' Clinic: "You've got to take control of your release points!" And I thought he was here to teach tennis.

In Crested Butte, Rhoads is still prone to fears and sensitivities about day care, rational or not. Lanie calls it a manipulation. I think of my dear, departed doctor, Al Grokoest, "How does a child apply? By crying or getting sick."

Pierce emerges from the kitchen with a large flower vase full of ginger ale. "It looked like a really good glass to me." Mark O'Meara was a stirring British Open champion at Royal Birkendale, a triumph of patience and hard work.

Back to work, I sat next to Chris Evert at the sushi bar in Orlando today. She was looking for real estate in Orlando, possibly for a new tennis camp. There is a wonderfully genuine warmth about her in person.

First heavy dew and early morning coolness on Long Island. Poor Lanie has a headache and complains, "I hate this place in the summer after we come back from the mountains."

After two and a half hours and putting one match point smash into the fence and another into the net, Grant White and I won the doubles tourney over David Willson and Tom Russo in three exhausting sets. The world turns from hosannas of hopefulness into agons of despair, and I sit, mildly curious as to how it will all turn out.

What a wretched season August was, laughing gulls diving down upon me as I jogged, trying to lurch towards Fall but stuck in summer's stasis.

Lanie and I viewed Mrs. Timpson's house, a red brick faux Georgian designed by Otis Chapman, a local architect of note, with a circular stairway, much imported wood from Carlie Timpson's years at Ichabod T. Williams, Importers, and a rather lovely gentlemen's dressing room. Through it all Marcelle, 99 and counting, slept, vivacious lady of New Orleans, now surrounded by rosaries and scapulae and her domineering West Indian maid Zita, growing acres of eggplant in the garden and filling in Mrs. T's martini glass with candle wax so she won't overindulge. Zita is a teetotaler, but Marcelle was not and must surely resent the loss of half an ounce per day. The late Carlie's take was, "As far as I'm concerned one of you is worse than the other."

Fires in the sand dunes and Bill the beach club manager tells me: "We had one. It was one of a series set by a guy at the Long Beach F.D. These fire bugs are strange cats. They set them and then invariably turn up to watch them. Some of them actually jerk off, it turns them on so much. Really fucked up."

AHN's latest streaming special, a live open-heart surgery with Denton Cooley, was a great success. Fighting a virus, I briefly blacked out at LaGuardia en route to Houston to be on hand and was ordered to bed. A line of violent thunderstorms blew up from the south. Rhoads entertained me delightedly, insisting upon a shower and astonished that I knew the characters in *Peanuts*.

Wonderful Woody Strebeigh at the yacht club's 90th: "I sank my first boat, then got a second and was sailing it one night when one of my brothers jumped in and then a second, and I looked up and realized we were on fire and sinking, so I jumped into the pitch-black water. There was no one about and it looked hopeless when this hideous blue stinkpot chugged up. The others climbed on board, and I said, 'No, I'd really rather drown.' And wouldn't you know, the next boat was a beautiful white sloop, so I went home happy, and Father rewarded our incompetence with the Sara III."

End of summer perfection, sitting in the ancient wicker chair I saved from Grandfather MacGuire's Saratoga house yard sale, watching both Concordes land within minutes of each other. Pierce and I lost by a hair to the Aldriches in the father-son swimming race. As I strolled out on the IOW evening, Incy Brooks and John Passaggio were walking dogs, Phil Thornton was skateboarding, Carter Brooks roller skated, and Rhoads and Pierce did their imitations of Arnold Schwarzenhager: "Hasta la vista!"

Pierce is a second grader with a pumpkin smile now whom I walk to the bus full of talk about the Sammy Sosa/Mark McGwire homerun contest. Then I was off to the Cleveland Clinic and on to Houston, where I dined with Will Winston and his lovely ma Susan Baker on bread pudding and a crabmeat omelet before heading on to San Francisco to beg for cable TV distribution. Morale in Orlando is awful, and the place is peppered with grassy knoll theorists of our imminent demise.

Back on Long Island the suddenly cool fall air streams through the windows, and roses are once more in bloom. Rhoads and I go for bike ride, and he flops down outside Bob and Margaret Randall's house. Their golden retriever emerges to lick him promiscuously and thump his tail happily on the macadam. That night the stars are high and brilliant, and I drew on my first cigar in weeks, minute beneath all I survey, but happy to be included, grateful to be.

After beating me in tennis and sipping on a Shirley Temple, Pierce looks at the label on the yellowjacket holocaust lantern that reads "Insect Pesticide Device," and asks, "Dad, can yellowjackets read?" Later:

"Hi Charlie Brown."
"I'm not Charlie Brown."
"OK. Hi Snoopy."
"Dad, I'm not Snoopy. Snoopy is not even real."
"You're not going to tell me YOU'RE real?"
"DAD, I'm real."

Off to Europe and MIP to buy programming, sell same, discuss co-productions and look for investors. How lovely to be back in London after so long! Supper at Greens the first night. I saw Brian Mullen in a taxi on the Strand. He and Liz are here for a stint with DLJ. A fun lunch with our old PR consultant Pippa Groves at Orso, Antonia Fraser smiling as I walk by, while Harold Pinter, beside her in dark glasses, glowers. As life goes on, I enjoy her work more than his, precisely the reverse of when I was 20. Beautiful Venice Canalettos at the National Gallery. Wandering the shops of St. James, I cannot help but think of how much Lampedusa loved these lanes and the shops therein: Lobb, Davidoff, Purdy, Poole. And a good dinner with dear Sara Poland, my old flame from Cambridge, doing well in real estate and design.

And then the Roman light . . . and the gentle nights of Cannes.

Back to New York in late October, I take my tuna sandwich to the park on a dazzling fall day to look at the East River. On Long Island how high the sky and quick sanded the marsh. Rhoads is three and a half and asking questions: "Is it chocolate? Does it have nuts? Daddy, are you sweaty?" Meanwhile Pierce is reading *Black Beauty* by himself while we are called to teacher conferences to discuss his inability to organize his book bag.

10/30: Golden mornings, golden days, even if darkness now be visible. Rhoads is Spiderman and Pierce Zorro for Hallowe'en this year. Rhoadsie struggles to see through his mask and cries, "Wait for me," as he runs as fast as his little feet will carry him.

Pierce and I drive to his occupational therapist in Rockaway Beach. When I asked him if he had special friends this year he answered, "I like everyone," with real sweetness. Rhoads is racing around the house acting out two and three person mini-dramas, like those my brother Peter and I used to put on at 50 Cedarhurst Avenue.

November is the color of paper and parchment as leaves wither, bleed, brown and crumple. The smell of the earth rises. We have a spirited soccer scrimmage pitting Dick Aldrich and me versus Russell and Pierce at sunset this afternoon. Pierce and Rusty won. I smoked a cigar that night and got a sore throat. When it persisted and I went to the doctor, I got a ticket for not wearing the seatbelt. The wages of sin.

I hate myself when I get cross with Pierce's inability to tell left from right, to tie his shoes, or to pay attention to his homework for more than three minutes. Pierce is so sweet and smart, funny and crafty, and yet there are parts of his brain that do not yet connect. I got up and covered Rhoads before walking into Pierce's room, lay down beside him and took him in my arms, sensed him stiffen, then relax, and sigh peacefully. I kissed him and wept during a windy, rainswept night, the gusts baffling the entire house.

I took the car to Hassel Motors in Freeport today and thought, as I always do, of Lee Peck as I did. He started it and raced hot rods as well, one of the coolest of the cool when I was growing up in Cedarhurst. He was lost at sea a decade ago with his sad-faced half-brother, Warren Crunden, in a heavy storm off Cape May when the boom hit him from behind, and he had neglected to put on his life vest. Lee was knocked overboard, and Warren dove in to help him get back. They got to the boat three times in heavy water but could not climb back in and finally drowned. Steedman Hinckley, the yacht club Commodore then, presided at the dockside service when the boat returned to its berth.

That night I woke and went downstairs to work, leaving Rhoads red cheeked and slumbering in bed. Next thing I know there was a thump upstairs and a woe-begone cry on the stairs as he slips down them eyes half-closed and finds me in my study, his look half-scared, half-proud of his adventuring. He runs into my arms, holds me tight and falls back to sleep. I will miss moments like these.

11/12: Four years ago we came into this house on a cold November night. In that time Pierce has grown up and is now bicycling to Taylor Foran's house on Bannister Lane and Charlie McClendon's on Sage Avenue. In 1995 Rhoads arrived and was instantly another source of great joy. Nowadays he tries to turn his bike in circles too narrow for him, so it falls down and he whimpers, but he bravely stands up to try again.

Rhoadsie explains his latest dream. "I like the good zoo, but the bad zoo is scary. The good zoo has seals and sheeps. The bad zoo has dragons." He began shifting in the night and by dawn his earache was full blown. Poor fella.

Lanie arrived back from Europe Sunday, two days later, strangely, than she originally said. Not in a good mood.

Pierce is a fidget at church but loves singing loudly, just the cantor and him! He asks if he can be "a baseball player and a priest." Why not?

*Waking Ned Devine* is a charming Irish comedy. Excellent cross-editing, Jackie's wife superb, and the naked motorcycle chase wonderful! *Charming Billy* by Alice McDermott is also a well told, but depressing Irish-American tale.

Holidays hove nigh. My business cell phone number was previously a private detective agency, and the calls toll in for that and also the state social services bureau. A drunk young man in a bar calls trying to find his father, hesitant older ladies search for an assignation, assertive younger women, pissed off men wanting something proven they already know is true, and innumerable clicks. One can imagine the real and imagined infidelities, frauds and fiduciary failures that so animate the human heart in conflict with EVERYTHING as it turns to the Central Florida Yellow pages listing of a defunct gumshoe outfit only to reach an unresponsive *moi*, who, however much I dreamt of being a Sam Spade or Philip Marlowe, am sitting mute and on Long Island.

At Rhoads and Pierce's student conferences the ample and irrepressible Mrs. Zaroff cries with schmaltzy but genuine joy as she describes how secure, friendly, and gorgeous Rhoads is. I try to interrupt the superlatives to identify a problem or two, but she is adamant: Perfection has been achieved, here and now, and she whips herself into such a frenzy about it that there is no escaping a bear hug and kiss before we leave. Whew. As to Pierce, his math and reading fine, but problems with focus and organization hold him back. His handwriting is shocking, even by comparison to *mine* at his age, chicken feet scrawls all over the page. Dear boy.

Thanksgiving to Kevin's where, by virtue of the lady who has helped Sally's family cook the feast for 35 years having fallen and broken her hip last night, we go to their club, Wee Burn, instead. Great fun and a long ramble back to the water when we return to Stable Lane. In the morning after the sun rose, clouds scudded, wind blew, and all was light, 23 days to solstice, 28 to Xmas, 35 to New Year's, markings of no particular significance, arbitrary as lines in the sand. And a hailstorm of honking overhead, hundreds of geese marking their way south.

11/29: A quiet Sunday, eerily warm. Lanie is taking the kids and neighbors to Atlantic Beach for a picnic. Alec Guinness' diary, "My Name Escapes Me," is a wonderful memoir. New Year's Resolution for 1999: "Re-read Shakespeare; especially the minor plays." St. Andrew's Day on the morrow, which I shall celebrate with a large single malt. And then to the feast of Saint Edmund Campion. Christmas around the corner. Let it start.

I got the geraniums done and had lunch with Treddy. It was so mild I just had to grab my golf bag and walk one final nine amidst the fallen leaves and rust-colored landscape, the tide high and cormorants eyeing me dubiously. Cormorants (Great and double-breasted) were flying in single file close to the water with slow-flapping wings and outstretched necks. They sit on top of CYC dock pilings in winter. Their very posture suggests a hunchback trying to sit up straight.

When seen passing diagonally at a distance close to the waves, the long wings of each seem to overlap those of the next in line, all rising and falling very nearly together. Often in the shimmering summer haze, which operates to deceive the eye, the spectacle will almost delude the credulous into the belief that they have seen the folds of a sea serpent rolling along the waves.

Cormorants don't undertake the crazy arial dives pelicans do; instead, they fish from the surface of the water, entering it head-first. They are expert at tossing a fish inconveniently caught a foot or so above their heads and receiving it into their open gullet. They are rank tasting, foul their nests, and greedy (Chaucer: "the hote cormeraunt of glotenye" in *Parlement of Foules*).

A few roses are still in bloom at Alistair Hanna's house on the IOW, from which my cousin Eileen McCarty was married when Uncle Buddy and Aunt Barbara rented it many moons ago. The red ball of the setting sun was soon supplanted by a glowing moon in the western sky, and winter nigh.

The Hebrew Academy of Long Beach (HALB) is trying to buy the Sheik property 200 yards down Sage Avenue for their new one thousand student yeshiva, and all concerned are up in arms. "We don't need an Orthodox Andover South in the neighborhood," says Steve Madsen.

M. Donald Grant is dead at 94. At Hobe Sound in the early '60s, after the perfidy of Walter O'Malley with the Dodgers and Horace Stoneham with the Giants had left New York City bereft of National League teams, he suggested to Joan Whitney Payson that they start a new one. "If I pay for it, will you run it for me?" She did, and he did. And nobody there could play that game for awhile. Don was the sportswriter Dick Young's favorite target. They thought he was a plutocrat and not the self-made Irish lad from Montreal who had done vaudeville at night while learning Wall Street from the bottom up. He could be brusque and stuffy, was a stern moralist, stubborn and had a temper, and was never forgiven for trading Tom Seaver. Perhaps I should have resented the fact that he had only the vaguest sense of who I was and called me "Mickey MacGuire," but, given my treasonous enthusiasm for the Yankees, I loved the name. And I remember all the good he did and tried to do. He gave many a second chance at Fahnestock, searched the bars for Dad when he went missing, and tried to help many others. He was tough on his own kids which led to the wonderful morning he sent a still single Patsy to the Club with instructions to write down the names of every eligible bachelor she could find. The list came back with the staff front and center: "Dario, Joey, Nino . . ."

He won the club golf championship in 1964 at aged 60, and, when my parents called to congratulate him, invited himself over to tell them about it hole by hole. Another memory: When Dad toasted Theresa at what would prove to be his last Christmas Eve cocktail party, Big Don came over and said, "You sonofabitch, you made me cry."

Two weeks later his beloved Alice passed along as well, perfection in its own way.

12/1: Lanie over dinner asks sweetly, "Jamie, what do you think about our marriage?" She has been angry and irritable since her return from Turkey. I say I think it needs work, we need to spend more time together, and she needs to devote more time to the kids. For her part, she feels we don't communicate, and that she gets no support. Plus, "I don't always want to feel like I'm the bad one." Why?

Rhoadsie is the bacon king, "Is it crispy?" And then later, appearing with Frisbee in hand, "Dada, can we play crispy?"

How strange to find a desert in December, even as the geraniums bloom and the golden sun rays flare over scarlet-tinged clouds, the water in the channel as blue as stone. The desert is within. Not December depression but the utter desolation of being unloved by the woman whom one most loves. And the breaking up of a family and two young sons.

12/14: Winter looms. June Finlayson goes to hospital for a loose pin in her hip. Bill Denson died Saturday after several strokes. A courtly southerner, our mayor, and hero to Long Island's Jews as the war crimes prosecutor in Dachau after WWII. Meanwhile, President Clinton lost more votes in the impeachment melodrama and launched a Wag the Dog attack on Iraq.

12/18: An awful day for our nation. I was sickened by the spectacle of the clerk of the House reading out the articles of impeachment. Pierce and I drove to his occupational therapy in Rockaway Park. He was in good spirits as opposed to yesterday when he cried upon learning that neither Lanie nor I would be at his holiday show. We put our own agendas first, and a little boy was hurt. I got home that evening and told him how great I'd heard he was from his Aunt Dean and Bibi. "Too bad you weren't there," he said non-judgmentally, in a voice that pierced the heart.

12/19: Solstice shadows. Today it was dark until 7:13. Lanie barred Rhoads from our bedroom for acting up. He cried most bitterly and tried to reinvade only to be repulsed by her, whereupon I took pity and went to his side. He crumpled into my arms and was asleep in seconds. Immediately, Pierce tried to invade our room and was only mollified when I promised to lie with him, which I did and then went back to bed after he had drifted off. At three Lanie and I were cordoned off in our corners, but the wind rose, and the house rocked and I remembered how it was in other times, our bodies intertwined or resting together, and then we touched slightly, warmed each other and lay close in what may have been nothing but could be a new beginning, maybe.

12/21: Pierce and I trimmed the tree. Solstice here at last, Rhoads is snoring noisily upstairs. We caroled yesterday in front of the fireplace at the Club. It was Terry Blanchard's last year after leading it and reading "The Night Before Christmas" for three decades. He and Wanda are retiring north to Newburyport. The last Advent candle was lit at Mass this morning. The boys and I walked afterwards with John Passeggio's cocker spaniel, Sally, and Ann Thornton rushed out from her house to give us presents.

12/27: Christmas at the Ranch: Yesterday evening we had a warm fire, a tenderloin for dinner, and afterwards Lanie asked Rhoads if he wanted to sleep with her (we're in the two-bedroom guest house), and he said no, he wanted to sleep with me. Whereupon Lanie said OK, gave me a decidedly un-pro forma kiss, loving and long, so much so the children giggled. After waking with the garlic and jalapeno grits to process, I made my way to her room around 5 a.m., where we slept entwined and made love in the dawn, softly and sweetly, finishing as Rhoads stirred. Let's pray we can turn the solstice corner. Lanie was off early to walk, possibly the most independent girl in the world, but let's enjoy what we can together.

Dr. Tom Patterson died this Sunday morning, aged 83. He was a good man who was infinitely kind to us when Pierce was a baby with ear infections. He opened his office on a Christmas morning, endeared himself to me when he had trouble with the ear thermometer ("The nurse usually does this.") but got Pierce better. Another of Lanie's Patterson cousins gone. Bert, Virginia, and Tom, with Don and Dot well into their 90s. Fred and Patsy are still going strong.

A good ride in the Renshaw Pasture later after building the fire, cloud cover trying to decide whether to go or stay away. Jim Bob the rancher talks of feral pigs growing to 400 pounds, his son's high school rodeo club, leasing land to hunters who cheat and ranchers who cut down the herd, and all the kids who kept going back to Dr. Tom Patterson long after they had grown up. An enviable epitaph.


## 1999

At age 46 I won the local club squash singles championship for the first time, beating Larry Phillips in the semis and my brother Peter in the finals, the former far fitter and ever so much younger, and my brother the superior player of the game, but I got hot and shot well.

I worked on the AHN digital strategy, rolling out multiple spin offs of our network as technology allows, if we ever have the money and the audience to justify it. "To walk hopefully is better than to arrive," said Robert Louis Stevenson. To walk hopefully *is* to arrive.

Optimism is creeping back in, possibly with the sweet smell of shampoo on the three-year-old's hair when he crept into bed with us at 3 a.m. Dreams, the very oxygen of life, fill the sore and battered shell of my ageing, oversized frame. Had I but nothing but dreams, and a wife and two boys who believed in me, it would be enough. But a shard of financial security would be nice too.

1/8: Bibi tells me that yesterday Pierce said to her, "My Dad is the greatest Dad in the world, but I don't think Mom is the greatest Mom." Bibi says she's scared to tell Lanie. The truth is that they simply don't see that much of her. She leaves early every Sunday, coming back at seven. And when she is in the house, she tends to stay in her private castle in the bedroom rather than interact with them.

1/12: Lanie tells our jolly, elfin therapist Dr. Lampert very movingly of her struggle to find a life for herself, of her parents' lack of relationship, and her feelings of hopelessness because she had never known how to relate, and even how she was spending more time at work and less with the children because she found it more "satisfying." Is it because it's more abstract and defined, and not as messy and personal? Dr. Lampert leans forward into his suede Guccis and calls her criticisms vague.

A dream I have had several times of late is driving along an access road on a western highway, and suddenly I'm not inside the car but watching it from behind and realizing I've lost control. Lampert says it appears that I have had a lot going on, but it just hasn't worked, and that I am restricted to a narrow emotional range. As an old girlfriend, Anne J., once said, "Even when you're here you're somewhere else."

A quiet Sunday in the blahs of January. A thaw is on and with it an all-encompassing fog, which, acting as a lens, brings the roaring ocean from beyond the beach a mile off right into our back yard. Lanie slept badly but, sitting at her dresser this morning, looks radiant. She was nominated to the Jung Institute board yesterday, the youngest person ever. A great achievement!

1/25: At a staff meeting in Orlando, Web gives a status report on Fox, Comcast, and Discovery's expressions of interest in buying AHN. Back home Rhoads has dozens of new words. "I waited for you Dad, and now you're going to stay forever and ever."

Al Finlayson is dead at 94. He had been ailing with a bad hip and reclusive for years, but I remember him golfing and gregarious when I was a teenager. June will have an easier time of it now, but she hung in all the way.

2/1: A raucous session with couples therapist Jonathan Lampert in which he hilariously punctures various shibboleths of Lanie's and mine:

"OY, get a new wardrobe, and stop the mumbling. . . . and as for you, Lanie, if you use the word 'grappling' one more time, I'll teach him the best way to poison—slowly. He's reaching out to you, and all you can say is that he's not reaching out the right way. What more can the schmuck do? It's you who isn't doing anything, except being superior, condescending, snotty and stuck up. And why? Because he's the closest thing you've got to your father! And you, Jamie, you just sit there smiling quizzically. Can't you say something real? Even shout? No wonder she wants to hit you!"

*Goethe:* Love does not dominate; it cultivates.
*Joyce: Amor vero aliquid alicui bonum vuit* (Love is genuinely wishing another's good).

Dusk
*Fog-shrouded and leaden*
*A tint of rose trying to break*
*Through the sepulchral gray*
*Night on its way.*

As Jung wrote: "Hurry is not of the devil but IS the devil."

Meanwhile, Rhoads is dancing and prancing around the Isle of Wight, merry and giggling by day and snoring at night. In the morning Lanie says, "I want to apologize for what I said about divorce. I didn't mean that. It was just sheer frustration."

2/5: A gray day close to freezing and windy. It was Pierce's first confession, and he asked to go to the new priest rather than his buddy, Father Paul, the pastor, "So I can get to know him, too." He trudged up the aisle like a trooper to Father Sean but could not contain himself returning, holding up his fingers and saying in a voice the entire church could hear: "Four Hail Marys!"

Meanwhile, Lanie took Pierce's old bike to the shop to fix it for Rhoads. It proved beyond that, and she sweetly bought R. a new one, on which he is pedaling furiously but not before telling the Israeli bike shop owner that the doomed bike was named "Spike," and kissing it goodbye.

I talked to Jack Bierwirth today, who remembered a similar wet winter when my cousins Mark and Matt McCarty came out of the marsh with a wood piling to add to the bonfire at Jack Jr.'s birthday, and the wood smoked and sweat forever antil the flames broke and sent a plume up into the sky for half a mile.

I'm enjoying Patrick Samway S.J.'s Walker Percy biography—successes, doubts, depression, bourbon sipping, self-description as "a horny impotent at 59," the trashing of semiotic thugs and Kierkegaardian impulses. All sound very human.

2/15: Pierce and I fly to Crested Butte to ski. Winter is wonderful here. My instructor urged me to lead with the bellybutton, a delightful concept. Pierce persevered but got altitude sickness on his first day. Then he got better every day going forward in the white glare and the newly falling snow. In the dawn the peak hangs there—a slab of rock—towering over a long Colorado valley, at the other end of which three college students were killed yesterday in an avalanche. Pierce pops in with the important questions, "Dad, why do you and Mom fight so much?" "Do you have any friends?" (He was shocked to hear of my seven godchildren). His sleep is agitated with grinding teeth and wound sheets, and in the middle of one night I leaned over and said, "Happy Birthday" (his 8th), and was greeted by a snore. We shopped the next afternoon, tobogganed in the evening and dined at his favorite boîte, The Idle Spur. He wore beads for Shrove Tuesday, consumed the world's biggest Sundae and was full of wit and fun.

Back at the condo we read in bed together. My eyes strayed fondly to his sun-reddened cheeks, the full and handsome head of hair, his bifocals and nose buried in a volume of "Scary Stories." He sensed my gaze and looked sideways, smiled and said, "Hi." A sweet voice with a slight catch in it. We hugged. "Daddy, I love you." We said our prayers then and went to sleep.

Pierce makes great new strides each day on the mountain. He insists on bombing down the slopes instead of turning until he crashes and burns. "I knew that was going to happen!"

So much more than I deserve.

2/18: Pierce reads the book of Genesis in bed after I catch him watching a bodice-ripper on TV. "Dad, what does 'rate' mean?" Rape presumably. Great. Asks me to tell him funny stories of childhood. Camping with my Dad on golf course. My pony Crow at Eaton's Ranch nearly rolling over on me. Sledding behind Sky's VW Beetle in a blizzard on the outer holes of the golf course, Peter falling off and getting buried in a snowbank. He has a raucous, mischievous laugh. Then, seriously, "Dad, why isn't there a White History Month?"

On the way home to New York Pierce is transported when we are upgraded to First Class, and we watch *The Mighty* while eating off linen and china.

2/25: Back home Lanie and I maunder on. I remember Father Vince Dwyer saying at Michael and Sydney McDonnell's wedding, "The cornerstone of marriage is the ability to forgive." I quote Rilke to Lanie: "Love consists in this: that two solitudes protect and love and greet each other."

Not much response.

A.R. Gurney's *Far East* not overwhelming but not bad either. The moral dilemma at the end of Act I was interesting.

3/1: Dull dawn with calls of crow and gull interspersed. The Fox deal is closing at nothing like the valuation we wanted, but at least it's a way forward. Our March is coming in neither like a lion or lamb. Rain spits and spouts from the south and then pours. The car dies, and I watch nervously as the lane fills with water while the tow truck hooks it up. The plugs and distributor cap are shot. So much of me is shot through the knees, the ankles and shins. Sometimes I wish I were an old man who sat quietly and said little. I make a fire and the sweet smell of smoke fills the room. Rhoads has helped build it, then clenches his fists and says, "Dad, this is about Bibi. She says you were gonna take me for a walk, and you never did." Lower lip stuck out for emphasis.

"That's because you fell asleep. Besides, it was raining. But I'll play a game with you."

"What?"

"I dunno. You choose."

He puts his forefinger on his nose. "TAG!"

And off we go.

3/3: Marcelle Vallon Timpson dead at 100. A vivacious lady of New Orleans, she was my best friend Lars Potter's grandmother, and a great bridge partner of my mother's. She gave me a kiss in front of a large group of ladies when I was eight, and I cried, "Massacre!" which she repeated ever after.

And Billy Talbert dead. Mr. Tennis. When he brought Pike and Peter back to Cedarhurst in the '60s what a thrill it was for us all to play with a national champ and Davis Cup captain. He was serious and could be quite critical but had an amazing life story as one of the oldest surviving diabetics and the first to insist upon living a world class championship, competitive athletic life. At the funeral at St. Thomas More, Tony Trabert remembered, "I met my idol when I was 11. After I began to win tournaments 10 years later, I said, 'Bill, I'd really like to pay you back.' 'Don't, but help the next kid who comes along.'" Austere and blunt, dogged and graceful. Peter told a great story of going out to Forest Hills one day during the many years Mr. Talbert ran the Open (*pro bono*). Suddenly the costumed figure of "Mr. Peanut" walked by, and his father's voice said, "Hi Pete." The regular inhabitant had called in sick, and Billy wanted to make sure the advertiser got his money's worth!

Lampert says my failure to engage Lanie's anger is a neurotic disorder. "Don't try to calm her down, just be there with her. And when you have to, like at the big client dinner, just tell her to leave. And never stop telling her you want to screw her . . ."

Expert advice at 300 clams an hour.

One's mind a riot of different strands of thought, feeling and sensation— the love of children and Let's Make it Better with Lanie strand existing side by side with the Let's Nail Anything That Moves strand and Who Cares? strand. Early songbirds sing in the distance, but two crows predominate on the lawn. The beautiful and predatory side by side. And here the rest of us are, too.

3/24: The Oscars were uneventful. *Shakespeare in Love* won best film, but *Saving Private Ryan* wins best director. Both strong, but *Shakespeare in Love* was the better movie, a real paean to the theatre, with an hilarious Stoppard screenplay.

Lanie starts our therapy session saying she feels sad and out of gas. She would like to feel she wants marriage to get better but doesn't. Lampert asks if she notices she always puts herself as an individual first rather than family, or even herself in relation to family? She acknowledges that.

She says she has gotten beyond vows. Our love is dead, she says, and thus so are the vows. And besides, she loves Christianity for the ritual, but other than that it's just a metaphor.

3/26: Spring breaking through. Could that be a metaphor? Rhoads is emphatic on his classmate Alana: "She's not my girlfriend; she's my *fwiend!*"

Lampert loves the metaphor of Lanie as operatic and me as chamber music inclined. He says Lanie will always have a wonderful, generous side but will also always have a miserable, "people are out to get me" side, and I have to deal with that.

4/8: Bill Gates become the wealthiest person in the world as his Microsoft stock soars.

4/17: Back to the hurly burly. Rick Scott's calls are not being answered by Chase Carey of Fox or Jimmy Dolan at Cablevision. Spring is coming to Long Island just about on time, however late love is. Sun rises red in the east above the marsh and three cock pheasant cried on my jog this morning. The sky is so blue one sees beyond it to a mysterious new dimension. The swan glide on Reynolds Channel's choppy waters, and soon, surely, there will be a green field we can refresh ourselves in, glorious grass, fragrant flowers, infinite sky, inexhaustible Spring!

4/25: Pierce's First Communion: 15 or 16 beautiful children, about two thirds Black, the girls in white with hair up and the boys in suits and blazers. Recovering from a rehearsal where he fell down while genuflecting, Pierce was perfect, happy and hugging all around. "Today, I am a man!" Mother would have loved it (and no doubt did).

5/10: My fifth grade teacher from London, Derek Sutton, is in town on his third farewell tour of the States. Fred Alexandre comes up from Wilmington for dinner. When I ask, Derek says he is a red wine man, but later confides since his epilepsy he has lost all sense of taste! He has also lost miles of memory, which made all conversation seem new and wonderful to him.

Dr. Lampert denied at our joint session ever suggesting separation for a three-month period as Lanie had claimed to me, and Lanie acknowledged this was so. Very strange. "I must have wanted you to say that," she offered. Never never land, but we agree to an assignment to imagine ways in which we could change for the better. Later Lanie was volatile at dinner, presumably because she had been caught out dissembling.

I seldom speak of it here but so much of my inner life has been formed by my training as an athlete and by the outdoors. The maxims of Outward Bound: "Today is the first day of the rest of your life;" "Your disability is your opportunity;" "To serve, to strive and not to yield;" "A mistake is something from which you learn nothing." One could write a sermon on each.

May: First fog, spring rain, wet ground, all apiece with the desperation of spring, the anxiety of being on the edge of failure in Freud's two anchors— work and marriage. The unspoken, unimaginable, yet faintly present impulses to self-destruct appear on the horizon of one's farthest feelings, still too close for comfort . . .

5/20: In a sweet, if inaccurate, but terribly earnest letter, Lanie reaffirms her wish to separate. It has been a long six months of struggle, and Lanie does appear to be a soul in suffering. She is terribly depressed, especially in relationship to me, and I see no ethical alternative, even in the eyes of the Church, but to grant her the relief she seeks. It could, one supposes, be temporary, though it hardly feels that way. I don't like to admit it to myself, and

I do love her, but in some respects it's amazing that we have made it work at all for nine years. It has often been a hard ride.

At our meeting with Dr. Lampert all is compassion for each other. Lanie says she has "no idea" how all this will go. "It's as if I have to get down to complete chaos and come back up again to see . . . ."

That night the children crawl into bed with their stuffed animals and begin to play. By morning, the spiders are weaving, and a Daddy Long Legs is climbing up onto the ceiling. Herons stretch their necks on the pond as I jog, three rabbits play on Eliza Chauncey's lawn as a robin eats worms nearby, the Concorde ascends skyward out of JFK at an angle of 45 degrees, passing by the effaced moon.

5/29: Perfect weather for Memorial Day weekend. The band from Saratoga Racecourse comes down at Sonny Staniford's behest to play for Babs' 70th birthday at the beach. Peggy Nicol and I dance it up as we did at dancing school in 1964, though no longer wearing white gloves.

Started tennis but not only does my game need work I need therapy on my finger, knee, toe and hamstring. A wreck!

First beach barbeque: the sun a red ball in the sky, kids organizing them-selves into a monster game of running bases. Smells of wisteria and foxglove and the stench of the channel at low tide.

This morning Pierce's bus ran late, and I took him to school by car. Rhoads and he carried on en route, kissing me to turn me into a toad. As we pulled up the school driveway to the curb I looked back, and Rhoads had opened the back door while the car was still moving. I slammed the brakes and he fell forward (having loosened his seat belt) and hit his tooth on the back of the front seat. Much blood and tears, and he cried and shook with fear. He only jollied up when we re-entered the driveway at home and both of us were splashed by the sprinkler I had set on the impatiens. Later, when I called Lanie, he said, "I'll tell her the story of the sprinkler," which he did with much joy. Then Bibi scolded, "Tell her what happened to your mouth," and he answered, "No, because then I might cry again."

An interesting teaching moment. He knew where to go to sustain himself, and where not to go as well.

The brook of the mind burbles happily around all sorts of stones and is not detained on its way. But the beavers build mud dams and clog the water's pure flow in the damnedest places sometimes.

Graf over Hingis in the French Open. Lemon Drop Kid in the Belmont. "Dad!" Pierce called out, "the funniest thing just happened. The Indians walked Hideki Irabu (a pitcher and notoriously easy out)."

6/10: First heat wave passes into cool overcast. Grass browns and the wild cherries drop their dried-out blossoms. It's only early June but feels as if whole cycles, entire seasons have played themselves out in the last two weeks.

Back home there are bird songs and baby baths, but the storms gather. Lanie is off to Texas for her boarding school reunion. I water the garden and listen to the sounds of spring and silence interweave. As much as I would like her to, I do not now expect Lanie to return to the marriage, and I'm not so sure I want to persevere either. I love the children and much remains to be done there. As to the rest, I don't know. A part of me is angry she dragged us through this. A part of me is crushed. A part of me is at peace with God's will, whatever that may be. And a part of me is exhausted.

6/25: Living in an aviary in the Isle of Wight at this time of year. A world of warbling. A four-year-old snores beside me, and an eight-year-old, filled with salt water and sunshine, scampers in the moonlight. Pierce swam in his first race today, put his head too far down and finished third. I took the boys to church, then played tennis with Jake Carpenter on the clay. The glamorous Bree Mortimer came in to babysit, always ten minutes late but disarming one with, "Mr. MacGuire, it's such an honor to babysit for you." Really? As they do with their other beautiful babysitters, Alexandra Leonard and Lindsay Payne, the boys beam at Bree and say, "Dad, you can go now."

Off to John Conway's surprise 70th, he, dear friend, dumbstruck in his early Alzheimer's when he walked in but then recovers to make several toasts. Then on to Cee Cee Gammon's and Jeb Belford's engagement party at the yacht club given by the Boturs. I remember the awful night Cee Cee's house burned down, and her Mom, Lisa, perished. May they be happy!

7/1: I took Pierce to a Yankees game, and he led the "CHARGE" and "GO YANKEES GO" shouts as well as "Take Me Out to the Ballgame," knew all the players and was busy making friends with the four black kids who crept down to the seats behind us and at first seemed startled by the pesky conversationalist who engaged them.

The next night Rhoads and I dance on the sun porch to Fatsy Watsy Waller singing "Until the Real Thing Comes Along."

A pleasant golf game with warm hearted Jim Higgins at Somerset Hills in Peapack, who desperately tries to make it an even match ("It's the salesman in me") to no avail. Afterwards, over lemonades on the porch, I confide that the last time I was here, in 1974, at Carter McShane's deb party, my brother Peter, Jake Carpenter and I drove home, went to swim in the ocean at dawn and got back to the house to see the nurse's car gone. Nanny was bawling in her bathrobe in the kitchen when we came inside. Dad had died in the night after a three-year struggle against prostate cancer. "I felt very strongly you boys had to go live your lives," Mother said. Jim grew pale as I reminisced. What could poor Higgins say?

In Colorado, Rhoads asks, "Dad, what is your most important job?"

"I don't know, Rhoadsie, what is it?"

"Taking care of me!"

Just so. And Pierce is a lovable, wisecracking, frequently toilet-mouthed, antic Little Leaguer, on top of enormous ranges of subjects mentally, with a wildly associating mind, while still a disorganized mess of a little boy. He hit a three-run homer yesterday. When I arrived in Crested Butte, I intercepted Rhoads wandering back from his swimming lesson. He kissed me and said, "That's the best surprise in the whole wide world." Then we played catch before going for ice cream.

7/16: Lanie was in Aspen for the night after a hike over the beautiful Blue Maroons. There was sad news as she arrived back. John Kennedy Jr.'s plane had been lost in fog off Nantucket, his wife and sister-in-law on board. Poor Caroline. Pierce cries in my arms as we sleep because I am leaving in the a.m. Lanie listens to my entreaties sweetly but without response. I rise at four in the morning to drive to Colorado Springs to jump start a new chapter, the road dark to Gunnison, and then on fire in the gorgeous western dawn.

8/4: I retake the house from our impeccable renters, Cathy Curry and Andres Gill, and am just working out a few chords on the piano when I hear cries of, "Daddy, Daddy!" and Pierce rushes in, leaps into my arms, and won't stop kissing me or let go. Then Rhoads floats in and takes his kiss more calmly and says, "If you don't work tomorrow can we take a bike ride together?"

On a clear August morning Rhoads plays happily in the sand and soon is lying belly down in the surf with Stephanie and Christian Tomasson, giggling, "O Man!" as the waves break over them. There is a super realistic clarity to the sightlines clear down Rockaway Beach and over to New Jersey.

Can consciousness be verified? Can two people look at the same event and see and feel it completely differently? Does the experience of the material world change from species to species? If so, is it not likely that the experience of other beings (e.g. angels) is also different, and that of a Supreme Being would be supremely, even unknowably, different?

Pierce sailed his own boat for the first time Monday. He had to bail water. Bibi is in a state over Lanie's and my looming separation. "I can't take it." Neither can I.

8/13: Treddy's 80th. A happy, happy night. Margie and Tim Carpenter gave a dinner party for two hundred at the Club. Many of Tred's childhood friends—Seth French, Henry Mellen, Worthy Adams—made it back. The Commandant of Marine Corps, General James Jones, sent a letter on recounting Treddy's heroics at Iwo Jima:

"His men exposed and under severe attack, with complete disregard for his own safety, Captain Ketcham moved alone over some two hundred yards of open terrain to a rocky crest. In spite of heavy mortar and small arms fire, he directed (by radio) accurate 60mm. mortar and artillery fire on four pillboxes. After destroying these fortifications, he led his company forward in another assault. The position was taken after bitter hand-to-hand combat. Although very weakened by his wounds, Ketcham personally directed a speedy reorganization of his company to successfully repulse a counterattack of some seventy Japanese. His skill, initiative and courageous devotion to duty in the face of enemy fire are in the highest tradition of the United States Naval Services.

"Admiral Nimitz' famous words, 'uncommon valor was a common virtue'— were about Marines like you: 'ordinary' men whose courage and sense of duty to their fellow Marines compelled them to do the extraordinary. It is part of what bonds us forever as a band of brothers . . ."

As Uncle Tim finished reading, Burtch Drake and some of the other Marines in the room (Jim Hellmuth, and Uncle Tim, who fought on Okinawa as well as Iwo) let out with "Semper Fi," and the place erupted into a standing ovation. Treddy was calm and poised but immensely proud and happy. Glad he "hung in," these last years, to use his phrase.

8/14: A night of encircling thunder and lightning lighting the sky, rain pouring down *rat a tat tat* on the roof, rattling it as the phosphorescent light surrounds us. Bibi is still highly upset. She says Lanie has written a note accusing Bibi of "blaming" her.

Pike Talbert and I win a doubles match against 18-year-old big hitters, Matt Schmeelk and Charlie Leonard, slipping on the wet grass. I see Seth French in the ocean, Treddy's childhood friend, up from Charlottesville for the party. I mention how good it was to see the picture of Froggie (his late Uncle John French's nickname) with Mrs. Payson at the Fasig Tipton barn at Saratoga this summer.

"You know, Jamie, I thought of Froggie a lot this week, because we were really his family, and I thought that Treddy was doubly blessed because he had Bombright (Treddy's younger brother, Bonnie), but then he had another family—the MacGuires."
And we had him.

Fox completes the AHN purchase and promptly fires Web, Joe and me. I can say with some certainty that I fought the America's Health Network fight with everything I had until we went off the cliff, so to hell with it, as Joseph Kennedy used to advise his sons. Pierce wins his eight-year-old mixed doubles tournament. His partner? "I don't know her name, but she's half Australian." Pike and Lizzie Talbert's daughter, Caroline!

8/22: First cool day after a night of wind and rain. *Rosa rugosa* and Montauk Lilies recovering nicely now. Lanie is visiting a very sick Mara—a fellow analyst who writes on incest—in Baltimore. The mood here is autumnal. Cloud of depression is descending, and one cannot submit. Also spanking big hard ons and no shortage of fantasies about where they could be put to use, but I am determined to keep to the high road and still hope things take a turn for the better.

To Saratoga with Pierce carrying his trophies to show Kip Elser. Eating at Sperry's with Josee and Rick Violette, he asks if crab cakes are white meat. The answer is, "Yes," since he won't touch fish, and he orders them for both his appetizer and main course. He ate half of one, then feasted at Ben and Jerry's on the largest chocolate ice cream cone in history, 90 percent of which ended up on his trousers.

Back home Lanie told me she had decided to leave work early Thursdays this coming year to pick the children up and would take them to school Fridays. Good. Then she had the inspiration to sleep outside with Pierce. "Is Mommy serious? I want to go!" They lasted about an hour or so when I was woken by, "Hi Dad," and a thump beside me. Rhoads arrived around two, and at six complained that Pierce was kicking him in the face. Lanie slept downstairs.

The next day she asks me how I'm doing. "OK. Why?"
"I dunno. You seem sad."
"I am sad."
"I am too. Let's talk about it."
Goodbye kiss and hug follow. Then exeat. Whither?

Why shouldn't I be sad on the edge of losing everything I ever dreamed of? Can I go on? Oh yes, trying to give two beautiful kids the world they deserve. Will it be fun? Not for a long time. And sadder still to hear how sad Lanie is.

On the job front I have leads but no income—Realhub, Communications Asia and another start-up still to be funded.

8/30: The Gospel yesterday from Matthew assured us we would all be given our crosses to bear, even as Jesus was. "He who takes up his Cross and bears it may enter the Kingdom of Heaven; but He who refuses it will not." Words to live by. Let me look to St. Edmund Campion and do it cheerfully.

9/1: Over dinner Lanie says, "I don't know what I think. Maybe we're doing this too fast. Let's not see Dr. Lampert. It's not helping."

When I suggest a New York date she says, "Maybe we should," and we set it for next Wednesday. We'll have to see what, if anything, it all means.

Other friends have serious problems with wives that are bi-polar or com-pulsive-obsessive. One actually accused him of sexually abusing his daughters and slept in their room for a year until even her family could see she had cracked up. He stuck it out, got her help and they flourish. So I know improve-ment is possible.

9/4: Big day for Rhoads. He went off the diving board for the first time, gently nudged by my younger brother when he hesitated. "Uncle Peter helped me," he explained later. Still looking more tadpole than human when he swims but enjoying himself thoroughly.

On Labor Day, Pike Talbert (ice-packed and back-wrapped) and I played the doubles finals against the Pohly brothers, Rob a former Yale number one, and Mike a good player as well. We had to be considered the underdogs giv-ing away 40 years or more, and I contributed greatly to that status by losing my serve to 3–4 *and* 5–6. Somehow, we climbed back into the tiebreaker though and won it going away. The second set was scruffier with serve breaks all around and Mike getting tight. We won 6–3. The tournament is now called the Wm F. Talbert Doubles, after Billy's friend Dick Schmeelk gave a cup in memory of Pike's Dad last year.

On the last point I hit a good lob that fooled Rob and went off his rim. Before anyone in the gallery could applaud a voice rang out, "Yes!" It was my eight-year-old fan, Pierce, who had just told Lizzie Talbert, "This is match point." When the spectators around him laughed, he broke into tears of embarrassment, but before I could leave the court, he had challenged me to a singles match.

Lanie and I go back to Zarela, where we had our first date. Later we sleep on 55th Street, together for the first time in '99, whole cylinders of brain chemicals going off inside my head. "Maybe it will all work out," she says. That will be my constant prayer.

She looks more beautiful than ever, her face still unlined, her body slender and eyes soft, voice melodious when she isn't tense, and her guard against me relaxed. Can we cross the chasm that has grown up? I hope so.

The boys chase the Monarch butterflies high into the sand dunes on the weekend, and reeds grow yellow.

10/6: Pierce's start in school is as troublesome as always: Lack of focus, misbehavior, missed homework, disorganization.

Summer shifts toward Autumn, hurricane season roiling the surf. Here ashore we are beset by fog and reduced visibility. Leave my family intact, that's all I ask.

10/7: Lunch with my childhood friend Susanna Porter, doing wonderfully at Random House. Tell her the long, strange tale of our near separation and renewed effort to work at marriage. In the course of narration, I say that I had

never had an affair. Susanna, listening intently till then, cuts in, "Did she have
an affair?"

"Lanie says she hasn't, and of course I take her at her word."

But something in the way Susanna says it, as if she might know something
I don't, lingers in my mind.

10/24: We dedicated the new Hunt Club squash courts to Treddy yesterday
evening. Our great friend, Percy Douglas, president of the University Club,
came out for the occasion.

It was a good night with an exhibition by world champion Gary Waite and
delicious grub and drink after. Even Lanie enjoyed herself at the Club, and
that's saying something!

10/25: Incredible moment in the economy when Spencer Stuart has over
100 executive searches ongoing for CEOs of dot coms. How can it last? Only
if these companies truly take off.

10/28: I went down to the unveiling of Kristen Jones' "Metronome," a
whimsical, steam-spewing brick inlay on the new building at Broadway and
14th on the south side of Union Square. Her parents and sister, Jeanne, my
old love, were there, beautiful blonde hair shorn short now. It was the first
time I'd seen her since 1987. Cultural Commissioner Schuyler Chapin dedicated. A happy occasion, and good lunch with Joe Tobin at Veritas after, in
from San Francisco, wonderfully direct about cousin Nion's hopes to buy
Chronicle Books: "It will just go to the highest bidder."

Lanie is in town for the night. Pierce announces he's too old to sleep with
me. Rhoads comes in at 5:30 hiccupping and tells me his dream with wonderful transparency. I ask him what he wants to be when he grows up. "Just like
you . . ." Ah yes. Poor deluded sweetheart.

Just like me . . . 47, fighting for my professional life, falling behind on
taxes. Not enough hours in the day to work, let alone parent or husband,
falling behind on the treadmill, and seeing the future through a glass darkly,
when I can glimpse it at all.

Hallowe'en: Rhoads is the Pokemon Pikatu. Pierce is an Alien, too old for
the kids' party, so he and his buds get caught by Fluffy Lynch invading her
Holly House property on the premise that a witch lives there. Taylor Foran
was good enough to mention this hypothesis to Mrs. L. who snorted, "Very
funny," before expelling them.

Jim Higgins was the last of our company to be fired from Fox this week.

11/2: Even as the Celebrant rather pathetically tried to lead us in "When
the Saints Come Marching In," yesterday I felt strengthened to be in the congregation's presence, and today, All Souls, comforted by how close they all
are, especially those I have loved and been loved by, even as the leaves turn
brown and fall, and the crows' heckling caws rise again.

The leaves are mostly off the trees, reeds and hedges thinned, in the morning there's a pumpkin-colored patch of sky out east where the sun struggles to lift itself, and I know how that feels . . .

11/10: I saw Dr. Lampert alone today, who made extensive encouraging comments on the progress that seems to have been made. Ascribed parts of it to my presenting as more manly and less "schmeilly" (Thank you, thank you, Doctor). When I spoke of waking up at 3 a.m. in a cold sweat and thinking, "I'm fucked," he said, "CEOs of the biggest corporations in America wake up and think they're fucked. It's widely reported. What you should be focused on is how successful you've been in going out and developing new interest in you."

Thanksgiving was joyous at Kevin and Sally's. Pierce and Casey exchanged exhaustive notes on Harry Potter, and then Pierce, seated at end of the table, yelped, "I don't want to sit here. The person who sits at the end has to pay the bill."

I took Pierce to the Giants game and gave him a good time while I inwardly wished we were watching on TV. Constant timeouts for ads, gross music and foul-mouthed fans. He loved it!

Went to a wonderful BBC Films/ Miramax "Mansfield Park" with Lanie and had a sweet night after. Then an interesting lunch at the Century with Christo who confides he has not always been as pure as the falling snow, "and I think that has made it better." Really?

12/6 Rhoads was a brave expeditioner on our last picnic outing to the beach. "You follow me!" This morning in bed he said, "Mommy's the queen, you're the King, I'm the Little King, and Pierce is the *slave*."

It gloomed over night, and rain rolled into a very late dawn.

12/14: An odd, disorienting time of year, one's mental processes increasingly befuddled, as if magnetized downward. Dark dawns, low light, money woes and children's health awry. Otherwise, no problems! Seem to be perpetually multi-streaming: Doubt, Faith; Hope, Despair.

*Spin* publisher and former roommate Nion McEvoy, in from San Francisco, takes me into a 24-hour record store in Times Square and buttonholes the 6'6" salesman.

"Young man, I need your help in locating a rap CD."
"Yessir."
"I don't know the name of the group, but I remember a couple of lines."
"What would those be sir?"
*"Back that ass up on it . . . let me run it up the hole."*
"That would be the Juveniles, sir. Shall I get a copy for you?"
"Oh, I was hoping it was the Mormon Tabernacle Choir."

12/23: Christmas at the Ranch after an eight-hour trip. Johnnie Marie welcomes us all most lovingly. Calves at the windmill, riding horses, smoking cigars with Will Winston, Johnnie cooking up a storm—meat loaf, tenderloin, grits, black-eyed peas, turkey, cranberry, sweet potatoes, bread pudding and all the rest. Walking in the winter white grass I interrupt an armadillo scuffling in the brush and lose my hat in the rising breeze. Lanie and I lope into the southern pastures, my horse Toby keeping a lovely lazy canter, and two white-tailed deer bounce up a hill across a dry creek bottom. Back inside, little Leland, Will and Suzanne's son, is the star of the show, just as his cousins were in their infancy, and all is bliss.

## 2000

1/1/00: Lanie was the Belle of the Ball on the Millennium's last New Year's Eve in her outrageously pretty dress at RHC-LBC dinner dance. "Peanuts" Charles Schultz retires, and the strip will go on for at least two years with old material. Good-bye Charlie Brown!

Pierce was a sweetheart when I introduced him to my squash opponent, Gordon Ogden: "Go easy on my Dad, because he has a bad leg." I had blown it out against Adam Savin and was lucky to be able to play at all, but I couldn't push off, and surgery looms. The next Tuesday, as I limped downstairs to taxi to the airport to San Francisco, he looked at me and said, "You know, Dad, you drive yourself too hard."

"Well, Pierce, sometimes you just have to . . ."
". . . I know, for the family."

1/10: AOL purchases Time Warner for $162 Billion, the largest ever corporate merger, and like so many, not a good deal for the shareholders.

1/22: Marriage improvement continues, mysteriously. Cold snap, and all of us cuddle. Bob Dalldorf brings his son, Robbie to play all afternoon, who could have been lonely otherwise, and Pierce says, "He's NICE," with real sympathy and sincerity. Rhoads reports with gloom, "Alana's moving." First crush. Ah.

Our horse with the Elsers, Skirmish Hill, races at Aqueduct in the aftermath of blizzard, and if there are 70 patrons in addition to NYRA employees I'm amazed. Far outnumbered by the swooping seagulls over the infield. In the grandstand the West Indian goat curry cart does much more business than the hot dog stand.

Test results in and I do need surgery. No surprise. Lanie stayed in town last night after a delicious dinner at Christers and a so-so Orpheus concert. The kids were raucous and charged up when I got home and are now asleep at 8:30 a.m. Pierce and I drive to New Hyde Park to get his first trumpet. He clutched it to his chest and promised to love it like his own child. He complains I'm away too much and says, "Daddy, I need to have my time with you." Helas!

Little Rhoads is now given to exuberant exclamations, to wit: "I have NO idea," or, "You're givin' me a nervous breakdown!"

Life is messy, complicated but mostly happy, in a zany way.

2/1: Duck fly off the frozen pond, pheasant track across the snow, sun rising by 7 again—progress! Pierce and I discuss our ski trip over his breakfast bar and banana. I watch him crunch his way across the icy surface of the snow to the school bus as the saintly driver, Cindy, waits patiently. I return inside to write when shortly after a voice upstairs cries, "Is anybody home?" Rhoads descends, cheeks ever so red, another Game Boy day ahead, gives me a kiss, takes his sippy cup, and begins to play, sitting in my lap. One feels unutterably blessed.

2/21: Crested Butte again: Pierce and I agree it would be better if Rhoads and Mom were here, and Rhoads was hurt, but in the absence of Lanie coming it was impossible to keep watch on the two of them. PP is raring to go and did well on the slopes. Afterwards, he approached and asked, "Dad, would you care for a game of Monopoly?" He promptly routed me at that. Darling boy, starting three things (Monopoly, TV and video game) at once, he starts to put on his sneakers instead of boots, then loses his hat. He had two dreams last night. In one he was skiing and trapped in an avalanche. In the other Rhoads had started skiing and flew off a hill and cried. "He was all right, but he fainted." Sounds of severe anxiety.

George Gilder: "If a brain cannot function without a human mind, how can a computer be expected to function without a human mind?" The overthrow of the Materialist superstition, although GG will inevitably be attacked as a sentimentalist.

Still, the inability to find "mind" in all autopsies performed indicates it is not in the brain; machines have always and will always need designers, and man too may therefore be the beneficiary of intelligent design.

Alas and alack. As I scan the Net for news (no newspapers of worth being available here) the resignation of our friend and neighbor Dede Brooks from Sotheby's after 21 years is unexplained but foretells bad news. Dede was a star at Farmington, the cousin of one of my best childhood friends, Tommy Dwyer, who died at his Citibank desk aged 36, and husband of Mike, an infinitely more gifted tennis player than I who was good to play with me for several seasons and then saddled me with the tennis chairman's job at our little club. After Princess Di and Dodi's fatal crash, Dede cancelled the Fayed auction against Fayed's will and said, "Sometimes your inner moral compass just takes over and tells you it would be wrong to proceed." Hope she has been listening to it . . .

Pierce confides to me at dinner, "Dad, you know, when we moved to Long Island, I thought I'd have to learn a new language."

Pierce handles the Houston slope with ease and later gets to the top of the more difficult Paradise. That night we eat in town and run into Sally, his summer camp director, six weeks shy of her second child, on her birthday at Le Bousquet. Pierce gives her a huge hug, doubly returned.

In my dreams I think I am back at 50 Cedarhurst Avenue, now somehow morphed into a combo of my great grandfather's place, Eastview, and his cousin Mother Butler's Marymount College in Tarrytown. Mother refuses to assign us rooms until she gets a count of house guests. At the same time the place and all its memorabilia is to be sold. "Mom can move in with us," I say to Lanie. "Jamie," Lanie says sweetly, "Your mother died five years ago."

Another great day on the mountain, cut short by blizzarding, so we watched the delightful "Eat, Drink, Man, Woman," by An Lee.

3/1: End of winter. Moderation if not mildness in the air, yet still aways to Spring. I'll be 48 years old on Saturday, older than all but Dad lived to be in the last, sad generation of MacGuires.

3/7: A pleasant birthday. First shad roe of the season for lunch and then drinks chez Thornton for FW and Alice Pearce. Lanie cooked a delicious turkey family dinner topped off by an obscenely good chocolate cake. Now light by six again and a succession of clear dry days means many walks to the water where the swan look curious and happy for the company.

3/10: Partial meniscotomy. Feeling no feeling below the waist as I sit in the recovery room, heavily medicated. Dreams and meandering mind all night. Mozambican snakes on the river. Don Pillsbury and I are pitching some arts group on the North Shore on the joys of chamber music.

Between the valium drip to "loosen me up" and the epidural in my back I felt nothing, and Dr. Riley Williams III, a thoroughly appealing Black orthopedist, did his job well. Dario waited an hour outside for me and faithfully got me my medicine and home, where Pierce wants to know all the details, and Rhoads comes in whimpering, "Daddy, I'm scared." Before long, he is eager to play with my "crunches."

The night before I had visited my old Portsmouth classmate Miguel Gomez, up from Costa Rica after eight years to have his gall bladder removed. He has a lovely wife, Ileana, with their third baby on the way. "*Jaime*, I can kiss you, but I can't make love to you." A tender greeting indeed. He was still in pain and will have to watch what he eats and drinks for the rest of his life. He still intends to play polo though, so his hopes are high.

Rhoads on a rainy March morning opens the bedroom door slowly enough for us to disport ourselves, looks at us with sleep-filled eyes and asserts, "I want to be in the middle." When settled there, he asks, "Why are you guys so naked?"

George Gilder assures us that the literature of our time is not being written in novels but in software in Silicon Valley and Seattle.

3/17: Dressed the children in green, and off to Locust Valley to take my 80-year-old cousin, Gen Moore, to Saint Patrick's lunch. Her "new" house now 10 years old though I have never been there. It's a pretty yellow cottage near Piping Rock. She is older, beset by essential tremor, slightly speech-impaired, and with the beginnings of osteoporosis, but wonderfully jolly.

Gen is the family historian and full of anecdotes about great grandfather Butler and other prominent early twentieth century Irish American families in New York. She scoffs at the idea of calling them the First Irish Families (FIFs in author Stephen Birmingham's pretentious phrase in his book *Real Lace*) and laughs uproariously recalling her Aunt Dorothy hiring a genealogist to trace the family's links to the Earls of Ormond at Kilkenny Castle. In due course the gentleman was sacked for lack of performance!

Fawzi Mustafa is OK after radical mastectomy. Brother Schuyler comes out of his thyroid operation well too. I fill my knee cuff with water and walk the garden with our gardener P.J. O'Rourke. Winter burn has claimed quite a few plants this year. We fill the kids' bike tires with air at the gas station, play Monster with the monsters, read Rhoads Maurice Sendak. He says "This night" for "tonight" these days, like a character out of J.M. Synge.

Money Hunt, Register.com, razorfish, etc. Where will it all end up? The market seems to be poised, wondering the same thing, but the hype goes higher and higher. At a healthcare conference in Miami everyone remains bullish on the web. I run into my old JV football teammate E.J. Dionne with his wife Mary and three kids by the pool at the Fountainbleu. Also enjoy a good dinner of stone crabs and snapper with Denis and Joanna Hector, my oldest and best Miami friends. Enjoying "Consilience" by Edwin O. Wilson though not persuaded by it. Forty million years of evolution has only brought the brain and mind so far, and there are whole realms of being to which we have no access yet and likely never will. It is the height of pride and self-delusion to presume otherwise.

4/3: Back to the still, still born spring. Pierce goes to grandmotherly therapist Dorothy Martyn who feels much of his anxiety comes from Lanie's and my tension. No doubt true. "I can see you want to make me feel comfortable," he tells her at their first meeting, the first nine-year-old ever to do so. I give him his first golf lesson that weekend, and Dave the pro cracks up at Pierce's running commentary on his putt's progress past the hole. I biked with the boys and at Rhoads' request arranged an April Fools "pwank" for Lanie. Later we look at pictures and Rhoads says with conviction, "That couldn't be when I was two years old, because I didn't get my curly hair till I was three."

The day starts in a delirium of depressed tremens and explodes into a rash of disorientation. There is Spring fever in the city's precocious microclimate, so far ahead of the suburbs. I fight through traffic to the Chamber Music Beginnings concert of Cuban and African music, and all is transformed as a sea of young black faces is stilled by the sounds, their bodies stop twitching and eyes light up. Afterwards I walk with heroic but failing soprano and Harlem School of the Arts founder Betty Allen to our education committee meeting and then enjoy the David Smith sculptures on Lincoln Center Plaza. Later I cooked out on the grill for the first time, and the next day I drove Rhoads to school, stopping to buy petunias for his class en route. He burst with pride and joy carrying them into the classroom.

Life laughs out loud at us, and we issue half-hearted, rather hollow chuckles in return.

4/14: Lanie is back, rested and happy. Rhoads has gone on a rampage and fallen asleep before dinner. He surfaces at 2 a.m., cuddles and is seemingly asleep when Lanie suggests we go to his room to make love. Immediately he cries out, "I wanna make love." Opens his eyes. So, we read the dinosaur book, and such are the joys. Over sorrel soup at dinner in their attractive Brooklyn Heights apartment with a wondrous view onto the harbor, a fellow guest asks Sir James Murray who were the world's most interesting people. Without a moment's hesitation he replied, "The Scots," with emphasis, a truly hilarious assertion.

Sunday, straight from Palm Sunday Mass, Pierce collected snails at the beach and raced them against each other. Songbirds and the sound of crashing waves lulled me to sleep later in the afternoon. Around five I walked around the Isle of Wight, the first soft evening of the year. Pierce and Lawrence were playing in the Madsen's backyard, the Bowdens were gardening, Ed Reitler was playing ball with his nephew on the field, the Keatings bicycling *en famille*, Tovy barking, a peaceable but noisy kingdom reborn in the Spring.

4/19: I read a well-crafted article by Jason Epstein on how the web will enable the return of small, autonomous publishers with a funny digression on Random House's six parking spaces in the courtyard of the Villard Houses, and when Cardinal Spellman arrived one day to offer his poetry manuscript, Bennet Cerf agreed to publish it "as a neighborly act and to protect our parking allotment."

Good Friday 2000: I closed on the lot next door this week for a shocking amount of money, but if we can make it all work, we'll have a nice piece of property to expand on. Ivillage is down from $120 to $10.

5/7: Consulting in the west coast tech bubble, I leave the squabbling entrepreneurs of San Ramon to get home in time to see Rhoads open his new computer game on his fifth birthday. Fugaisi Pegasus romps in the Derby, and the Bowdens and Burgers come to dinner, Margo excusing herself early and wobbling out. Off early in the a.m. to NCTA in New Orleans again, too rushed. The outpouring of mourning at Cardinal O'Connor's death was moving, especially among the Jewish leaders to whom he reached out. When I call home from the raucous cable convention Pierce tells me of his single and run scored in his team's come-from-behind Little League victory, and Rhoads gets on and sings, "Hello Daddy, best Daddy in the whole wide world!" Wrapped around his finger.

I was driven back home from the airport by a Rumanian cabbie who tells me his story: here since 1982, lost his love when she went to Germany in '80 and fell in with a pimp, married and had a kid. She is separated now and he still loves her but she won't give him the kid he wants to heal the hurt, and he's not sure he can look at the pimp's kid and what will happen at that child's wedding when the father shows up and my cabbie breaks his neck. . . . Meanwhile he has a 25-year-old friend in Rumania who will give him a kid but he's still obsessed with the other woman . . .

The poor guy sounded deeply wounded, talking this through at 1 a.m. as we sat in my driveway, and I wanted to bring him up to talk to Lanie. Terrible pain, and one felt as a priest, but not much more to say except urging him to keep going forward.

Sweet dark scent of blue-gray lilac perfumes the room and intoxicates the air as the May rain falls and the breezes blow. Chris MacGuire attends Pierce's school concert and listens to him play the trumpet. Saturday was Casey's First Communion in Rye, and she looked angelic. Lanie is angry and was throwing up all night. She apologizes but Pierce is tense as a result.

5/17: I said goodbye to Sam Pekarne yesterday, a humane and gentle man and a good dentist. Rhoads is up all-night rushing in and out, wanting to play "Freddy the Fish," whatever that may be, merry little maniac.

The Chamber Music Society's free Beethoven cycle is a great 2000 gift to the city with Alice Tully Hall crowded with folks who seldom come to concerts. In my row there was an Orthodox Jewish family with seven kids, three under four years of age, and they were all serious and most attentive.

We had a family dinner for Rhoads' fifth birthday with much hide and seek outside. Later Pierce discovers "The Spy Who Shagged Me" on cable while the grown-ups eat, and his Aunt Julie Roach-like cackle (which Dean compares to his father unfairly!) shakes the house. Moronic Austin Powers scatology, perfectly age-appropriate for the audience.

5/24: The lights of Broadway dimmed last night for John Gielgud, dead at 94. He acted till the end, though retired to the country. "I can't bear to come to London anymore; every street is filled with memories—Peggy (Ashcroft), Ralph (Richardson), Olivier, etc. All gone. Thank goodness Alec Guinness is still going strong."

Grandson of Kate and grandnephew of Ellen Terry, he had the history of the English theatre in his genes, and a particular love and attention to set design, costuming and make-up. The TV special "The Ages of Man" was inspirational to me in the '60s. And what a thrill it was to come down from Cambridge and see Ralph Richardson and he do Pinter's *No Man's Land* with Denis Hector in from Stuttgart in 1974. His late work, whether as Arthur's butler, the snobbish Trinity don in *Chariots of Fire*, Jeremy Irons' father in *Brideshead* or *Prospero's Magic* was exceptional, yet all of his work was exceptional. And he was a hard worker. Valete.

At Little League beneath the Atlantic Beach Bridge, Pierce makes two good plays in the field and beats out a grounder for a single. One Dad, short, pug faced, in black shorts and t-shirt starts conversation with, "What do you do, like Wall Street?" I cringe inwardly but he turns out to be a hell of a nice guy and second-generation meat distributor at the Gansevoort Street market. Another Dad runs a gas station on West Broadway, and the coach is a lawyer at the Queens County courthouse. I am the only one without a key chain fixed to a belt strap, a knife or other tool, tattoos and a beeper.

Barry Humphries as Dame Edna had me in convulsions of laughter at the Booth. Then Lanie and I went to a very good film of Hamlet in modern dress, set in NYC.

Driving to church on Sunday morning I see Bob Baldridge, Priscilla Schmeelk, Sue Gatehouse and Art Murray. A story in each. Bob is older but over his severe shingles of a few years back, after which he had to give up jogging. Priscilla is a force of nature and frequently very funny. She was Dick's secretary at Salomon Brothers originally and now the mother of two and stepmother of many more. But it hasn't always been easy. Suzie is our slightly daffy neighbor and fragile soul, but unfailingly cheerful and especially generous to my adoring children. Artie is getting close to 70 now and looking fine.

First morn in June and the orange orb burns through a cloud wall to the east, rising over the now green marsh. Two swan feeding on the hassock, a gaggle of geese on Crooked Creek, a pair of duck rise off the water in tandem reminding me of a famous photo of long ago of Pete and Dolly Bostwick taking a fence together on horseback in Aiken.

Yesterday was spent in a dentist's chair having a new crown drilled, designed, ferruled, collared, clad, machined, impressed and the rest. I felt like a refugee from *Marathon Man*.

Rhoads strikes gold at church by rummaging beneath our pew until he finds someone's long ago thoughtfully adhered chewing gum and spun it out in messy threads.

Jeff MacNelly, a son of Cedarhurst and my Camp Monadnock counselor, died at Johns Hopkins Hospital where he was being treated for melanoma. A genius and three-time Pulitzer Prize winner for his cartoons once Neal Freeman began syndicating Doug Martelle and him, but also a sweet man with a wonderful, slightly off-center, satiric wit. 53. My brother Kevin's Lawrence School classmate. Far too young.

Dorothy Martyn tells us some of Pierce's game narratives: "There's a little boy who really wants him to win . . ." and, "This player has a secret weapon."

"Can you tell me what it is?"
"His family."

Father's Day 2000: Lanie feels the return of feeling, she thinks. We are all red as lobsters under a broiling sun. Rhoads swims the width of the pool for the first time. At home we grill steak and the boys run races on the IOW ball field, when not petting our newest neighbor, Peter and Ince Brooks adorable spaniel puppy, Charlie.

The next week Rhoads races for the first time, solo, and does an interesting roll before the finish line. He grins delightedly at the applause for a first-place finish. That night he and Pierce serenade the MacMillens with trumpet, song ("It's a Small World") and an improvised play. Rhoads loves it but interrupts himself frequently to inquire, "Now what do I say?"

Lanie, asking after Skirmish Hill, means to say Hair House, our former nag, but misspeaks! "How did Whorehouse do?" The Jockey Club has gone pretty far with sanctioning names, but not there, yet (though I do remember a Puerto Rican stable slipping by a claimer called "Ess & Eff" some years ago).

Claudia Shearer's Mae West homage great fun. "Do you believe in love at first sight?" "I dunno, but it sure saves a lot of time."

July: To Crested Butte and our tenth anniversary.

Is it true that organically we are wholly different every 10 years? But what of looks, mind, memories, genes and even archetypes? The 80–90 years allotted us is still too short to achieve what's needed.

*The Patriot* attacked from the left and right, and not as good as I remember the Francis Marion *Swamp Fox* series on Disney, but good enough for the kids to love it.

Father Jim tells us to find Peace in the everyday at Mass at Mary Queen of All Saints, the sweet Catholic church in Crested Butte, strengthened by the simplicity and gentleness of the local mountain people's western Faith.

Messaien's *From the Canyon to the Stars* fantastic at Avery Fisher Hall when I return East. And a miraculous run on the 6 a.m. beach the next morning. Nion's marriage is sadly over. My cousin Steve Ryan and Lynni are splitting too. I was an usher at both weddings and these, plus Kip and Rhetta's divorce, make for a crappy year. But we all have to take care of our children.

7/28: Consulting for Cable Asia, WorldLinkTV, Gilder, BH.com. Who knows what is next?

Won the first renewal of the Seabright tennis match in the Millennium 7–2, with Pike Talbert playing a tremendous match. Both teams pledged to each other we would keep this, the oldest inter-Club match in the country, alive for all of the twenty-first century. They will come after us next time!

Hilary Northrop's 40th was a rock and roll dinner dance at the Cedarhurst Yacht Club, Bill Miller buying the excellent wine. The next day Rhoads and Nicky Hsieh scared Bibi to death when they tell Nicky's Mom Manali, "We're going to the back yard," and walk all the way to our house. June Finlayson was gardening as they strolled by and told me later, "I thought it was a bit strange."

"It was my idea," Rhoads said proudly.

8/8: Alec Guinness died yesterday at 86. I had selfishly hoped for one more book. In addition to being a brilliant actor he was a civilized, well-read mind and self-effacing spirit. I had the honor of meeting him while he was doing his last play with Ed Herrman in London, *A Walk in the Woods*. Valete.

There were rainbows at dawn in Saratoga, seen from the Reading Room lawn, colors radiant against dappled cloud puffs and a soft blue humid morning sky.

Lanie slices her arm on a sun porch louver while I was north, and Tyler's granddaughter (Nina Mullally's daughter, my schoolmate when young) looks after the kids as Mike Lawrence drives Tyler and Lanie to the hospital.

Later in August we have a sweet time at Glimmerglass seeing *Salome* and hearing my buddy Susan Kinsolving reading "Constellations." Our marriage seems restored, and yet, I sense emanations as we sleep at the Otesaga Hotel.

And the season of rain swells on with endless cloudy skies, wild cherries purpling the white garden chairs. The end-of-summer sun descends, and darkness falls by 8:30 on August 22nd. Sea birds fly out of the Madsen's marsh, and gulls cry noisily overhead. Yesterday's blue skies are gray today, and rain is forecast for tonight. Rhoads woke up with tales of a dream of being confronted by a crocodile who threatened him, Pierce and Lawrence Madsen. "What did you do?"

"We jumped over his mouth!"

We saw a pretty good *Julius Caesar* in the Park, David McCallum the best thing about it.

8/20: Rhoads breakdances to the Dixieland Band in his first visit to Saratoga, throws in some Korean shadow boxing and adds, as he swirls in the dust, "I'm crazy!"

Labor Day: Four-time Olympic Gold Medal Winner Janet Evans exhorted the kids to excel at their awards ceremony at the Beach today. We gave an engagement dinner for Nick Hayes and Lisa Simpson last night, Ambassador Ralph Earle branding Paul Gigot, "a right-wing nut." Diplomatic!

The next morning, I walked Pierce and Rhoads to the pond for their first day at school, the sun burning through the haze, the trees still green, years rolling on. Rhoadsie scrambled up the steps as best he could, and Pierce, growing impatient, trampled over him! Happy days. Pierce has eleven girls and nine boys in his class this year. "I hope you make friends with a few of them."

"They're all already my friends."

Later that night, after reading my younger son to sleep, I woke at 3:30 in the morning as a cloudburst cacophonized the rooftop, and the rising wind ripped rain through the open windows. Closing them throughout the house I could see the showers skip off the lane, the lawn, and even the field beyond.

And I could also feel and then see the lightning, and then the thunder that followed it. It was as sensuous a storm as one could smell, and I lingered there in the dark, savoring its scent, all else still in the silence now.

Flawless September evening, blue skies above the marsh, sea birds feeding, shadows lengthening on the lawns . . . a sweet and delicious dinner of turkey loaf and spinach salad for the family, followed by a "new" dessert that proves to be ice box cake. Memories of Theresa! Recalcitrant Rhoads, still saying "'member" for "remember," is put to bed with difficulty. Lanie stirs in the dawn, and we cuddle and stroke . . . the sun rises and dew sparkles . . . one wishes every morning could be so unhurried and sweet and hopes anew that marriage can go on forever.

9/11: Pierce, nervously, after Lanie yells at me when I suggest she take a computer course: "Dad, are you and Mom going to have a fight?"

"No."

"Good."

So we drove to the shore for the final time as the orange sun settled into the mist, and we watched the children slide across the sand, no trace of sadness in their saunterings to pool, sea and sandlot field, playing ball, skimming shells on the sea surface, climbing high into the lifeguard chair and jumping to the sand beneath. All young, spirited, part of the herd, hurrying nowhere, and sure, as we all are, to get lost at points along the way.

9/ 20: Rhoads' chatter about school and Pierce's pride in his buzz cut made me feel infinitely better.

10/10: Last swim in an ocean filled with leafy seaweed. Al Gore sighing, hyperventilating and hyper-gesticulating in debates.

On the Saturday night of the second weekend in October, a front blew through, and temperatures fell into the middle thirties, putting a hint of frost upon the impatiens that had been over-fertilized in May before anyone understood how rainy a summer it would prove to be. Now they began to look rust-tinged at the root instead of green, and the grass developed a top-furze at the root as did the clematis. But the Montauk Lilies thrived, and the marsh turned a deep shade of yellow and then quite red, which heightened the contrast with the ibis and heron, swan and duck that overflew it.

Yom Kippur in 2000 AD was a sun-stunned silence on the suburban streets as school buses stayed home and worshippers walked to shul.

Stand-up comic on Al Gore's sighing: "He reminded women of why they got Caller ID in the first place."

10/12: Sleepy-headed Rhoads, in the throes of morning languor, stuffed his fists into his pockets and shuffled toward the bus, curls blowing in the breeze, looking for all the world like his Uncle Peter at the same age. Rhoads exclaimed, "There's something in my shoe!" Indeed, there was. A cricket! And we laughed as we ran to the bus after extricating it.

10/15: Another perfect October day. On the tennis court a hunter wasp landed on Ed Yodowitz's shorts, long and multi-legged. Jack Bierwirth assured Ed that they only ate insects (yesterday he gave me some aged firewood and showed me a leafy snug hole in the wood pile that had been a mouse nest).

Rhoads biked to the yacht club and encountered Michelle Warren and dogs, who asked him who he was. "The littlest MacGuire," he called out. "It seems to be his identity," she remarked, sagely amused.

I went to Belmont for the Breeders' Cup Preview Day with Bill MacMillen and Greg Morton. Mac, 87 now and stooping slightly, said of Greg, son of his dear friend Warner, "He looks just like his father; his habits and interests are just like his father's; and when we're with him it's as if Warner never left" (Warner died at 51 but lived large, and Greg, a consummate chef and caterer, has carried on). At the track Hall of Fame trainer Johnny Nerud of Dr. Fager fame came by. "John and I are the same age and have been around the races together for over 50 years," Mac said with Scottish understatement.

"Not much time left though," the Nebraska cowboy said with a grin, and Mac concurred more grimly.

In the setting sun hundreds of insects are visible on Sue Gatehouse's lawn. Danny Lavezzo, the major domo of P.J. Clarkes, is dead at 83. A blessing perhaps in that he had been stroke-ridden and wandering around in a great-coat even in summer of late, but his iconoclasm and sense of a funny story will never be replaced. His gruff, soft touch made PJ's the joint it was, and hopefully may be again.

That old Monday morning habit got me out of bed at 4 a.m. (actually it was Rhoads sleepwalking, saying with great certitude, "It's MY Gameboy.").
I brought him to bed, and he cuddled close.

Pierce's misbehavior warranted three trips to the Schoolmarm in one day, and he confided to the lovely Elizabeth Glazer, "My Dad's going to yell at me, and my Mom will want to sit down and talk about it for an hour."

Rhoads came to bed in the early hours Wednesday night but snored loudly, so I carried him to his room. Stumbled back in at 6 a.m. and protested, "I woke up in my room. Why?"
A grievous affront!

10/23: The *Lion King*. The Walt Disney theatre magnificently restored. Julie Taymor receives criticism by some of my avant friends, but she has done great work for kids here, and it resonates.

Rhoads brought in stuffed animals this a.m. and said, "Mama Bear wants to sleep with you, Baby Bear wants to sleep with you, and I do too!"

10/26: I woke weary, sun only very slowly seeping south of the bedroom at 7:04 in this last week before the clocks turn back. "Do you want me to put the children on the bus?" Lanie asks sweetly, having not gotten back from *Fidelio* until past midnight, and I say no and rouse to wake, dress, comb and feed them. Then back to bed in the fog-shrouded dawn, a few sun strands highlighting the yellow and rust covered leaves, as sweet a way to start a Thursday morning for two busy people as could be imagined.

All Saints, 4:48 a.m.: Pierce goes on a Dennis the Menace spree, dumping newly bought bubble bath down the drain, spreading Lanie's bath crystals on the floor, throwing cereal around the TV room until it looks like hamster litter, cutting his hair with scissors and breaking the light bulb in the bathroom by jumping up and slapping it, "shaving" and leaving an exposed blade on the floor. Then, after the Hallowe'en Parade at school, he jumps into a leaf pile and emerges sans glasses. Despite all, Lanie is calmer and loving. A miracle. Onward!

11/1: Lanie totals the jeep turning onto Sage Avenue too quickly, as a pregnant driver, one of Jim Daly's daughters-in-law, coming on is looking at a map to find the Daly house. All are safe, thank God.

11/8, 5:55 a.m.: Still no President! Gore 249 and Bush 246, with three states left to call—Florida, Wisconsin and Oregon. Both are at 48 percent of the popular vote though Gore has a 200,000 vote lead. Urban democrats,

Labor and some Naderites appear to have swung toward Gore late, and he deserves credit for that. Bush coasted and should be castigated for so doing.

In the worst abuse of the electoral process in history, all of the networks called Florida for Gore early. Around 9:30 p.m. they reversed themselves.

11 a.m.: The Democrats are flying in 75 lawyers to Florida, Professor Dershowitz and Rev. Jackson preceding them with invective.

Jogging down Sage Avenue this morning, ruminating on the diabolical potential of the election from every side, and contrasting it with the beauty of the November dawn, duck kerplopping off the pond and fluttering into the air, a black Town Car sidles up to me and its impeccably liveried driver bids me go 'round to the passenger side. It's Fluffy Lynch, aka The Witch of Holly House, looking lovely at 84 with her fine features, immaculate coif, dark glasses, and laden in mink, en route to Bermuda.

"Good morning."
"Good morning. Jamie, I'm sorry I haven't gotten back that paper of yours.
    I've just been too busy. I'll do it on the 17th."
"No rush. It will take me another two years." (In the event it took four to write
    the Club history I had asked her to contribute to).

She laughed warmly, we said goodbye, and she was off. Ending of an era. Known to the young as the recluse she has become, she is in fact a sweet-natured, beautiful and generous soul, of character and breeding as we used to say, and for me a link to a life long past, however seldom I spy her these days.

11/10: Election Update. Gore dispatches Warren Christopher. Bush sends in Jim Baker. The battle is joined, and troublemakers abound. Bush's lead is reduced from 1,770 to 365. Lanie is angry and adrift about it all, in her operatic, mineral bathed glaze.

Thanksgiving 2000: Freezing weather brought frost and Lanie woke exhausted and sick, throat closed. Connecticut would be a bridge too far. A shame, but she has been on the downward slope.

I took the kids up and they rejoiced to romp with their cousins, Tyler, hair as eccentric as Pierce's, and beautiful Casey and Clay. Rhoads said Grace, and Pierce shocked Casey by asking whether her parents had told her about the birds and the bees. Later there was football on the golf course on a gorgeous day. When we returned home Lanie was fully recovered. In the aftermath I worked with Pierce on the Birds and Bees, but suspect I was too theoretical.

11/30: On this Saint Andrews Day I do feel kinship for James Boswell, who suffered from fits of depression so deep they could only be relieved by insensible drunkenness, whereupon in his euphoria he would get laid with a lady of leisure and then be beclouded by feelings of guilt over his wife and bairns in Scotland, and repeat the cycle, save for an occasional trip to Tyburn Tree to witness a gory execution, after which he would feel just fine, for a while.

12/10, 6:20 a.m.: Back home from the cable TV convention in New Orleans. I bought our Christmas tree with the boys yesterday, set it up and then we played football in the back yard. Court struggles over the election drag on but are closer to the end.

12/12: I sent Pierce to bed for making a mess of the kitchen with play dough for the second time tonight, and as a result he wakes in the morning of his own accord and happily rested for the first time all year. His inner clock does not click in at night, and his mind races.

Two very bright and well-intentioned orthodox Jewish neighbors, Aaron Felder and his father Simon, come to see Bill MacMillen and me with their Internet health payments business plan, and I write my Gilder plan for 2001.

12/14, 5 a.m.: A very dark and rainy night. Slow falling rain with no letup in sight. The very heavens weeping in catharsis. Vice President Gore went before the nation with family and the Liebermans beside him and, more than graciously, indeed, valorously, conceded. "And this time I will not be calling him back." He was the winner in the popular vote by 300,000, loser in the Electoral College by 4 (271–267).

Bush addressed the nation at 10, asked for conciliation and our prayers, a good start.

12/26: Christmas in Texas, icy-limbed mesquite standing stolidly in the pastures. A winter storm roared out of the east.

Comedy of ranch life sweet as we hunker down for third day of exile with roads all over north Texas too dangerous to drive on.

*Chapter 5*

# Losses, 2001–2004

Resolve to make it better for and with Lanie, family, country and God for 2001. We'll see.

1/9: iTunes is launched.

John V. Lindsay is dead, mayor of Fun City in the '60s. That was an exciting election, too, against Democrat Abe Beame and William F. Buckley on his right. Lindsay was a terribly handsome, terrible mayor. "Mayor *Linley*," as Transit Workers Union head Mike Quill insisted on calling him in his hard as nails Irish brogue, as he brought the city and Lindsay to his knees with an extended, paralyzing strike. Lindsay brought in bright people, but their policies undermined and sent into exodus the City's outer borough middle classes. He was a nice man. When my best friend growing up in Cedarhurst, Lars Potter, returned Margie, beautiful, tall like John, and dark brown-haired, to Gracie Mansion at 3 a.m. and somewhat the worse for wear one night, the detective on duty made him wait after Mrs. L. came down, gave Lars a dirty look and got Margie. Then the Mayor descended in his paisley bathrobe. "I'm not very happy about this," he began so the ladies upstairs could hear, without bothering to conceal a sparkle in his eye and proceeded to ask Lars how his studies at St. George's were going. They had been at one of Howard Dean's toga parties on Park Avenue before stopping at Mike Malkin's for several Black Russians after. Enough to make anyone sick.

A wonderful moment re-entering the Stable Lane house from the airport at dark: a sparrow nestled in the Christmas wreath on the door is startled and takes flight. Rhoads calls Christmas "the best ever" and that makes it all worthwhile.

1/26: Billy *Elliot* a touching little film about a Newcastle miner's son who discovers a love of dance. *Crouching Tiger, Hidden Dragon* another success for An Lee, whose *Ice Storm* I admired in its very coldness. A pair of hooded mergansers on the pond, teal and blue heron.

2/6: We went to Pizzelati Lumber in Inwood to acquire linseed oil and talked of old times in the IOW. I showed Pierce how to oil his baseball glove just as Dad showed me, and his father had shown him.

Rhoads with conviction: "Bibi says you and Mom should come home every night. I get scared when you don't, and I want you to."

2/23: Pierce's 10th birthday spent at Mars 2112, a theme restaurant with rides at Broadway and 51st Street. He and Rhoads loved it, and the next week we went south to Lago Mar in Fort Lauderdale with the Hectors, where we enjoyed the little resort, cool mornings, green palms, wide beach and pelicans flying overhead.

3/4: 49 today and all is in transition. Mom used to say that Life Began at 40. How about 60?

3/10: Then skiing in the Berkshires with Pierce the Younger, pushing the envelope at every turn. Finally defeated by Lucifer's Leap but recovers and improves. We move along, enjoy ourselves and get back to Long Island to see tufts of green emerging in the Isle of Wight's salty air.

3/16: Meditating on his favorite subject, Rhoads today asked, "Why can't Mommy have milk in one bosom and grape juice in the other?"

3/25: Underwhelmed by re-reading *Dubliners*. The narrating persona is often priggish and overwrought. And yet out of it emerges, at the end, "The Dead," a masterpiece of description and introspection, and the knowledge that we can never truly know the mind of another. Also admired the frank description of Gabriel timing his movements to nail Gretta—why is it always the man in our evolutionary plan who has to initiate?—only for the memory of Michael Fury to intervene, and Gretta to descend into mournful sleep.

Then Joyce's great act of imagination: Gabriel's imagining his Aunt's approaching death, and all of theirs, himself joining the legions of the dead, even Michael Fury in his country churchyard, in beautifully poetic, deeply affecting language.

3/27: Lanie is off to Europe. I reviewed my grade school report cards. I seem to have been on target until 6th grade when I veered off course. "Irreverence and smirkiness in tone can be amusing in small quantities, but there is a time for sincerity too," said Harvey Murdock, a tweedy Californian sailor, who was earnest and well-meaning in his gay way.

Other recurring themes include being too boisterous with smaller boys and hyper-critical. Pierce is showing these signs as well. The kids wouldn't sleep last night because I was working hard and did not read them a story or say prayers. Incredibly, they said their prayers together on their own. When we were young it was Nanny who taught us our prayers, and Mom and Dad, however Catholic, NEVER said them with us.

Father Paul at church quotes the former Archbishop of Canterbury: "The world is like a department store where a mischievous soul has snuck in and rearranged things so that all the most worthless things are the most expensive, and that which is truly priceless costs nothing at all."

All this put me in mind of my first years at a Catholic boarding school, Portsmouth Priory in 1966–1968:

We weren't due at Portsmouth until 6 p.m. my first day that September, but Mother was an early bird and got me there by noon. When we got to St. Bede's she knocked on the housemaster's door, and a mellifluous voice bellowed, "COME." I opened the door and saw a middle-aged man in the Benedictine black habit with precisely parted but thinning grey hair seated at his desk. He was holding a black lamb and feeding it milk from a baby bottle.

"Come in, dear boy. Why hello Joan, so good to see you."

We sat on the sofa, as Father Hilary continued to feed the lamb.

"Very rarely a ewe will have triplets, and then there's no room at the inn, so we have to feed the odd man out. It's even rarer that one of them be black. His name is Formosa. Here, why don't you feed him? I'll look for your room assignment." He plopped Formosa on my lap and gave me the bottle before I could protest. After a minute he looked over and said firmly, "Jamie, one must support the head while feeding."

I did as I was told as he consulted his list. "Ah yes, just as I thought. Murray. Marvelous!"

Father Hilary—sun-tanned at the end of summer and surprisingly strong, carried my bags to my room and gave me a quick tour of the surroundings. Saint Bede's was the first piece of modern architecture to be built on a campus that had previously been burdened with stolid neo-Gothic red brick buildings, the first stage of a grand design that had happily been halted by the Depression. St. Bede's was made of redwood and fieldstone with large plate glass windows surrounding an inner courtyard that suggested a contemporary cloister. Father Hilary said something that sailed way over my head about it being a "Fifties restatement of International Style," and that his friend George Nakashima had designed the wonderfully abstract but tree-like wooden furniture. I just knew I liked the sense of openness and the abundance of natural light in the building.

I remember every detail about the first time I entered the church at Portsmouth, from the flagstone floor to the sculpted redwood beams, to the spun-gold wires that ran from the cross above the altar all the way up to the chapel's rafters. It was patterned on the sixth century Church of San Vitale in Ravenna, commissioned by the Emperor Justinian in Saint Benedict's lifetime.

Inside there was a sense of soaring verticality as one looked up at the great, laminated birch arches that supported the chapel tower. In January wind roared off the water and buffeted the building so that the chapel creaked and shuddered like an old ship as she tried to turn into an increasingly hostile storm.

We went through all the new school year rituals, the orientation meetings, the endless lists of very rigid rules and nearly non-existent privileges. Then classes began and with them crushing homework assignments and endless study halls, the hours of the day crammed with obligations from before dawn until ten at night.

In those days everyone else seemed to know the routine and I was constantly struggling to figure it out. I always seemed to be spilling cereal on my shirt or walking around with my tie sticking out of my open fly.

In the junior common room of St. Bede's I got to know some of my classmates. Bacardi was a scrawny and sarcastic Cuban, Raho a tough, stocky Greek-Italian, and Branson a black Boys' Club Boy of the Year scholarship winner from Columbus, Ohio. They lounged around the common room, discussing the merits of The Animals' "House of the Rising Sun" versus The Kingsmen's "Louie Louie" or the Dixie Cups "Chapel of Love" which Branson endlessly mimicked in falsetto.

Fierce literary argument also raged. Which was the coolest—Green Hornet, Metamorpho, or Spiderman?

At one point I asked, "Has anyone read *The Caine Mutiny*?"

"What kind of comic is that?"

"It was our summer reading assignment," I replied wanly, and from the way everyone else's eyes glazed over I could tell I had betrayed myself as the uncoolest of the uncool.

The most interesting thing that happened late that year was the night the Prior, an Englishman named Dom Aelred Graham, taught us how to meditate during his weekly chapel talk. Dom Aelred was a well-trained Thomist theologian who could usually be counted on to speak on some subject—how God brings good out of evil, for instance—sufficiently abstruse to lose most of us in the first five minutes. He had written a book called *Zen Catholicism*, and that evening he told us, "Put your hands together, and extend your fingers fully. Feel the pulse of one hand beat to the pulse of the other. Breathe in and out. Pay attention to your breath. Let your mind go still. Focus on a word or phrase. Let your minds relax and journey into a zone of contemplation."

The first reaction to these instructions from 220 teenagers was a good bit of giggling with frequent farting noises thrown in. But then everyone got into it, and the chapel went quiet. I remember having a detached floating sensation and, despite the increasingly bitter cold outside, felt warmer inside than I had all Fall. It was over very quickly. Then Playboy Playmates and Miss Subway bathing beauties swarmed back into my head, but that was a zone I wanted to find again. "That's the best thing that's happened at this place," Tommy said. We talked about it a lot after lights out and soon were exchanging D.T. Suzuki's books on Buddhism and C. J. Jung's *Man and His Symbols*.

1967 was a year when fifty thousand demonstrated against the Vietnam War at the Lincoln Memorial, but five hundred thousand marched down Fifth Avenue to *support* it. A vastly outnumbered Israeli army beat off the surrounding Arab forces. The Shah of Iran crowned himself, but King Constantine was kicked out of Greece. The witty Surrealist painter, Rene Magritte, whom Father Hilary called a minor genius, died. China exploded an atomic bomb. Christiaan Barnard performed the first heart transplant operation in Cape Town. And Mohammed Ali was indicted for refusing the draft with a naïve eloquence that spoke for many and infuriated more: "I ain't got nuthin' against no Viet Congs."

I had no idea how I fit into any of it.

In my second year we read from *Beowulf* and Chaucer all the way to Eliot and Pound, although Fr. Damian lingered lovingly on the sprung rhythm of Gerard Manley Hopkins:

*The world is charged with the grandeur of God.*
*It will flame out, like shining from shook foil;*
*It gathers to a greatness, like the ooze of oil crushed.*
*Why do men then now not reck his rod?*
*Generations have trod, have trod, have trod . . .*

In History of Music, Father Ambrose illustrated from the piano and with rare recordings how Gregorian chant and the melodic, one-voice music of the troubadours gave way to the *ars nova* in which two or more melodies could be combined, leading to the establishment of polyphony and counterpoint, and the flowering, in the sixteenth century, of Orlando Lasso, Josquin des Pres and Palestrina.

Bill Crimmins' course in Medieval History was more high-spirited, focusing on battles from Constantine's victory at the Mulvian Bridge in 312 through the Crusades to the fall of Constantinople in 1453. Crimmins also covered the rise of the religious orders and the growth and schisms of the Medieval Church; but with his own innate humanism he would point out that the Council of Trent (1570) had declared: "Whoever does what within him lies, God will not deny the necessities of salvation." His excitement with History's sweep was infectious. And along the way Crimmins gave bonus points for victories in athletics, which our first year was problematic since we had a *defeated* season in junior varsity football. In the last game Coach Crimmins stood on the sideline saying, "Just one victory will save the whole season." As the long afternoon waned Crimmins shifted to, "Just one score . . ." Finally, he pleaded, "Just one sustained drive. . . ." It was not to be, but he never gave up hope.

The courses Father Hilary taught that year were geared at the upper form students, but he led morning and evening prayers for everyone in Saint Bede's and gave us all talks on the need to cultivate an inner dialogue with God while living fully in the world around us. He emphasized the hopelessness of our situation unless we acknowledged our inherent sinfulness and urged us to be open to the mystery of God's saving Grace. "Thou hast made us for Thyself," he would declaim, "and our heart is restless until it rests in Thee." And as if to underscore the point he scrupulously followed the monastic horarium of prayer despite his many other duties at the Farm and in the School.

At the time, of course, I wasn't at all sure what Father Hilary did mean, or what Grace really was, but I knew he thought it was important, and that therefore I should try to understand it. He took an interest in each of us personally but had at the same time an innate sense of discretion and recognized the need for boys to work through adolescence on their own. On one occasion that Fall, however, he intervened.

I suppose he had spoken to my mother after my dismal first report card had gone out in October, and that she had mentioned my father's deepening depression. All I know is that one day he came astride me as we were walking to lunch, took me completely naturally and companionably by the arm and said, "I thought we might offer early Mass tomorrow morning for your father, that rather heroic figure."

It was not necessarily the first phrase I would have used to describe Dad, but Father Hilary putting it that way made me think anew. And I did serve his Mass, before dawn had broken, in a side altar of the school church. I had been an altar boy for several years in the little parish we went to on Long Island, but serving Hilary in the pre-dawn of the Rhode Island winter in Pietro Belluschi's understated masterpiece, the other monks saying their private Masses at side altars nearby, was a more ethereal and profound experience. I couldn't help notice the small sculpture of a salamander to the side of our altar, and, after we had finished and were walking to breakfast, I asked Father Hilary about it.

"It was recovered from the ruined Abbey of Cluny and sold by a Parisian dealer to Father Hugh at Portsmouth's founding for the express purpose of linking the new monastery school in America with the most famous monastic foundation of the Middle Ages."

Once again, the message was transmitted: Time was eternal, the present temporary, always informed by the past, as it led to a future, yet unseen.

A new era began the winter of 1968. When we came back from Christmas vacation, we were only dimly aware that a former seminarian-turned-senator was challenging a President of his own party over the government's Vietnam policy. A hirsute French teacher named Mr. Cable began wearing a *McCarthy for President* button on campus. At first, he was the butt of gentle jokes.

But when Eugene McCarthy, with little funding and no establishment backing, polled more than 40 percent of the New Hampshire primary vote that February, the campus was electrified. Throughout New England students galvanized into a "Children's Crusade." Mr. Cable, Father Hilary, Bill Crimmins and his striking but histrionic wife, Anne, gleefully joined the fray, driving us into neighborhoods of Tiverton, Fall River, and New Bedford we had never seen to collect petition signatures from and pass out bumper stickers to people we had never met. Whereas days before Tommy, Porter and I had been lamenting our animal state after reading *Lord of the Flies* or perfecting our existential funks whilst laboring through *L'Etranger*, now we found ourselves mad with meaning.

So did someone else. As soon as McCarthy proved there was significant support for an anti-war insurgency, Robert Kennedy threw his hat into the ring as well. Now the junior senator from New York, Kennedy had infinite finances and even greater ambition. Democrats were divided by the development. E.J. Dionne, a year ahead of us, saw McCarthy as a saint and Kennedy as an opportunist (as if that were unusual for a politician); others perceived RFK as the candidate with the necessary bucks and clout to run successfully against LBJ. We spent hours arguing about it in common room bull sessions.

Then in late March President Johnson, looking old and beaten, wimped out of running for re-election. What had been a civilized campaign disintegrated into a cat fight. Although Kennedy had attended Portsmouth for three years, the campus was solidly behind McCarthy. Father Hilary was the principal exception.

"Senator McCarthy has demonstrated moral courage of the first order, but he is far too inscrutable a personality and a politician to attract national appeal," Hilary said. "Kennedy, on the other hand, represents an identifiable liberal tradition that can reach across ethnic and interest groups to build a winning coalition."

My brother Schuyler married his childhood sweetheart Dean Tyndall that winter. He had returned from the Army in Germany in time for a raucous Thanksgiving engagement party at my parents' house. When he came in the front door from Fort Dix still in his uniform, a cheer rang out through the house, except in the corner where one of my best childhood friends stood. Carolyn Carpenter, whose brother George had died the previous January in Vietnam, burst into involuntary tears. It was heart-wrenching. After a period of commiseration superintended most sincerely by my mother and the other guests, the party went on, and the wedding in February was no less festive, too festive for a 16-year-old inexperienced with alcohol. I had brought my first "A" in an essay—on *The Merchant of Venice*—home to show off, but before I could I had barfed all over it. My father had to help me into the shower to clean up after the festivities. I had a lot to learn.

When in March President Johnson mandated that all computers purchased by the Federal government support the ASCII character encoding, no one noticed. We were more interested in "Danny the Red" and his French compatriots occupying the administrative offices of the University of Nanterre and setting off a chain reaction of demonstrations that would culminate with one million marching through the streets of Paris, and a countermarch of De Gaulle supporters shortly thereafter. Columbia University students occupied their administrative offices and shut down the Morningside Heights campus as well.

That was a bad spring. I had screwed up, as was so often to be the case, in my studies, and to make me focus on them as opposed to the presidential campaign Father Hilary sent me down to study hall again. When I returned at ten one night, my roommate that year, Sandy Grant, opened the door for me. He had a strained look on his face.

"Have you heard the news?"

"What?"

"They got Martin Luther King."

"You're shitting me."

"He was shot outside his Memphis hotel."

I went into my room in silence, in a world that seemed even more messed up than usual. That night I thought of what King had said in a sermon I had read in the papers just two months before:

"I don't want a long funeral. Say that Martin Luther King tried to love somebody. . . . Say that I was a drum major for justice. Say that I was drum major for peace, that I was a drum major for righteousness, and all the other shallow things won't matter. I won't have any money to leave behind. I won't have the fine and luxurious things to leave behind. But I just want to leave a committed life behind."

I promised myself that night I would try to do the same, though I had no idea how. The next night, in a debate on a college campus far to the south, Julian Bond asserted that Dr. King's death proved that America was not worth saving. Tears streamed down William F. Buckley's face as he argued in opposition, but there were few students anywhere who would have agreed with Buckley then.

My admiration for Bobby Kennedy began to grow when I read what he had to say on King's death at a rally in Indiana.

"Martin Luther King was shot and killed tonight. . . . Aeschylus wrote, 'In our sleep, pain which cannot forget falls drop by drop upon the heart until, in our own despair, against our will, comes wisdom through the awful grace of God.'

"What we need in the United States is not division or hatred; what we need in the United States is not violence of lawlessness, but love and wisdom, and compassion towards one another, and a feeling of justice toward those who still suffer in this country, whether they be white or black. . . ."

The advance man for one-time segregationist George Wallace's campaign arrived at Portsmouth the next week. Marvin George, an African American football prodigy from New Orleans, and a bunch of us decided to picket the speech. We made signs, marched around the auditorium and then out into the open air, leaving only the Headmaster, two or three other faculty and a handful of students in the place. Later Father Leo accused us of violating the Wallace supporters' freedom of speech.

"What about our freedom of speech?" Marvin asked.

"You don't have any."

"You mean this isn't a democracy?"

"That's exactly what I mean. This is a school, and those of us running it are *in loco parentis* to you boys. That means we make the rules, and yours is not to reason why. And furthermore, we offer hospitality to our guests, even when we disagree with them."

"We were courteous," Porter interjected. "We left him alone."

I tried to focus on my studies for exams, but after the long winter the weather was finally good, and I loved spending every moment I could out of doors. I played varsity tennis that year, and I can still smell the fresh salt air whipping off the Bay as the wind played havoc with the balls. You learned to aim your toss about six feet west of where you really wanted the ball to land on those windy days, and then watched the gusts bend it back. The wisteria that grew on the Manor House trellis perfumed the surrounding air. Summer was coming, but never quite arrived. I sat in classes and dreamed I wasn't there. I couldn't wait any longer, but I had to, because summer was far more patient than I.

We were drinking beer at a 21st birthday party for my brother Kevin and his Georgetown friends outside the little yacht club on Long Island two weeks later. Suddenly a girl burst from her Mustang and cried, "Omigod, I can't believe it. They got Bobby." It was the night of the California Primary, and, as Robert Kennedy had exited his victory speech in the Ambassador Hotel ballroom in Los Angeles, Palestinian Sirhan Sirhan had shot him as he passed through the kitchen. I rushed home. My mother, who had angrily called

Kennedy a carpetbagger when he came to New York to run against Kenneth
Keating for the Senate, was in tears in front of the television.

It wasn't until the following morning that we learned that Bobby Kennedy
had died. In the days that followed we lined up before dawn well east of Park
Avenue so as to file past his casket at St. Patrick's Cathedral. Later we staked
out a place on Fifth Avenue where the hearse would pass by on its way to Penn
Station after the Requiem Mass, surrounded by people of every color singing,
"The Battle Hymn of the Republic." Women cried freely; men hid their tears
behind sunglasses; even the cops on duty took frequent swipes across their
faces with their meaty forearms. City bus drivers pulled over to the curbs and
idled so that passengers could pile out and stand on the sidewalk as a sign of
respect. Whatever one might have thought about Bobby Kennedy's opportun-
ism, he had possessed a magic for setting others on fire with the possibility of
building a better world, and of uniting them momentarily, albeit by his death.

Nion McEvoy and I spoke on the phone and asked each other, "When does
it end? When does all this shit end?" And, over my parents' objections, on
a steamy Sunday soon afterwards I jumped on an early train to Washington
and joined the Poor People's March. The Mall was packed with protestors,
many of whom had been camped out in Resurrection City for weeks, and the
Reverend Ralph Abernathy appeared in coveralls, pledging to carry on Dr.
King's crusade. "We shall overcome," thundered across the nation's TV sets,
hundreds of thousands of black and white Americans with arms interlocked
singing as loudly that night as they had the day King gave his "I Have a
Dream" speech five years before. But there was a sadness to it all that would
take decades to erase.

But back to the twenty-first century . . .

3/30: Yesterday, I put Pierce on his school bus and took Rhoads to #4
public school for speech therapy testing. He is a happy little fellow who thoroughly enjoyed it all, and his lovely lady interlocutor, Dr. Devine, confided in
advance of the official results that he was "learning beautifully."

April Fools: We moved a woodpile to a better site and then took the kids to
the Club to shower. Schuyler compared Rhoads to our childhood dog, Paget,
who exulted in his monthly bath by running around hilariously as did R. in the
locker room, putting on paper slippers, applying baby powder, weighing himself,
wrestling with Chris MacGuire, and then scooting around ever more mirthfully.

Then to Cedarhurst Park where Pierce's team, the Cardinals, lost 4–3.
P. made good contact with two hard grounders and made great plays in the
field at 2nd base (my old position). The other day he looked at a photo of me
in second grade and said, "Dad, you look just like I did at that age." And the
similarities only start there. His irrepressible, silly, scatological, sometimes
smart ass take on life echoes my own at his age.

After a dinner filled with too much of Mina's Club gossip (shades of Mother's table!), Van Burger sits down in the drawing room after and begins quoting from Verdi's *Nobucco* in Italian. He has a rich retirement ahead of him.

Easter, 4/6: The Ranch is gloriously green this Easter dawn, a pair of cardinals singing in the full-leafed mesquite outside the guest house. I was up early, walked the road up to the highway in the moonlight, and my rendition of "Jesus Christ Is Risen Today," drove the cows off into the pastures below. Down in the pecan grove there are four handsome colts still suckling their mares. Over in the game preserve, Jim Bob says there are 600 lbs. wild boar. Inch worms everywhere, spinning silk from the mesquite, beetles, multi-colored bugs, the woods alive, and under the grass carpet an array of red, yellow, blue and orange wildflowers. Riding in Pasture 4 my sturdy horse Rust, 16–3 hands, lopes easily in the honeysuckled pastures. Pierce and Rhoads share Chief, and Lanie, with her beautiful seat, lopes along on a nameless Palomino.

Pierce and Rhoads enjoying their cousins—gentle Jay, towering above them and soon off to U. of Kansas, and precious Leland, making various noises but still short of speech. Lanie has suffered a nervous attack and has been bouncing twixt bed and bathrooms.

Otherwise, sweet, though distant, her feelings bottled up for the moment, but soon to explode. Sunrise blood-orange east of Denton on our last morning, I have the strong feeling this is the last visit I will make to this beautiful place.

*Plainsong* a good novel of the plains by Kent Haruf. *Speak Rwanda* an OK, multi-voiced narrative of the genocide.

Meanwhile, back on the Isle of Wight, spring came with buds bursting, and Rhoads and I scootered to the CYC. A rabbit crossed our path, and Rhoads cried happily, "One of my favorite *aminals!*"

Pierce hit a towering triple in Little League yesterday, knocking in a run and then slid into home on a subsequent grounder. Teammates lined up to shake his hand and high-five, and Pierce glowed.

5/26: A giant gone from my life. Dr. Benjamin Berliner, pediatrician, teacher, orchidist, environmentalist, human rights activist. Along with Jerry Maisel, my doctor, with bushy hair going steel gray, penetrating eyes, a craggy, wise face. He had a strong connection to Mother. Ben came to Dad depressed in his bathrobe downstairs after visiting me sick in bed and shouted, "Why don't you get out of this house and do something for yourself and your family, Phil , LIKE A MAN!"

At that point Mom, who had doubtless encouraged or assented to this intervention (a generation before they were so called) came to the door of the den and said in a quavering voice, "Ben, if I had it to do all over again I wouldn't change a thing."

And with the passion of an Old Testament prophet he glared at her and him and said, "You fool!" and walked out on them both.

Dr. Ben saved my eldest brother Philip from an asthma attack at 3 a.m. when Mom and Dad were in Florida. He told a crying Theresa on the phone, "You stay with that boy until I get there." She worshipped him ever after.

As for me, when I was four or five, I had a double hernia, a tonsillectomy, a follow up operation for scar tissue, and multiple ear infections. I missed much of school, but on Christmas Eve it was all transcended, because my two heroes, two Jewish pediatricians in a still sometimes anti-Semitic enclave of Long Island, starting out their practice and in debt, closed their office early to come see me, because I "had had a tough year." They were welcomed as the family they were, ushered into the living room reserved for special occasions, drank bourbon and smoked cigarettes. I sat on Ben Berliner's lap in my pajamas and bathrobe and felt utterly loved.

As I still do thinking of him. Like Martin Luther King, he led a committed life. May his memory be an everlasting blessing.

5/30: First Sunday evening beach barbeque, Pierce and Rhoads climb on the lifeguard stand, playing with Benton Madsen and Cuffia Reitler, Lanie and I walked down the beach, chatted with Bob and Linda Foran, a lovely couple we have done too little to welcome after they have beautifully restored their shingle style house on Bannister Lane.

This morning I jogged in a gloriously fresh breeze, showered and dressed the kids, put them on the school bus, waved and they waved back, Rhoads blowing a kiss goodbye.

5/31: Heartbreaking moment on the IOW as dear Daphne Hellmuth rhapsodizes to me of all the possibilities the field adds to developing our house and property. All my dreams! Yet I know the marriage is ending, against all my hopes.

6/5: Pierce got his yellow belt in karate last night, a great event for him. Big, lovable kid growing into his body.

The moving vans pulled up to Holly House yesterday, and men were lying idly on the grass outside as I drove by. Fluffy Lynch was at the gate and I stopped, shook her hand, told her I would miss her, and could not resist a swift peck on her cheek. "I'll miss the whole area," she replied. "Jamie, is that what I'm paying for?" Pointing to the guys sleeping. "Shall we talk to them?" "No but thank you for stopping."

Rhoads at dinner: "Mom, you know Dad has a name sometimes for you when you scream. He calls you, 'MOMSTER.'" Then, he added, "When you and Dad fight, I feel like you wish I wasn't born."

6/21: Bibi tells me that Lanie yelled at her on the street, falsely saying Bibi had told her both the washer and dryer were broken. "Fire me, Lanie," Bibi answered, "It might be a blessing in my life." Lanie backed off, but Bibi says she was so depressed she could not work. "She should concentrate on Pierce and Rhoads!" she says.

Sophocles compared love to a piece of ice held in a child's fist: The harder you hold it the quicker it melts.

But the children are a joy. Rhoads does a couple of his newly acquired front flips in the pool at the beach and Pierce heads for the surf. Later Pierce throws his board on the shore and the waves grab it, but Rhoads saves it for him and plants it safely on the sand. That will be their future, one breaking into new frontiers, the other cultivating the known world. They *will* take care of each other. Later we enjoyed a sweet night together, watching the Yankees and munching on charcoaled veal chops.

July 4th: Fireworks drifting north with the wind, spewing the burnt casings on the ground, the sand dunes erupting into fire.

*Rosa rugosa* and wild rose trimmed, crab apple succumbing to gypsy moth, cardinals flitting from bush to bush.

Goran Ivanisevic, a qualifier, wins over Pat Rafter in the fifth set, 8–6, in a classic Wimbledon final!

A Priscilla Schmeelk tennis memory: "When I first came out here everyone brought one ball to the doubles match and the WASPS all initialed theirs so that by the time you were finished playing your thigh was covered with ink."

Roseate tern diving down to challenge us. Doves fly in. Cicadas sing in the cooler dawns. And the sea! Kudzo washes ashore in the end of August glow of red clouds and pastel blue skies. A setting sun highlights the white sand, jelly fish late and miniature.

9/7: Quiet days even as the difficulty of unemployment and impending separation weigh in. I cannot remember a time when I felt more peaceful. One must be sober and stoic.

9/12: Yesterday was a terrible day. Our Pearl Harbor, only far worse. Four 757s were hijacked in mid-air. Two crashed into the World Trade Towers; one into the Pentagon; one into a field in western Pennsylvania, apparently its intended target of the Capitol aborted by passengers who rushed the terrorists that took control of the flight. Downtown tens of thousands trekked through the streets to safety, my brother Schuyler evacuating the Federal Reserve Bank to walk across the Brooklyn Bridge to the Long Island Railroad.

The rest of the family safe as well, thank God. I saw my old schoolmate, David Moran, now of Dow Jones, heading north on Third Avenue. He had not gotten to work yet. "Is 200 Liberty Street OK?"

"Jamie, I don't know if there is a 200 Liberty Street."

200 Liberty was OK. Brian Cullen was saved by being 20 minutes late to work due to carousing late the night before and watched the towers fall from his subway stop. Young Timmy Grant walked down 90 stories. Lindsay

Herkness was not so lucky. He was in early and on the phone to the Union Club squash shop making his evening game and saying he would stay put because it was the safest building in America. And Kevin O'Rourke, of the NYFD, died fighting his way up to save people.

Belinda Morrissey's fiancé called to say they were being evacuated. He is now missing, and Bebe is down there searching for him with her Dad. 2500 Morgan Stanley employees alone are among the dead, and we will know many by various degrees of separation.

I met brothers Pierce and Peter for lunch with Becky, who had fought her way from Christie's. Then we heard that the "letter" subways were running. and I took the E train to Penn Station. Got home around five and Bibi said I had to tend to Pierce. He was standing in front of CNN on the tube, watching the planes hit over and over, his face taut and eyes over-flowing. We drove to the beach on a beautiful, blue-skied, stunningly still day and took a last swim. Then we played ball on the sand and talked. He had many questions but seemed to relax a bit. Rhoads was unaware, lucky little fellow.

Very still, very starry night. Fighter jets passing by from time to time. Still deathly quiet as day dawns. A very occasional plane. No trains or sirens.

9/13: Today the kids all wore red, white and blue to school, and on the Isle of Wight ball field there was a ceremony where we held candles and sang. Ralph Howe, a hero of amateur squash and tennis past, is here from Florida for the USTA National Grass 60s with Dennis Lynch, up from Seabright. They helped lead us in singing, "God Bless America."

It was touching how many calls came from around the world this week. Sara Poland told me that for the first time "The Star Spangled Banner" was played for the Changing of the Guard at Buckingham Palace yesterday, the Queen attending.

My own memories will be of the two swims Pierce and I took near dusk, freighters on the horizon, surf jumbled, wind blowing, some jelly fish in the water amazingly late, sun sinking in the western sky, beginning of the migration as the occasional Monarch butterfly blows past, Pierce propelling his body through the water, keeping his mind off the darkness.

9/17: Tens of thousands are still stranded around the country. In the, "I thought I had problems department," a beloved Isle of Wight neighbor tells me he has a $400K payroll to meet each month and has been cheated by a partner. Meanwhile his wife is not at all well and their recently adopted child may have developmental issues. We must be strong, all of us.

9/20: The dimensions of the attacks are only now taking shape. Bush's talk to Congress declaring the War on Terror was effective. I ran into Randy Jones, stockier now than the sleek and handsome boulevardier of 20 years ago, on First Avenue en route to a funeral. "Having a tough time," he said in his ever-genial voice, "Marsh McLennan lost 350 people."

The President's best line: "The Terrorists follow in the path of Fascism, Nazism and Totalitarianism. And they will follow in that path all the way to where it ends: In History's unmarked grave of discarded lies."

9/22: Last night we told the children that we were separating just before dinner. Both cried, Rhoads so inconsolably that Pierce took it upon himself to explain. "I knew this was going to happen," he wailed bitterly. Indeed. I tried to emphasize they were not to think it any fault of theirs. It didn't work. Later we went for a ride on the swings, Pierce and I played catch and Rhoads clouted a home run in the gloaming. Later, over a turkey dinner, Rhoads insisted on saying the blessing: "This is a different blessing than I've ever said. God, why did this have to happen? Why can't both my parents be here at the same time?" Lamentations.

Sunday Rhoads told Bibi and began to cry, and Bibi told me, "I cried too."

9/27: Yom Kippur. We must atone for our many failures and ask God for his forgiveness and his mercy. We must seek to change ourselves from within even as we battle for justice without. And we must pray, and, most especially, love our children.

9/30: Our lovely Isle of Wight neighbor Sheila Brown McCarthy has died suddenly at 75 after bravely fighting cancer. I first rode on my bike to her house in Spruce Street in the village of Cedarhurst to see my classmate Tommy 40 years ago. One of Mother's favorites, always sweet, always good, always bearing up in straitened circumstances bravely until she and Jack found each other.

Father Rahilly wept in his sermon recalling Kevin O'Rourke and Belinda Morrissey's fiancé. A sense of sadness pervades the time, hanging like a mist.

10/1: Flip Tyndall died this morning, my sister-in-law Dean's Mom, ailing with Alzheimer's for years. Wonderful Grandma to Chris and Tim, she took them every weekend. She coached sports years ago at Lawrence School, but as her illness progressed she uprooted next door neighbor Dede Brooks' tulips and went out at dawn to collect all the newly delivered newspapers in the neighborhood. She was a sweet, if occasionally bitter, lady.

Another neighbor on the Isle of Wight, dear Mary Murray, died suddenly of cancer as well. Three in the same week, just a fortnight after the World Trade Center attacks.

In DC at lunch with Chris Buckley. I tell him my sad tale. Sympathetic, but, journalist that he is, Christo asks, "What's Lanie's version?"

"Thank you for asking, Christopher. Lanie's version is that on any given day I'm entitled, inflated, narcissistic, charming but shallow, alcoholic . . ."

"But JAMES!" he intones ironically with a grand sweep of the arm, "Those are all of your GOOD qualities."

I am touched at how deeply courteous my fellow travelers are to each other. The soft reassuring accents of the New York Irish conductors. 51 Dads, mostly cops and firemen, were lost at one Queens parochial school!

Jennifer says she has heard of many couples trying again since 9/11 and hopes we will too. Sweet. Rhoads' front tooth comes loose and after we make him go to bed Pierce helpfully sneaks into his bedroom and helps him pull it!

A wonderful celebration of Richard Wilbur's 80th with readings by Tony Hecht, John Hollander, Sandy McClatchey, Derek Walcott and Rosanna Warren. Good to see them all again, and the Kinsolvings. As I grow older Wilbur's craft and sterling sensibility appeal to me more and more.

Sumner Redstone is a mogul now, and I have to disclose my long and intimate relationship. When Phil used to take Vicki Tyner to the drive-in in Lynbrook in the early '60s Peter and I came along and sat in the back seat while they necked. And who owned the enterprise? Sumner and his Dad.

10/23: The iPod is introduced.

10/24: Pierce says to me indignantly re his desire to have his own on-line access: "Dad, I assure you I have no interest in becoming sexual prey." Good.

10/31: Deep, deep silence out here by the shore. The kids played catch outside and scampered happily to the school bus with Hallowe'en costumes packed in their knapsacks.

Around the village, just as one feels sorry for himself, Elaine and Tom August lose their troubled son to a knife fight in a Florida bar. John Conway, Alzheimer's advancing, now led around by Mom's old nurse, Josie; Art Murray, who just lost his wife Mary, can't wait to offer his condolences to me, and John Emery, struggling at home himself with wonderful but still imbibing Patsy, offers his good wishes, asks me to defend Nick Benvin and says of some of Nick's critics, "They seem to confuse arrogance with class."

All this going on during an intensely beautiful November weekend.

11/18: Last night was Nick Benvin's 50th anniversary at the club. A tremendous turnout of 150 to greet him. Fiske Warren said in his quiet way, "There's a good feeling in the clubhouse tonight." Nick spoke wonderfully for one so monosyllabic by day, as did Dee Dee Baker, Daphne Hellmuth, Emma Miller, Carl Saling, Bob Hart and Cindy Benvin. I looked out and saw Patsy Emery, Margie Carpenter, Van Burger, Sylvia Lynch and Helen Corroon. I could see their parents and, in some cases, their grandparents hovering above them, and I felt very much they were all with us that night, applauding along for someone who worked sixteen hours a day seven days a week for half a century, who could be gruff, but never ever said no.

Thanksgiving: Kevin and Sally's celebration was a joy as always. Clay and Rhoads compete to manufacture the biggest Sundae. Friday, we went with Jay and John Saling to Radio City Music Hall for the Christmas show with tickets given us by Steve Finch. My grandfather Casey's favorite show of the year. Drinks at the Talbert's beautifully renovated house Saturday. Lanie is due home from Paris tomorrow.

Doing homework with Rhoads this weekend I asked him, "What's a word that describes you?" He thought about it and answered with a smile both shy and proud, "Speedy." It's true, too. He's fast and quick.

12/2: Enron files for bankruptcy.

12/4: Farewell to the Whitmans at the MacMillens on Saturday night. Sandy was serene, leaning on his lovely wooden cane. Sylvia is increasingly in the throes of aphasia, bent over and speech becoming difficult. Two of Mom and Dad's best friends and wonderful to us since we came back. Good that they will have help and less to do in their Essex Meadows retirement home in Connecticut.

Pierce the elder told funny stories of the prior generation's ideas about dieting (Missy Ryan switching from vodka and coke to vodka and diet coke; Ray Stein smoking four packs a day, but, when he got a sore throat, changing to menthols for a bit).

Pierce the Younger took a squash ball slammed into his forehead by a player at Gold Racquets as he sat in the gallery most bravely. Abject apology from the poor fellow who was attempting a retrieve off the back wall.

In the midst of much pain, still the capacity for joy, as in seeing the harvest moon rise behind the old stables on a December night.

12/10: Rhoads reacted to our new reality by punching (his teacher's version) or mistakenly running into (his account) a classmate during soccer. When he arrived at the principal's office sobbing, Mrs. Glazer asked him, "How is everything?" and he answered, "I'm scared of divorce."

"You're already living through it," Elizabeth said, "So it won't be any different."

"YES, it will be different," Rhoads answered passionately, "Because Daddy's not coming to Texas for Christmas."

Lanie moved out of 55th Street, and I moved out of our bedroom and into the den downstairs.

On Friday when I got home Rhoads was laughing, and said, "Dad, guess what? Pierce punched me so hard in the stomach I almost threw up on him, but instead I did something even more powerful."

"What was that?"

"I farted."

And at our MacGuire men family dinner he says Grace, "Dear Lord, this Christmas, please let us all be together . . ."

12/21: I spend the night with two darling boys, playing with new electric toothbrushes from Ann Thornton, singing Frosty the Snowman in French, challenging me to checkers and chess. Contemplate my sinfulness, selfishness and general shittiness and wonder if I can ever change from the inside out. Can I somehow convert these cries *de profundis* to an Advent hymn?

12/23: I gave the boys the best Christmas I could and sent them off to Texas at 5 a.m. Returning home, I walked to the water and read. Coffee from Burundi and a Wisconsin kringle. A 6'4" man in London has been prevented from lighting his shoe on board a plane. Hope all are safe.

David McCallum at the Warren's cozy town house party: "Is she unhappy with you or just unhappy? In my first marriage it was years before I understood how many affairs she had had, or how many jobs I had lost. (Jill's agent would call and say, "David never works without Jill.") She was forever after me to go to a psychiatrist, and I said I really don't want to go, but eventually I did, and after ten minutes the shrink said, 'I think you need to get divorced.'"

12/25: I called the Ranch and Will answered as ever, as Jim Bob shouted hello in the background. I cooked breakfast for my childhood friend, Ross Savage, in from Minneapolis, whose Dad is dying in hospital here of Alzheimer's and prostate cancer. We then had a wonderful lunch at Sky and Dean's and a walk on the golf course after.

12/30: The kids are home and happy. I drive to East Hampton for New Year's with Rob Barnes and Chris Coy. At Mass the Monsignor preaches the four rules he was given when young by his first parish priest:

1) *Accept challenge and pain;*
2) *Stay close to people;*
3) *Know that you make a difference; and*
4) *Live until you die.*

Good advice at the end of a lousy year.

12/31: Fun at Chris and Joanne Coy's house in Sag Harbor. Superlative spread by Joanne, her sister, and Donna Zakowska, Roman Paska's longtime companion. I got Rob home in my role as designated driver by 1:20, not an inconsiderable feat! Then I drove home at 6:30 a.m. on an utterly open, frozen road. Doc Savage is dead. Ross and and his sister Joy are here to take charge.

The pictures on the wall gaze down upon me: Mother, who endured loneliness, a husband's serial sadness and alcoholism, and early death from smoking and prostate cancer, only to uphold his (considerable) heroism forever. She looks lovely and non-judgmental (which she wasn't always!) and deep. Grandpa Casey looks slightly more ready to assess the odds.

Have I honestly dedicated myself to doing all I could for Lanie and our marriage?

YES, AND I HAVE FAILED!

## 2002

January yawns into the slowest of gears after ending the most painful of years. I have never felt so blocked.

*Lord of the Rings* with the boys was stirring, but I loved *Shipping News.* Perhaps the redemption of the wounded is of particular importance to me now! Julianne Moore wonderful in voice, the music Celtic and landscapes brooding.

1/6: I made a fire and cooked for the kids, played squash with them as well, and on Sunday morning, in a pink dawn, Rhoads wakes up and asks, "Dad, when you were young, who was your hero?"

Without giving it sufficient thought, I say I don't know, maybe Mickey Mouse or Mickey Mantle, and he answers, "Well, YOU'RE my hero." I don't deserve it.

Pierce the Elder at lunch: "I can't believe you only saw Dad drunk five or six times. He would arrive home from town and call out, 'Hello Muzzy,' in that joking voice, and her face would fall."

Jane Clark, at dinner: "I don't think our parents could speak to each other the way we do." No doubt, given hers and ours.

January darkness outside and despair within. I have made a mess and must struggle on. I think of the months and years Dad could do nothing, and Mom had to wait it out. Not happy times, and yet happier times did come. All I have to do is look at Pierce and Rhoads to know that I have everything to live for. Tonight we will light the fire, sit around the dinner table, sleep under the same roof, and somehow things will get better.

1/17: Went to Ground Zero. Long lines of tourists outside Saint Paul's Church waiting to walk to the platform to see the rubble, now three stories down. Construction workers and heavy machinery everywhere. Jolly crowd at the burger joint where Jim Higgins and I lunched and touching messages of condolence from around the globe hanging on the sides of buildings everywhere.

1/21: Duck dinner at the Thorntons and lots of football on TV. Bachelor calls have replaced those to Mother on Sunday night. Kip unhappy to be alone, lamenting the inability to achieve settlement with Rhetta and missing his kids: "When you're out, you're out."

Dr. Michelle Warren, distinguished endocrinologist, on medicine at dinner: "It's a terrible time . . . the HMOs have bought our silence, and a few unqualified but highly opinionated celebrity doctors have stolen our voice."

1/29: Last night Pierce slept with me because he had the flu and was still miserable. Feeling competitive, Rhoads insisted on crawling in wearing his new boxer shorts and red pajama tops as well.

2/11: A great Superbowl as Belichik's Patriots shuts down the Rams. Would that the Giants had kept him! Good meetings on Cable Asia. Yesterday I toured Bayswater and Far Rockaway looking for signs of its resort prominence in the

1870s. None left. When I was young, I rode my bike there to dear Dr. Fink, the dentist. A child allowed to do so today would be taken from his parents who would be had up for willful endangerment. Nowadays Far Rockaway has only a burnt-out shell of a downtown, no movie theatres, few shops and most of those loan sharks or check cashing outfits. St. John's Church looking pitiable now, a temple of some kind. The office building where Debbie McTigue's Dad worked is a public services building. But the Russell Sage school and church still massive and its Tiffany windows beautiful. Across 878 I poked around the lanes where the first families of the Lawrence resort settlement lived—the Hards, Lords, Rutherfurds and Stevens. All have streets named after them though any trace of the old homes has long been replaced by post-War split-level homes. It was a melancholy but oddly satisfying tour.

2/16: Rhoads performed splendidly on International Day. It was Ireland this year (I continue to be delighted whenever Pierce wears his 2000 Israel t-shirt around town!), and Rhoads finished his dance with such a vigorous two step that he fell over backward and lost his bowler. There were blessings the kids had posted on their classroom wall. "May you have your loved ones close to you." Just so.

And a good skiing weekend after in the Berkshires. It was Rhoads' first time, and he narrowly missed deballing a very large man whose legs he went in between when he lost control on his first downhill run.

3/3: Anticipatory anomie of my 50th birthday. It rained all night and I played "War" indoors with Benton Madsen, Rhoads and Pierce. I bathed them and settled in for the night. Tomorrow I'm 50, a financial failure, or a future success? Or both?

A birthday gift most precious was the pair of swans who flew down the Causeway in sight of our house and over the marsh, huge hurling winged beasts making their way to water.

3/6: I walked the Isle of Wight and found early signs of Spring. Mary Millett's daffodils are in bloom (she was Dr. Allison's daughter, and moved away 20 years ago), as was the forsythia and Carnelian cherry by Penny Coe's kitchen, also gone from us alas, her emphysema winning out. Larry Blatte, her successor as Mayor, and the other Orthodox village trustees were most gracious when they came to her house to pay respects. Daphne Hellmuth's groundcover was ablaze, though she and Jim will be in Florida till mid-April. And so, the cycle renews.

3/10: Hilarious and profoundly happy 10th year reunion with Sy Fliegel, with whom I wrote "Miracle in East Harlem." Still at the top of his game, making schools better, fostering charters, opposed to vouchers. Carlos Medina is promoting school choice in Chile while Cole Genn, John Falco and others of Sy's old gang are charging around New York still doing the best they can to create good schools.

And a good lunch with Ray Domanico too, who ran the Center for Educational Innovation in those days and is now working for another education reform outfit. Dressed in black with buzzcut white hair. A stunningly beautiful day in Soho.

Dinner with Nion McEvoy en route to Europe, the divine Jennifer Davis and Hall Powell at Union Pacific. And the next night a sumptuous dinner at the Racquet Club for me, generously arranged by Kevin and Pierce. Four of my brothers and their wives, Tim and Chris, Brook and Bill Maher, Susanna and Jamie Clark, the MacMillens, the Crimmins down from Rhode Island, Kip from South Carolina, Denis from Miami, Matthew McCarty. What a night!

It was a year when, after three years of the most intensive effort possible to muster body, mind and spirit to preserve a marriage I had been faithful to throughout, I had to admit defeat. My business life crashed as well, and I approached financial ruin. Our beloved country, and the city of my forbears and my birth came under deadly attack; the leadership of my Church was revealed to be sickeningly asleep, if not complicit, in grave sin; and the world was wholly indifferent to my art.

And yet this night I was secured by the love of family and of friends.

I started the next rainy, windswept day with a jog along the East River. At home on Long Island that night there was lots of homework, a warm fire, baths, stories, prayers and bed. A beautiful sunrise and jog on still wet roads the next morning. Then our first game of early morning catch on the front lawn while waiting for the bus. Rhoads is now old enough to grasp several. Thrilled, he asks, "Can we do this every morning you're home?" Of course, we can.

The Met in the first sunny day of spring.

I find myself spending more time in front of the mesmerizing picture of Saint Joan by Jules Bastien-Lepage (1848–1884), painted after the loss of Lorraine to the Germans in 1871 during the Franco-Prussian War. In the picture Joan of Arc stands in her parent's green garden, pink-white roses blooming by their house, her eyes transfixed receiving the vision, and SS. Michael, Margaret and Catherine watching over her from behind. Stunningly beautiful on so many levels.

3/22: At Smitty's Superette on West Broadway, the main provisioner of our little Lawrence backwater, Antoinette, doyenne of the cash register, says to a customer, "JOE . . . You don't notice he ain't been here for two months? His wife caught him cheating—an older woman—and he's out. She served papers on St. Valentine's Day. What do you think of that?"

On the weekend I play extended catch with Pierce, whose skills have improved mightily. Rhoads romps home from Nicky Hsieh's with an athletic grace I never had. Together we watch the Oscar's as I daydream—

4/10: Lanie's 49th. I had Rhoadsie call her, he in an especially happy and grinning mood. Windswept day with a stiff easterly breeze. Pierce is grooming himself with a comb in front of a mirror, using his towel to conceal a considerable erection after showering. Growing up.

Pierce is in his absent-minded professor mode. He gets on the school bus to go home but then remembers his trumpet lesson and scrambles off with his book bag but leaves his jacket and trumpet behind! The next day we cannot find his baseball glove (turns up two days later after a Little League game in his bicycle saddle bag). To his credit, Pierce goes through life undeterred by the absence of hard wiring most of us have been given and loves beating me at squash on Saturday. When he hits a ball out of court, and Treddy, watching from the gallery, gropes downward to throw ball back into court, Pierce sweetly asks, "Should we let him bend down like that?"

And Rhoads is yearning for a Dalmatian puppy. He also says he only wants Benton and Christina at his birthday because he's sad about Grandpa. I suspect this is a symbolic association connected with Lanie's and my separation. "Mom says she doesn't like you even one tiny, teeny bit," he reported grievously the other night. It bothers him.

4/28: Must appeal to our better selves, as G. Washington did to officers considering mutiny for non-payment etc.

5/6: Yesterday was Rhoads' seventh birthday. He woke up early, singing like a lark. He wanted to go to Benton's but it was only eight, so we walked to the Little Beach. He communed with the swans and seagulls, duck and geese on a cloudless, high-skied spring morning. Then to the yacht club listening to the songbirds atwitter. Rhoads was thrilled with the conceit they were singing just for him. He made friends with the dogs and their walkers out and about. "Mrs. Lynch, do you know what day it is?"

"Your birthday."
"Right."

Peter Boneparth jogged by and greeted him with a Happy Birthday, learned from his son Neal, Rhoads' LWA classmate. On the train to town later in the day Rhoads spied J.P. Sletteland, his summer tennis counselor, with girlfriend Alison. "J.P., what a surprise!" And to Pierce's embarrassment he talked with him for the duration of the journey, generously received. In the city he gets saluted by a sidewalk vendor, picked up and hugged by a burly cop, loved the Pokemon Store and ESPN SportsZone, and was a very happy child by day's end.

5/15: Seeing Rhoads wake, eat breakfast, skip, then run across to Benton's driveway on an overcast May morning makes me feel it's all worth it. Even the most quotidian tasks are a deep pleasure so long as they bring children joy. Pierce and Taylor Foran are building a baseball field on the lot next door!

*Unfaithful* with Richard Gere and Diane Lane was haunting.

John and Dede Passeggio's spaniel, Sally, was electrocuted chasing a squirrel under Mrs. Chauncey's ancient second house on Albert Place, hitting a live exposed electrical wire this week. The community mourned. Treddy was the exception: "I didn't know what to say. I can deal with conventional grief, but dog grief is another matter."

"Weren't there dogs on Iwo?"

"If there were, we would have eaten them."

5/24: Beloved friend Gael Crimmins: "You cannot be the guarantor of another's happiness. That's THEIR responsibility."

And Bill, my Portsmouth coach, teacher and a second father in so many generous ways: "Are you still in love? Because that's hard."

When he said it last summer I was, and it was hard. But now of a sudden I realize he was speaking from his own first marriage experience and am ashamed of my obtuseness.

Memorial Day weekend I cooked veal chops outdoors. Pierce rode his bike to the village and back for the first time. Then he did not want to sleep alone so all three of us cuddled, and in the dawn as I rose Rhoads opened his eyes and murmured, "Hi Dad." Ever so sweet. I lay back down and gentled him to renewed sleep before shaving and going for the papers. The songbirds sang matins, and all was bliss.

The next morning Pierce woke at 5:30, showered, ran out for a bike ride, played basketball, and ran back asking if he could wake up Rhoads, which he did with his Palm Pilot, and then fed him breakfast, Rhoads enjoying the gentle fraternal interaction hugely.

Pierce makes a falling down catch in left field to win his Little League game at the Atlantic Beach Bridge field. My old Cambridge buddy, Haleem Lone, one-time East African junior tennis champ, comes out for a day of tennis, and he and Pierce hit it off.

*Y Tu Mama Tambien* was sexy and sensual, primitive in parts, but won me over.

Charlie Seitz drives me to the airport and tells me his grandparents, the von Balthazars, owned the coaching inn where Dee Dee Baker lives. Charlie has been driving 50 years now and remembers taking Dad to Belmont Park.

6/11: Rhoads on Father's Day night: "I like sleeping with you because then I feel safe. But I'm trying to get you and Mommy back together, because then I'll feel safer."

A tall, elegant egret is feeding in the shallow water of the beautiful marsh.

6/20: Last day of spring. We return Pierce's trumpet to New Hyde Park, then dine at the yacht club on Malcolm MacLean's excellent flank steak. The next morning, I jogged and then drove to the beach for my first ocean swim. Wonderful! But I was saddened to see only one cygnet surviving on the pond.

6/24: After years of struggle, the Hebrew Academy of Long Beach's attempt to build a yeshiva near the Isle of Wight was eventually turned back because the Village did not have sufficient sewer capacity, and the Environmental Protection Agency forbade it. Many other natural and environmental groups had opposed the plan as well. A coalition of village residents, Christians, Jews, both Reform and Orthodox, had also worked hard to preserve the zoning, and there now exists an organizational structure, trust and good will to fight off other attempts, if it is ever necessary. HALB has found a more suitable and legal site in Woodmere.

7/1: Pierce, watching Wimbledon, "I want to plan my own future. I want to go to the junior sports program for two more years and then turn pro." By the end of the next day, after one clinic and two hours in the water, he was ready to become a surfer.

7/6: Now Pierce says he won't go to Colorado without me, but he must. Hard. We have a great night at Yankee Stadium in the oppressive heat with Jennifer Davis and her kids, Jack and Lily, Rhoads leading the cheers. I played in the Moorhead Cup for what may well be the last time versus the Oxford-Cambridge team. At fifty I still know what to do, but my body does not obey my brain! Rhoads was counting the bursts at the fireworks, leaning back into me, and forcing me to lean back into Jennifer, fireworks bursting overhead. Bliss in the summer night.

7/13: Helene Stehlin's 85th at the beach, and she tells me I have square shoulders, just like her Joe, "a great compliment." Joe and Helene were friends of Mom and Dad's, and he a longtime tennis chairman. Indeed, it is a compliment, even if Eileen Curry, my cousin Eileen's aunt, once in her charity called them, "the two stupidest white people on earth."
I liked them both.


7/24: My slightly subversive and very funny, extroverted America's Health Network buddy, Paula McClure, is dead of a brain tumor in Dallas, aged 40. She had been hosting "Good Morning Texas," and developing an African American beauty products line. Paula was herself a beautiful girl with wonderful *joie de vivre* and warmth as well as the usual neuroses of talent. Of all the America's Health Network performers she was the most entertainment oriented. We almost got into trouble but held back (Tiger Woods was her true target!) A terrible shock. Hope it was not painful.

8/1: When we were young and living in the big house on Cedarhurst Avenue, my parents were often away in Florida or the Caribbean, and we children would take our meals with Mary, Myra and Theresa in the small dinette area by the kitchen. And often in the evening the other girls who worked in the surrounding houses would come by after dinner for a cup of tea, a smoke and chat. One night a plane flew over low en route to Idewild, and I made the Sign of the Cross. The girls looked at each other around the table and smiled kindly at me. "Sure," said Nanny, "I think myself he'll be a priest."

And I thought I might want to be. But part of the deal as it was explained at catechism was that you had to feel called by the Holy Spirit. However much I might have wanted to be, I never was, no matter how hard I prayed I might be, in accordance with Sister Mary Albert's counsels, and so it came to pass I pursued another path. It was a good thing.

8/3: A 50th birthday reunion with Nion McEvoy at his Deer Park retreat in Utah, Walter Chatham and Joe Tobin (one year shy). Overlooking old pines and a wide valley. Great fishing and hiking to Lake Blanche and fellowship and laughter, and no drugs, little drink, but great food at this halfway house, golden western sunlight breaking through the Douglas firs.

It made me think back on my last years at Portsmouth with Joe and Nion, two of my best friends. . . .

The summer of 1969, after sitting a disastrous Math 3 exam, I went out to California to work in Sun Valley repairing ski lifts and building cross country skiing trails. I never quite got there. Instead, I settled into the comfort of Nion's cousin Joe Tobin's Hillsborough home. We frequently sprinted down to San Francisco, explored the Haight and took in concerts at the Fillmore, listening to Santana, Spirit, and the likes of Joan Baez singing her salute to Ronald Reagan:

*He's a drug store truck-driving man,*
*You know he's the head of his own Ku Klux Klan. . . .*

More than once, we arrived home after dawn after hearing the Grateful Dead sing the last of several encores:

*Lay down dear brother,*
*Lay down and take your rest,*
*Won't you lay-ay down,*
*Upon your Savior's breast. . . .*

The Summer of Love had been declared dead, but alternative papers and radio, new music, hip clothing stores (later that summer Don and Doris Fisher would open the first Gap store on Ocean Avenue) and idiosyncratic people were everywhere. If it was utopian to think there might really be a Revolution, ample evidence abounded that there were already nearly infinite mini revolutions. One night, Joe took me to a near-by neighbor's house for dinner. The Randolph Hearsts had four beautiful daughters at the table that night. One of them was a sweet blonde 15-year-old named Patty, today the wonderfully resilient Patricia Hearst Shaw, whose defense fund Joe would found after her kidnapping and repeated rape several years later.

Today a lot of people say that in the Sixties people did what they did because they were idealistic. I want to believe that but would also say that we did much of what we did because we were self-indulgent and not always very honest, especially with ourselves. Sure, you can say we did drugs to attain a higher consciousness, and we broke laws to achieve social justice, and we called our parents' generation "pigs," because we were creating "more viable commitments," but from this vantage point it looks like we were doing whatever we felt like.

It didn't seem that way then. I headed back east to attend a musical camping weekend rumored to be happening on an upstate New York farm. The tickets cost $15 at the local record store in Cedarhurst.

We drove up to Woodstock in Mark O'Neil's magic VW bus. He had rigged up its own loudspeaker and siren system, with which Mark expertly bluffed his way through crowds and check points, claiming we were an emergency vehicle.

"Cool as the breeze," Chris Coy called out emphatically as we made our way in.

By the time we had established our campsite on Friday afternoon Woodstock was a sea of people, the second biggest city, in all of New York State. We wandered over to hear Richie Havens start off the festival, singing the lines of "Freedom" interwoven with "Sometimes I Feel Like a Motherless Child." We found seating near the top of a natural, grassy amphitheater, crammed with sweating bodies. Most were sporting long hair, bell bottoms and t-shirts, but near us was a group of young Italian-Americans from Arthur Avenue in the Bronx wearing chinos and white short-sleeved shirts with slicked back hair, eating lustily from a mountainous hamper of fried chicken, pastry and soft drinks. The rest of us had ladled ourselves a cup of the tasteless, runny, macrobiotic couscous that was being served for free by scrawny hippie girls down the way. Porter Carroll halfheartedly claimed it was delicious, but after the second soggy slurp, I couldn't help envying our Bronx friends.

We sat peering down the hillside trying to see (our neighbors had also brought binoculars, which looked uncool but was certainly sensible; so many things that looked uncool have turned out to be sensible). Country Joe and the Fish got the crowd dancing on its feet when they played "Rock 'n Soul Music," shouting, "Sock it to me, sock it to me, sock it to me . . ." Then Arlo Guthrie strummed his acoustical guitar and sang, "Coming into Los Angeles." He was followed by Shana Na singing, "At the Hop," and then by Country Joe McDonald shouting into the microphone, "Give me an 'F,' give me a 'U,' give me a 'C,' give me a 'K,' and what have you got?" Nearly a million people in the audience told him what, and then he asked four more times and was answered by thunderous screams of "FUCK." Then he started in:

*Well, it's one, two, three,*
*What are we fighting for?*
*Don't ask me I don't give a damn*
*Next stop is Vietnam. . . .*

The whole festival rose up and united in the chorus then and brought Woodstock to one of its early peaks. That night we walked deep in the woods, hearing the music rise and fall in the distance, bouncing off the trees and the stars.

It rained harder and harder. Crosby, Stills and Nash sang "Wooden Ships," The Who screamed, "We're Not Gonna Take it," and Joe Cocker belted out, "With a Little Help from My Friends."

Then the deluge began in earnest, and people tried to take cover, tried to move past each other, slipped and slid and finally rose in a great chorus to propitiate the rain gods with a chant that reached to the heavens. It didn't work. It poured and flooded, and after that the mud flowed into the makeshift tents and soaked us all.

The next day it rained some more, but no one cared. Ten Years After sang, "I'm Going Home," and the Jefferson Airplane played "Volunteers." Max Yasgur, the farmer whose land Woodstock was held on, stepped up to the microphone and said, "I'm a farmer, and I don't know how to speak to twenty people, let alone half a million, but I just want to say that for a crowd of kids this size to come here, listen to music and have fun, and only fun, is wonderful, and God Bless you."

Sly and the Family Stone played, "I Want to Take You Higher," Paul Butterfield played "Love March," and we stayed up through the night listening until Jimi Hendrix rang in the druggy dawn and the end of Woodstock with his electric, stoned-out "Purple Haze," followed by his jagged guitar solo of the "Star Spangled Banner."

During the course of the night, I got separated from the others, and our camp had been broken up by the mud streams rolling through it, so I hitchhiked home, and in the process partnered up with a stringy blonde-haired, Indian head-banded girl named Vickie who was searching for one of her sandals in the mud. We looked like refugees streaming out of a Balkan war zone. The first seven miles took us eight hours, but then the car we were riding in started to move.

When we got to New York I bought her dinner in a vegetarian restaurant in the East Village and took her to my aunt and uncle's apartment on the upper east side, who were supposed to be out of town for the summer at their rented beach house on Long Island. I demonstrated my savoir-faire by trying to enter her before she had gotten her pants fully off, and she wasted no time in letting me know my technique was seriously wanting. It was my first night.

In the morning, my uncle showed up to collect the week's mail. He wasn't happy to see us.

"Good morning."
"Good morning, Uncle Buddy."
"How soon can you be out of here?"
"Right away."

We grabbed our knapsacks and split. At Penn Station we turned to each other to say goodbye, before jumping on different train lines, she to Long Beach and me to Far Rockaway. Despite my maladroitness Vickie was kind. Her last words to me were, "Be good."

I wonder where she is now.

A couple of afternoons later the bus dropped me off at the top of Cory's Lane, and I walked down to the Portsmouth gate. I had been summoned back to make up my catastrophic math exam. For the next two weeks I lived life on the monastic model, a curious contrast to Woodstock, both counter-cultural lifestyles, one energized by the search for a new Way, and the other stabilized by fourteen centuries of experience based upon a seventh century's saint's strict yet loving rule.

Father Hilary was on his annual holiday in Italy, taking the waters at Montecatini. It was left to Father Andrew to take on my nearly hopeless cause. He had developed a bump on his forehead and a nervous twitch that jerked his chin sideways every thirty seconds, but his remained one of the most elegant mathematical minds that I have ever known. His ideas came out in torrents and then would hit a snag, but he recovered, carried on and got me to understand what had previously been unfathomable. Frequently he interrupted his lessons to recite one of his endless series of off-color limericks:

*There once was a lass from Abyerstwyth*
*Who took grain to the Miller to make grist with,*
*The Miller's boy Jack put her flat on her back*
*And they mingled the things that they piss with.*

Within two weeks of this regime, he had raised my final examination from 31 to 99. The school refused tuition for the crash course, and Father Andrew appeared embarrassed when afterwards my Mom insisted on sending him a Steuben ashtray as a gift.

What I really remember about those two weeks was rising early in the height of summer to attend Mass (excepting those days when I over-slept and Andrew had to come wake me). We would study math all morning. Then I would swim in the Bay with Father Damian and eat lunch in the monastery in silence as a spiritual text was read by one of the monks. After a twenty-minute period of recreation in which the conversation could range from the day's news to astronomy, archaeology, cartography, eschatology, and the relationship of alchemy to medieval theology, there was a period of prayer. Then I would have a shorter math tutorial in the afternoon and be free to play tennis with Father Bede.

Vespers were at 5:30. In the evenings after dinner we would sit and chat in the calefactory, giving me the chance to hear each of the monk's own unique life's story. Father Wilfred had lived in Greenwich Village near e.e. cummings and danced with Pavlova. He was now a *Rouge Dragon* and the country's foremost heraldic artist. Father Thomas had been ordained in both the Methodist and Episcopal churches before making his way to Rome. Dr. Lally, a retired layman in residence, had taught my father in the 1930s and written an impenetrable study of Lord Acton's opposition to the nineteenth century doctrine of papal infallibility. Father Ambrose was the radiantly kind, genuinely modest and supremely brilliant concert pianist who had given up fame and an international musical career to experience God and teach English and music to nitwits like me.

I sat with them at meals. On those mornings I woke up early enough I assisted at their Mass, and I sometimes stayed to listen to their night prayers echo up into the distant rafters. I wanted to know what drew them to that life. In a way I wanted to be drawn to it to. But I never was drawn. It seemed to me then that spiritual sensations are most often impossible to articulate or to communicate to others—silently experienced impressions that waft away on the air.

How wrong I was, but that took many more years to learn.

Father Andrew was the most brilliant and bizarre of them all. He could rage with language worthy of a sailor he had been in war time one moment and drop to his knees in front of you asking for forgiveness with abject humility the next. One day at the end of class we as usual ended up discussing things far afield, and I asked him how he had come to Portsmouth.

"Before the war I'd been a teacher and started a school in Cambridge. Systems analysis and statistics were both passions of mine, but the problem was I couldn't see much meaning in them anymore. There was a storm rising in me, and this was the one choice I could make to quell it, some of the time. I am a monk and a mathematician and, by definition, I have one foot firmly in faith and the other in reason. When I solve for 'the equation of life' and I insert the variable of God, it works. Conversely, when I remove the variable of God, nothing works."

His honesty was disarming. Were all revolutions inside the mind only temporary? Tommy often spoke about using Zen to defeat the ego. I had come to the conclusion that you were lucky to wrestle it to an occasional draw.

When I left the monastery and took a small Newport Aero plane back to LaGuardia, the only other passengers were Jimmy and Candy Van Alen, condescending from their Bellevue Avenue "Cottage" on their way to the second U.S. Open, where Rod Laver would complete his second Grand Slam, this time as a professional, as opposed to his amateur triumph in 1962. Van Alen had saved the Newport Casino from developers, founded the International Tennis Hall of Fame there and revolutionized the sport with his inventions of the tiebreaker and the Van Alen (no let) Scoring System, about which Laver and John Newcombe would later somewhat ungratefully remark in their Aussie accents after a few beers, "You can take VASS and stick it up your arse."

James Van Alen smiled benevolently as we taxied up the runway and complimented my early Jimmy Connors metal racquet, while Candy recited all the upcoming week's parties to him. Theirs was a different world.

I wondered then if, of all the counter-cultural adventures I'd had that summer of 1969, those two weeks of studying with the monks hadn't been the most amazing of all. And the words from St. Benedict's Rule still echoed in my ears:

*Seek peace and quiet; be much more of a listener than a talker; listen with reverence; if you must speak, speak the truth from your heart. In other words, walk in the presence of God under the guidance of the gospel, in order to see Him who has called us to his kingdom. To start with, ask God for the help of His Grace; then never give up. . . .*

It's easy to circumnavigate years of one's life telling stories that pop out of a brain that probably pre-selected them anyway. Wasn't it George Orwell who wrote that he considered autobiographies to be almost always lies, because they inevitably concentrated on the triumphs of a man's life, whereas, in truth, 95 percent of anyone's experience consisted of failure and humiliation?

The same could be said for an age. People romanticize the Sixties and wax nostalgic about the drugs, sex, rock and roll, and so-called freedom. But all those things involved as much pain as pleasure. Many of the rock stars died young. Sex was often tortured. The apostles of drug use became their own most compelling rebuttals. We want to believe the Sixties were about unconditional love, giving Peace a chance, Flower Power, and selfless idealism. However, wasn't there also a lot of egotistical attitudinizing, selfishness and unadulterated indulgence? And, if we were really honest, couldn't we say we had felt lonely, uncertain, foolish and miserable much of the time?

I think so.

At Commencement in June of 1970, Father Leo omitted his customary thanks to the Student Council. Our valedictorian, Michael Garvey, began his address, "We have failed," and expanded on his theme persuasively.

You might think that out of all these experiences—the good ones as well as the bad—might have come the beginnings of wisdom, the ability to sift through systematically, analyze what had been, and see where to head next. But it didn't work out that way. Not for me anyway.

Nion and I were lying on the lawn at Dumbarton Oaks one hot DC day early that summer, and after a long silence he said, "I've thought of postponing college so that I can go to the International Zen Center in Switzerland and get into it all more deeply."

"Really?"

"Yeah, it just seems like we're all trying to go too fast. Everyone is living like we're running out of time. And I want to oppose that."

"Sort of like joining a monastery, isn't it?"

I had read learned or simply smartass articles in newspapers and magazines saying, on the one hand, that we were right to be radical in the Sixties because there were horrific societal injustices that needed to be redressed; and we had to overthrow an oppressive power structure so as to create an idyllic new order. On the other hand, there were articles that said we were spoiled schmucks in the Sixties, subverting an Establishment that had created unparalleled prosperity and opportunity for those who flocked to Freedom's shores. We were self-indulgent, narcissistic, and so forth.

And you know what? They were both right. It wasn't worth bickering over anymore. There were more important things to deal with in the future than in the past, and it was time to move forward.

The existential stance I had been attracted to felt oddly empty now, with an endless war in progress against an often-invisible enemy and a society whose structures—material and spiritual—were increasingly bedeviled from within. Instead, I had new sympathy for a fourteen-hundred-year-old way of life a few men and women were still willing to surrender themselves to, to follow lives of obedience, poverty and prayer. It occurred to me then that what monks do is not merely admirable, but crucial to the life of the Church and society as a whole. A monk or nun who attends his vocation provides *all* of us an example. And that is what Hilary, Andrew, Leo, Ambrose, Julian and the others at Portsmouth—eccentric, odd, conflicted, deeply flawed, devoted and amazingly generous as they were—had staked their lives on doing.

And how could I not try to take those examples into account as I tried to figure out my own path?

I thought of Father Damian reciting the motto of Monte Cassino: "*Succisa, virescit.*" "When cut down, it will revive and flourish." I didn't know how, and I didn't know when; but I suspected this was so. I wasn't sure of what someone like me, who could never take a vow of celibacy, or anything else, was supposed to do about it.

And yet, even then, in 1970, I knew something was there.

Back to 2002—

8/12: Lanie upsets the kids with threats of moving. Dinner with my cousin Father Luke Travers at Orso, who says the quality of priests has gone downhill with too many pietistic losers content to finger scapulas and not enough brave hearts trying to move spiritual mountains. That is the issue. Bishops have been too willing to claim credit for vocation numbers that comprised well-meaning but mediocre or ill-meaning and perverted aspirants.

Luke also speaks of a paranoia among priests now, which must be difficult.

8/23: Rhoads is so upset at Lanie's threats that I should move out he refuses to leave the house and his voice breaks. Still wants us to be together, sweet boy.

Saratoga fun at Casa Elser, godson Christopher working hard at Fasig Tipton, partying hard as we all did at his age, and waking up from couch where he was sleeping to take a leak at 4 a.m., then falling into my room (formerly his) and flopping on the bed. Barry Donahue was uproarious in his one-day attack. The MacMillens were complimentary of my driving skills when I took them to dinner. "If Cable Asia Network isn't funded soon, I'm available."

Rhoadsisms: At the toy store he cracks up the girl at the cash register by saying, "Well, since you don't have Matrosauer, not that I'm blaming you or anything . . ." but immediately she composes herself to give his request the serious consideration it deserves. Grace in the afternoon.

Then that night he asks, "Dad, what would happen if you and Mommy died?"

"That's not going to happen, Rhoads."
"I know, but what would happen?"
"You'd go to live with Uncle Peter and Aunt Becky and Casey and Clay."

A smile slowly spreads across his face and he says, "Cool! But can they move
to this house?"
And Pierce a kick to play with in our first handicap doubles tournament.

9/11: One year later. I made the kids watch the news. Neil Levin's face
on the screen, the director of the Port Authority, an alumnus of Lawrence
Woodmere Academy, where the kids go, and whose wife, Christy Ferrer, I
was a houseguest of the Donahues with last March in Palm Beach. I put the
boys on the bus and went to jog the hurricane surf beach. Some surfers were
outside, but when I swam, I stayed in for the body surfing. The waves were
rolling, and I misjudged the undertow. Suddenly I was swept to the jetty and
had to decide whether to take the last stone or continue out to sea. I panicked
at the unknown and grabbed for it. I was bashed thrice into the stones until
I got my grip and worked my way down, focused on keeping my head high.
Meanwhile my body was sliced up the right side and bleeding from foot,
knee, thigh, waist and elbow. Stung but did not need stitching. Bibi was frantic when she saw the bloody towel and afraid something had happened to one
of the boys. It was a silly ass misjudgment for a 50-year-old and contravening
all I have ever counseled my children.
    9/16: Yom Kippur. Showers on a strange in and out day. I stayed with
the boys all day and then left for town before Lanie returned. I walked
the city and saw cops posted outside the Central Synagogue, where Allard
Lowenstein was memorialized decades ago, and where Jeremiah Kaplan worshipped in Macmillan days. The police were on hand to prevent a disturbance
on the highest holy day. I went to bed feeling more a weary soul than a body,
and dreams were filled with African genocide images. Eventually I took small
comfort in reflecting, "Hey, it is Atonement Day, and the Zeitgeist commands
us to feel this way." Doesn't it?
    9/30: Molly Wilmot is dead. And where do I begin? I remember when she
and Paul took their first Saratoga house by the railroad tracks outside of town
and worked their way up. Oversized white glasses, amyl nitrate dinner parties with Cynthia Phipps and Virginia Guest. Her sexy niece Nina Bushkin
arrived at the Reading Room one summer falling out of her dress and into the
loving arms of Toby Charrington. I was jealous. (Later Nina married Alan
Jay Lerner).
    Molly was famous for the Venuzeulan freighter that landed on her Palm
Beach doorstep the day after Thanksgiving in 1984. She entertained the crew
royally and *tout* Palm Beach who came to witness her agony. Why hadn't it
come to grief next door door, *chez* Kennedy? "It wouldn't dare."
    And she guarded that story, threatening to go to court when she didn't like
the stars Disney attached to the film version. The obit said it was Melanie
Griffith and Bette Midler, but the one that drove her nuts was Phyllis Diller.

Mollie had horsey features and oversized glasses, but in all fairness, she was better looking than Phyllis. And often funnier, especially in her cups. Which was usually.

Many wonderful personal experiences such as her rejection of my Brazilian friend Michael ("Johnny Rio") McGrath and the ensuing near-carnage on North Broadway, her many escorts, and the monumental face-off one August night between a Mollie hell-bent on smoking and a much larger Jessye Norman determined to prevent same. A wonderful piece of God's work, and I will miss her.

10/10: When Jennifer looked deep into my eyes and said, "YOU'RE my family," it was almost enough to turn me in favor of incest.

Off to Singapore and New Zealand for Communications Asia Network, in which I have invested too much time and money and may well come a cropper, but I must go the last mile and see. Tommy Dietrich took me to the airport en route to Asia. He had grown up in the Williams carriage house, now the Shaik's and was full of stories of two butlers, five maids, and after Christmas the whole entourage going down to Lake Wales, Florida for the winter. In WWI the original Mrs. Williams (Sam's Grandma) used to take the limo down to Fort Dix every Sunday loaded with food and candies to Tommy's grandfather, a Polish immigrant called into service. "I took your Dad and Dow Ferris to the Stork Club in black tie on Saturday nights. And Helen Maitland (Corroon) would ask me to come inside with her to the local bars. She was wild!"

Young Pierce is hiding critical school reports in a yew bush at the back of the garden!

Lunch with Pierce the Elder, who remembers Mother taking her taxes to her accountant one year and recounting her trips to four hospitals for all of us (I was getting a double hernia at Long Island Jewish, Kevin's hand was being operated on at the Hospital for Special Surgery, Dad was getting elec-tro-shock treatment at Payne Whitney, and finally Mother checked herself into the Leroy sanitarium, where shortly thereafter Peter joined us, in what remains the only recorded early arrival of his life). In that same year of 1955 came Doctor MacGuire's death, Dad's crushing, continuing sickness, and many other challenges. At a certain point the accountant's secretary began to snivel and then to weep uncontrollably, and Mother joined in despite herself. They recovered, but at the end the secretary lost it again and blurted out, "Mrs. MacGuire, I hope next year is better."

11/5: Back in New York in time to sup with Philip Goelet at Felidia, tast-ing Sardinian wine, who says VC money has disappeared. He encourages me to pursue Chinese horse racing! Then Chamber Music Society and Spoleto impresario Charlie Wadsworth walks by, and we have a pleasant chat about French music, a better conversation.

11/11: Mild November weekend. I took Pierce for his trumpet Saturday and to play squash later. Rhoads played with John Sipp and Benton Madsen. I went to church early and let the kids sleep in the next morning. Agent Peter Miller calls twice to say I am a brilliant writer, and he wants to represent my novel. As usual with agents this devolves to mean the reverse, but they can't help it, and it bucked me up for a bit.

Pierce is acting up at the brink of adolescence and his mind is ever twisting: I rein him in but feel like a heel for so doing.

11/15: Lunch at the Century with C. who tells me he is the target of a paternity suit (a child of two) and is taking legal action to make settlement and end blackmail. The girl's idea was that C. could split time between two households. "Not on the cards." Sound familiar?

"Two years ago, in my own difficulties, I remember you telling me you had not been as pure as the falling snow, and you thought it had helped."
"Senator, I would now like to amend that statement."

11/16: SARS virus appears in Guangdong.

11/25: President Bush establishes the Department of Homeland Security.

11/29: Great Thanksgiving with boys. And a good night at the Long Beach movies with Harry Potter. Rhoads was thrilled with the evil "basilisk."

12/5: Cable Asia stalls, and all looks bleak. I meet a nice and sexy but thoroughly Presbyterian girl who feels remorse at letting herself go. The managing editor of *Quest* suggests Hilary Geary instead! (soon to be snapped up by Wilbur Ross, whose charms are obvious).

12/10: Lunch with Jennifer Caeser, Eddie Uhlmann and Taki at Swifty's, the *Quest* brain trust. Taki has come straight from judo and is considering how best to eviscerate Lloyd Grove, who has printed what appears to be an anti-Semitic Taki quote from Chuck Pfeiffer's off the record Christmas lunch at The Brook. Taki seeks my counsel whether to kick him in the balls ("very painful and leaves no mark") or slap him in the face ("far more humiliating"). I am of little help in these weighty questions.

Eddie's story on Mortimer's. Glen appears one night with a new tie. "It's beautiful Glen, where did you get it?" Before he can answer George Miller cuts in, "He made it upstairs, on the Loom of the Fruit." Banned.

And another story of Claude Beer leaving Maxim's in a huff after finding a pubic hair in the famous noodle soup. Maitre D' Roger follows him to offer him abject apologies and catches up to him at Billy's in the Rue Valery. Bursting into his assigned room he finds Claude chowing down on a beauteous victim. "But M. Beer, only half an hour ago you complained about ONE hair . . ."

"Yeah, and if I find so much as one noodle here I'm walking out of this place too . . ."

12/16: The boys and I bought and trimmed our Christmas tree, hung the wreath, and went to church. "The Church is either dying or being born anew," Father Rahilly said, and that sounds about right.

Pierce and Rhoads' school concerts were a treat. Pierce played great trumpet on the Big Band and Flintstones numbers, and Rhoads loved singing "Feliz Navidad."

In the mornings Rhoads likes to wait for the bus outside the front door and lean into the whistling wind, gazing for the sight of it. "A boy's will is the wind's will, and the thoughts of youth are long, long thoughts."

12/24: Quiet. Shopping done; calls completed. I shook hands with Dave Johnson, old friend and racing announcer, at the coffee shop on First Avenue and rested a moment before launching into the new light of Christ.

12/26: A good Christmas. Father Rahilly mercifully had lost most of his voice, and Rhoads ran up and down the aisles during Mass. Bibi gave Pierce and him too much money, but that is how she is. To the MacMillens for drinks in a smaller group, the family for tetrazzini at our house, all home early and put the kids to bed by ten. I rose at four to hang stockings. By then the ground was covered with snow. Rhoads came to rubbing his eyes around eight, and we woke Pierce before opening presents. Game Boy 2, magic kit, Space Gun, Slinky, Yugio cards and many stocking presents. French toast and bacon breakfast. Lanie arrived from the city, and I played squash. Afterwards a wonderful day and lunch at Schuyler and Dean's.

At the table Rhoads proclaimed, "This performance is dedicated to Gordon and Treddy," and sang "Feliz Navidad" again. I drove the twins and Julia to the Woodmere train station in the blizzard afterward. Then I went to smoke a cigar in front of the fire at the RHC, the last year that would be legal. I got home just in time for the electricity to go out. Both boys hug me when I get home and Pierce says, "I know this is ridiculous, but can I sleep with you both tonight?"

Delighted that they did and drove them to airport for their trip to Caso de Campo in the 4 a.m. pre-dawn.

12/30: My resolution for 2003 is to be the best Dad I can be.

Our traditional Christmas lunch at the Oyster Bar with Miles Chapin, both stressed by respective marital difficulties, but he is stoically soldiering on and hopes to save his. In the end he didn't, alas. And Treddy's annual Brook lunch an oasis of male friendship to round out the year.


## 2003


1/8: Snow and darkness until 8 a.m. Rhoads is recovering from strep. Both boys are rambunctious with cabin fever. As Rhoads snores I pray, not for wealth or love, just to carry on, to fight another day, that God will unite me to his Will, that He will in Mother Teresa's phrase "Call me to fidelity, not to success."

"Blessed are the merciful, for they will obtain mercy."

1/17: Coldest days of winter on the Isle of Wight as the Sipp house ascends and Mrs. Chauncey, 101, sleeps much of the day. Jack McCarthy, a childhood friend of my mother's who lives next to the Passeggios, fights bone cancer and cannot make it to Florida. Three squad cars are outside Ellie Snyder's house. I thought Mrs. S. was buying the farm, but it turned out to be her son Phil having a stress episode. He is up all-night caring for his infirm mum and needs a rest.

My attempts at post-marriage relationships are friendly but ultimately failed. Don't want to hurt anyone, and sometimes I wonder if I'm really ready. I contemplate a season of abstinence and purification. Whatever the season of purification, there must be a season of more money making.

In *The Courage to be Catholic*, George Weigel makes the arresting point: "Any properly formed priest who on a daily basis (1) celebrates the holy sacrifice of the Mass; (2) reads the Divine Office; (3) spends one hour in contemplation of the Triune God; and (4) makes a thorough examination of conscience cannot, CANNOT be a sexual molester." But how far those seminaries must have fallen to turn out those so ill-formed.

When I think of what a great experience it was to ride my bike down to St. Joachim's in the village, wait for Mr. Barry the caretaker (whom Nanny called "Andy") to open the church in the still dark, and dress in my cassock and surplice before Father Franz came in. I helped him vest, got the altar ready and carried out the cruets. Then I led him out to the altar and responded to the Mass in Latin in front of a congregation of ten or twenty at most, predominantly women. Nick Benvin's mother Anna, who spoke no English, was always there. It was special and deeply reverent. Father Franz was not exceptional in any way, and his sermons were mumbled and monotonous, but he was kind and a good priest, and I felt close to him. The idea of him committing any kind of abuse or even cruelty was unthinkable, and I honestly think I would have trouble being in the same room with someone who had robbed a child of his innocence, trust and faith in that fashion without wanting to snap his neck.

Vladimir Feltsman was magnificent in *Masterpieces of the Russian Underground* at CMS. Gerry Levin, ex-head of Time Warner, is now in California after dumping his second wife of 34 years, and says he wants to "find the poetry again," advising his new gal pal on an alternative health venture. In truth, he was always out trying to screw others and climb over them, like Nick Nicholas, while positioning himself as the ethical high ground.

2/3: Space Shuttle Columbia was lost Saturday as heating resistance panels failed. Seven souls gone.

Good fun at the Saint Nicholas Society to hear Christo "Van Buckley" accept its Washington Irving Award. I sat with Sam and Susan Williams, Schuyler and Catia Chapin, Treddy, and the senior Buckleys, getting on but in good form.

Rhoads was a darling flag bearer in a yellow scarf for Switzerland at International Day.

2/6: The way kids move you—Rhoads and Benton have a fight and part badly. Rhoads stalks in but then has a change of heart and says he wants to call. "You can wait until tomorrow." "Nah, I better do it now." Later, as we go to sleep, he complains that Mrs. Appel wouldn't let his friend Brian wear his Fang costume for Hallowe'en, because it wasn't "pleasant." And as he does, he makes quote marks with his left hand. Little wise guy side emerging.

2/8: Good snow days with the kids, sledding in Rye, Rhoads saucering down delightedly. That night he went to sleep in Clay's room and called out her name when she tarried in the loo. She returned and they began exchanging scary stories. Clay delicately told one of a child's head being cut off, where-upon I heard the scampering of feet on the hallway floor, my door opened, and a flannel pajamed, curly-haired tyke snuggled into bed beside me, and sang into a deep slumber. And I was grateful for the gift of parenthood and wondered what else could be so profound.

A loving union with another, of course. But these boys must come first.

2/25: Cheery night at Peggy McEvoy's 64th with Nion in town, Hall Powell, Roger Greenwalt, Landi and Michelle. My second NYC family.

2/27: Dear Fred Rogers is dead of stomach cancer. An ordained Presbyterian minister, he saw television as a ministry, and made "Mr. Roger's Neighborhood" a daily lesson in love and affirmation to young people. I sang "Won't you be my neighbor?" with both Pierce and Rhoads, and they loved it. I remember touring WQED, the Pittsburgh PBS station, in the late '90s to explore some unorthodox distribution deal for AHN and was shown the "Mr. Roger's" set. It was tiny and ever so simple; yet so much good flowed from it. Can't we try, and be his neighbor forevermore?

3/6: Interesting 51st birthday if only for the lack of activity. Lunch with Jere Crook at a Vietnamese place and dinner with the boys, including a Carvel cake Lanie thoughtfully bought ahead on Stable Lane. Calls from Barbara Crane, Nion, Kevin, and John Egan.

Next morning the boys were delighted when I roused them for Ash Wednesday Mass and, in response to requests on why, explained the significance of the day, but in the early morning rain mispronounced "Ash" as "Ass," to their ears at least. Much merriment!

3/9: Rhoads gave me a Paul Klee drawing he had copied and shared his "Switzerland Skies" from International Day. Pierce spent both days of the squash doubles tournament with me at the Hunt Club and solidified his friendship with Taylor Heath.

Taylor's Dad, Freddie, and I advanced to the finals against my nephews, Tim and Chris MacGuire, who had beaten us 3–0 last year, when we tried to hit hard with them. This time we took pace off and lobbed. We made too many errors in the first and lost, but came back to win the second 18–17, clearly getting on their nerves. In the third I had a run of nine winning shots, despite a crippled back, and in the fourth we trailed 8–3 but kept working it, and finally took advantage of errors to reach 14–12. Fred erred for 14–13, a furious point followed, ending with Chris and Fred at the tin, and Chris winding up for the winner overmuch so his shot tinned. First doubles win at 51, an uncharacteristic hug from Fred (the baby of the family when I was playing sports every day with his brother Steve), and Pierce and Taylor mobbing us with joy as we came off court. All six brothers have won that tournament now, and five of us have been singles champions too. Not a bad day for a tennis player.

Forbes party for Heidi Klum at 66 last night, the Jean-George hors d'oeuvres and Krug flowing. "Heidi was pestering me for your number," Chris Buckley emailed after, "But of course I told her I would never betray you." Normally I prize loyalty . . .

3/15: Yesterday came the call to present myself Monday in DC for the Middle Eastern gig. I talked to Broadcasting Board of Governors chairman Ken Tomlinson and other key guys at length. We'll see.

3/23: U.S. invades Iraq.

3/29: Long Island is greening as spring approaches, but the ground is still cold. I enjoyed Robert Duvall's "Assassination Tango." Lanie to Europe and the kids ask repeatedly, "You really are going to be with us every night for ten days?" Such a small thing, but it means so much to them. Where else would I rather be? Which has been the hell of the last two years.

3/31: March is ending raw, but there's enough sun and rain to get the grass green. First shad roe, first steak grilled outdoors. A few shoots up in the garden but no buds. Birds back but no swans on the pond yet. This may be the last continuous stretch of time I ever spend in this house, but, "God never smiles so much as when we tell him our plans."

4/1: After telling Irish jokes to great hilarity, Pierce and Rhoads run to the bus stop. Suddenly, Pierce runs back, looking stricken. "What's the matter?"

"I had the TV remote control in my pocket." An absent-minded professor. He will have to work with that forever.

Georges Simenon wrote 700 novels—one, fully edited, every two weeks. He sat at the typewriter for nine hours straight or until 80 pages were done.

Two bottles of burgundy per sitting. He slept with 12,000 women, 8,000 of whom were whores. None of these milestones have I approached.

Ed Reitler's poignant story of Lane's breakdown after they traveled to Russia for Cuffia. Unbeknownst to them, Lane was pregnant. and inoculations caused her miscarriage. Heartbreaking.

4/10: Six inches of snow in April! Waiting for signs of a Russian spring, but so far the only forecast is rain. Three consulting proposals out, waiting on Washington and a book proposal as well. The tank is on empty.

In an especially severe anxiety dream, I am a corporate grunt again late for a critical meeting, but I can't remember where it is, how to spell the person's name in the directory, and can't hear out of my deaf ear what the operator is saying.

Wake up late and have to rush the kids to school. Lanie is 50 today.

A good night at Dario's stag squash dinner in Woodmere. Croatian delicacies abound. "Sarma" (stuffed cabbage), octopus and potatoes, gnocchi, veal, asparagus, and beef. Dario a life force, he, Lilly and their daughter Melissa entertaining Millard Atherton, Art Murray, Brendan Contant, Ed Reitler and Steve Bromley.

Spring arrived, and the children larked around on green grass, trampolines, baseball diamonds and bicycles. The house is full of kids, as it was on Cedarhurst Avenue, even a Heath. Happy days.

4/16: The Human Genome Project is complete, a huge accomplishment.

4/14: If God has a plan, he is keeping it quiet. But beauty emerges. Christopher MacGuire is engaged to lovely Rina McCreery. He proposed on the roof of her Greenwich Village building, and she said yes right away. Joy all around.

Sights and sounds abound: The light on Crooked Creek is puzzling the MacMillens . . . looks to me like a dock light of Mr. Solomon, the guy who lives next to Steve Owen. Sylvia Lynch driving her maroon station wagon down the Causeway to run her Labrador, Max, at the yacht club. Soon she will put flowers in the dog statue mounted on her hood.

The swans, thought gone, now back, but nesting in a safer section of the pond.
Patrick Kerins, master painter, attending his several IOW client houses.
John Passaggio, jaunty in his tweed hat, walking his new spaniel puppy, Biz.
Phil Snyder driving, hunched forward tensely. Steve Finch fiddling with tools in his driveway.
Debbie Drake painting the marsh in her studio. Mrs. Chauncey's daughter Kelly, now old herself and blind, here from Norway to visit her centenarian Ma. Art Murray gardening.

Good Friday: After the services, Treddy and I dine on shad roe. The kids are in Texas with Lanie.

Walk and talk with Jack Bierwirth, encountered bicycling by the yacht club one spring evening, wearing grey flannels, checked shirt, tie and windbreaker. Tells me he has a wild turkey, thinks it's a tom, feeding on his lawn every morning. There's another on Longwood Crossing.

4/28: A wicked rainstorm, and then in late afternoon two rabbits nibbled happily by Mom's stone rabbit now at the back of our garden, ducks waddling, cardinals darting in and out, a grey looking swan gliding on Reynold's Channel's grey still water, and one snow goose among the many Canadians feeding on the Madsen's front lawn.

4/30: Rhoads' big night at baseball. He got on base every at bat, once by half sliding under a tag into first. In the last inning Neil Boneparth hit a homer to tie. After two bingles, up came Rhoads, who cracked a high line drive deep to left and ran around the bases to win the game. He was so happy he spent the evening calling all of his MacGuire cousins and Uncles to tell them of his triumph. "Who shall I torture next?"

5/5: Rhoads' REAL birthday. I had the whole weekend with them as the apple tree ripened and the lilac blossomed. The boys trampolined, Rhoads had his First Holy Communion, and then said a beautiful grace with Treddy, Sky and Dean.

5/9: To Dallas for an alternative education conference and then back to hear Rhoads sing, "It's a Grand Old Flag." R. waves to me with a toothy grin from the stage.

5/12: Over to Phil Snyder's to see his new editing rig. His room is eerily unchanged from childhood, with Choate banners and the Hewlett Fire Department Essay award he won at Lawrence School. He shows me a seven-minute film of brother Rob monologizing how he feels trapped in job and in life with his dying mother. Mrs. Snyder is bedeviled by strokes and other ailments and now suffering from Alzheimer's. Bright, sensitive, nice guys, more stuck even than I at the moment. Bob Baldridge remembers Rob going on a rock tour with Tommy Hitchcock III during college and coming back wasted from drugs. "It took nearly a year, but big Phil and Ellie nursed him back to health." Then Bob says he was shocked to learn Phil hadn't worked for five years. But his mother is demanding all of his time.

After supper, bath and bed, Rhoads looks at me and says, "Dad, I love you. I wish you and Mom didn't have to divorce. Mom says you might have to move. Can I come with you?"

The pity.

Later, Rhoads was delirious with joy throwing balls to Huschi's dog, Noah. That night he fantasized about having one of his own. He also asked for a little brother. Said he would be lonely without one. Indeed, it is time.

He tells me that Lanie has threatened to move kids to Brooklyn if I move out, and he and Pierce don't want to go. Another struggle.

6/6: Days of rain and gallant Eithne Wrenn, my Irish third cousin, died this week in Dublin in her mid-80s. Derby and Preakness winner Funny Cide worked five furlongs in an eye popping 57.2 before the Belmont. He is either a freak of nature or got loose from Robin Smullen. We'll see Saturday.

6/8: Funny Cide fell short, alas, after leading for one and a quarter miles, whether because he couldn't grip the track or had been worked too fast earlier in the week. Rhoads cried out, "Daddy," when I came home from dinner, wet and cold after Belmont. He bounded down the stairs, thanked me for coming home, and cuddled with me all night.

6/30: Sophie DeSanctis's baby will be the fifth generation of that family I have known—Maggie Eaton ("Gaki" to her grandchildren), Aunt Kitty, Katherine McCallum and Sophie herself. (Luca was born healthy and beautiful).

7/4: Rhoads a funny little fellow body surfing on the 4th of July. He got racked up by a riptide and emerged gasping, but not frightened. "I got SMEARED." Pierce is off to camp for the first time. I hope he loves it as much as I did.

7/15: The kids are off to Colorado. Bibi called today to catch up on news and vent on how Lanie had blown her stack before they went away. I said I knew, because Pierce had told me and how he tried to calm her and was told to shut up. Bibi said how much it disturbed her when Lanie, returning from two nights in NYC in a bad mood, would begin yelling at kids even before she got in the door and then withdrew to her room. "I wish I didn't have children," she has complained to Bibi more than once.

Bibi says, "You have to be the mother *and* the father."

July: Franny Reese has died in a car crash, her driver at the wheel. A great lady and always the most unassuming person in any throng. She would stand in back of the Lawrence School assembly next to her Nanny, Gebbie, wearing no make-up and a plain house coat as the other Moms were decked out in lipstick, rouge, jewelry and lime green. She was active at the Church of the Transfiguration, the retreat House of the Redeemer (in her childhood neighborhood on East 95th Street), led the fight against the GE plant at Storm King and ergo pioneered the entire Hudson River Valley Conservation movement. Late in life she still taught Sunday School at the Church of Mt. Zion in Wappinger Falls while attending to a host of other good works.

The summer Dad died she gave me intros to Joshua Vanneck (Lord Huntingfield today) and Godlieve Van Heche as I set out to Cambridge, and they were wonderful to me. Modesty was her hallmark except when it collided with righteousness, but I have a singular memory of her, still playing tennis in a pleated skirt, when Johnnie and Hope's then young ones approached her on the lawn outside the tennis fences. She dropped to her knees and stretched out their arms and they ran to bury themselves in her enfolding arms. She was that kind of dame, and I doubt we will see her like again. Pierce adds that when she would hit a deft shot her husband Willis (Mesier Livingston Reese, professor of International Law at Columbia) would cry out in his high-pitched, "OH! Mummy!"

At times I cannot help but feel that some some women scent in me the pheromone of failure.

Treddy always seems slightly energized by death. "The end of an era," he'd cry and enjoy the reception after. He didn't mourn much. Having seen so much of death (70 percent on Iwo Jima), to him it is the natural order. And what one should do is celebrate what has been.

Mrs. Reese was an ideal, the kind of person one would like to be if he could be. In my case, of course, I know I could not, and will have to do the best I can with what I've got.

I received Pierce's first letter from camp, all three magnificent lines of it. Leslie Berriman calls and says borderline personality disorder is one of the most difficult to have a relationship with. But I chose it! And Lanie was full of beauty, goodness and intention to love for a long time, and I was the beneficiary of that.

Homelessness dreams, I am in the garage apartment at 50 Cedarhurst Avenue, mucking around with a computer. But it's not ours anymore, nor Nanny's, it's the new owners', and I'm trespassing. Where am I?

7/26: I serve as Master of Ceremonies for the Hunt Club's 125th, a rousing party with over 600 revelers, bagpipers, Bob Hardwick and his band, good speeches and much dancing deep into the morning, and a robust Hunt break-fast after. David McCallum arrived from shooting his NCIS series in LA at 1 a.m. and reported, "I've never seen so many gentlemen with dinner jackets off and soaked dress shirts from summer dancing who of course felt the need to hug me to their salty wet bosoms . . . and the sweating ladies generously smeared their lipstick across my face . . ."

Blessed days with boys during the summer whirlwind. Rhoads and Benton are inseparable but for a brief spat. "I got bored and called him a moron, and then he called me a moron, and then we fought, and then I said I was sorry."

Sir Walter Scott not only invented the modern historical novel but one of its enduring themes: The idea of cultural conflict. How to carry it forward?

Which side is superior and which deserves to lose is NEVER fully resolved. Therefore, Scott originates the idea that modern man may be able to hold in his head two inconsistent ideas at once.

Can I therefore chart a plot that takes place in the mythic past and the improbable present at once?

8/14: After lunch in Millbrook with the Hectors, we go to the Giants sum-mer camp and hit Saratoga in the blackout. Rhoads launched the parachute Denis gave him wherever he could and finally lofted it onto the unreachable roof of the Elser house, where Christopher tried valiantly but unsuccessfully to recapture it.

Unlike the rest of the Northeast, the racetrack got its generator up in nine minutes, and Bobby Duncan showed Pierce and Rhoads how to start a race from the seven-furlong slot. Tennis with Casey and Clay on Saturday. Pierce played wonderfully well on both sides. On the way down, Rhoads asks, "Dad, if you had one wish what would it be?"

"That you and Pierce had a happy life."

"But we already have a happy life, so let's wish for world peace."
Let's.

8/20: Mars rose yellow and red in the southeastern sky in the constellation of Aquarius as it approaches its closest encounter with Earth for the next five to six thousand years. It seemed to glitter there a bit as it sat there strangely over the yacht club. Difficult to see for the trees but it was a stirring, brooding sight. The wind had blown up by the beach and I sat there staring at the saw grass.

9/15: "He whose deeds exceed his wisdom, his wisdom endures; but he whose wisdom exceeds his deeds, his wisdom does not endure."—Shlomo Dov Goitein.

9/26: Peter de Krassel arrives from Hong Kong ebullient and certain the Chinese Government will invest in Cable Asia. After six years of such predictions, I have to write it off mentally as the disaster it has been but still preserve my interest. Meanwhile, George Plimpton dies in his sleep at 76. In his last Page 6 appearance he denied playing tennis with the midgets from Clyde Beatty's Circus at Maidstone! At Elaine's, the aforesaid was berating a Times reporter to get the obit *above* the fold. Dinner with Clarissa Bullitt, whose Dad ran the bulls with Plimpton in Pamplona. "We're doing this dance," she says. So?

Roshashona, and hundreds of Orthodox Jews at Lawrence basin and also at the water's edge of the Woodmere Country Club, casting bread upon the waters. Life in Town resumes as brother Pierce suggests lunch at Alain Ducasse's Mix. A regal lady glides by. "Hello Jamie, did you read that the Pope made 71 new Cardinals?"

"No, Mrs. Buckley, I think it was 31."

"I'm SURE it was 71."

"No, Patsy," says costume jewelry king and noted ecclesiologist, Kenny Jay Lane, smoothly interceding from the rear, "It's only 71 if you count their children."

10/1: October morning, marsh golden, leaves thinning on the trees. The paper has a story on Almost Paradise, a beach in nearby Rockaway with fine diving and abundant sea horses, starfish, blenny fish and even the Lion's Mane.

10/3: Little headway in business, eczema inflamed and reading Edmund Wilson's *Upstate*. Uproarious accounts of jousting with Nabokov and Mrs. Van Wyck Brooks "in her quiet way." Penny Whitehead makes a cameo. Wilson a magnificent stylist and genius though clearly impossible. I cherish the image of him engaging Wellfleet's sole taxicab to drive from Cape Cod to Talcotville (north of Utica!) and back twice a year.

A cold was coming on and bloomed in the night. Impossible to swallow or breathe properly. But pleasures with the children, watching the Yanks win and Giants lose, visiting Jim Thornton to see the raccoon he had caught outside Mrs. Chauncey's garage. Very still and miserable looking. He set it loose five miles east. Many possums about as well. Hard to compare with the 300-pound tiger the cops found in a Harlem apartment this weekend, along with a four foot lizard. The owner said he was creating his own Garden of Eden, before being bitten. Neighbors had complained for years of a strong urine smell and the renter of record, his mother, had moved with her daughter to Philly to get away.

Pierce has four discipline infractions and an equal number of academic derelictions. He is unhappy. There is a hole in his closet door, a broken swing, charges on my AOL account, and stealing Rhoads' video games to trade in for those he wants. 13 years old, and ever in a mess. He got a good grade on a social studies paragraph, after I made him rewrite it for the third time.

The locust hum rises. Mars, past its azmith, declines, and the sun is again the reddest star in the sky. The white pit bull with the limp hiding in the marsh darts across the predawn road. And the mind tries to organize it all.

Symbolic disappearance of Waterford crystal glass given me by Gerrie McCormack as wedding present for Lanie and me: Martha the Maid admits breaking it. No matter. It tells the tale. Alas.

Rhoads and Benton play all day, Game Boys attached. Pierce is striking out in school, but in the 97th percentile in standardized tests.

10/16: A flock of white sea gulls flapping their wings as they soared above the now russet-brown marsh on a still October day.

Bob Hart and Hank Rowley are playing golf, both so handsome and vigorous well into middle age, and now doddery. Bob's Parkinson's is proceeding, and his tremors are increasing. Sue Gatehouse looks pale as a ghost leaving her house this morning. She has been a recluse all summer.

I played baseball and soccer with the boys all weekend. Pierce loves to use his body; Rhoads is a gigglepuss who laughs so hard he almost falls down recovering from a feint. I work with Pierce on his homework, and he begins to calm down and focus with someone beside him. He's like one of those high-strung thoroughbreds Sunny Jim Fitzsimmons would partner with a goat in the stall to keep it company.

Sadnesses: The joy of watching Rhoads run with his friends Thalia, John, and Tyler, gleefully to the Big Slide, the Mystery House and the Carousel at the school fair, the sheer happiness of his being only offset when he fantasizes about Lanie and me being together again. "I love you more than anybody, except Mommy." I am grateful for that last and genuinely sorrowful that his idealization of our all "being together again" cannot be. Dear little boy, and I will miss him terribly if I go to DC.

I tour with Pierce to Groton, Portsmouth and St. George's. Perfect late fall weather. The Groton Circle is quite beautiful, the Gothic Revival chapel surrounded by Georgian brick effective and enjoyed remembering *The Rector of Justin*. Pierce is smitten by the Harry Potterness of it all and wants to go. He also likes Portsmouth.

My biggest fear is that his inability to organize and focus will prevent him from getting the work done.

Lampedusa: "I would have sacrificed 10 years of my life for the privilege of an hour with Sir John Falstaff." What he valued in the English: "Reserve, self-control, ironic sense of humor, 'fair play,' and sympathy for the underdog, understatement and self-deprecating humor." What a civilization we have lost!

"Dicken's Kingdom is a Magic Realism." Is this the first use of the phrase? (1962?) If so, it would change with Marquez et. al. A Palermitano, one of his ancestors exiled by the Bourbons to Santa Margharita between 1820 and 1840 for a "misdemeanor," (i.e. riding naked through the streets of Palermo in his carriage).

Bibi on the notion of Pierce ascending to boarding school. "When he goes away, I grieve for him, so I'm going up there INVISIBLE."

A great book conceit: "BIBI at Boarding School."

Scary moment on Stable Lane this morning when, coming back from jogging, Suzie Gatehouse's post-op day nurse says she has looked all through the house, no one is there, and the back door is open. Has Sue high-tailed it to the marsh? Tyler Mullally is striding out from her cottage in her bathrobe, and I am there sweating, but it turns out the nurse went into our house! And in the end, she finds Sue, frail and resting.

The Lunar Eclipse tonight was eerie and beautiful. Hallowe'en! I remember the solar eclipse as a boy at Monadnock when the cows on the Russell Farm headed back to their barns, sensible creatures that they were. I wonder in the night if, per the "Elegant Universe" doc on String Theory that Pierce and I watched on PBS, if we are not all wandering among 11 dimensions, infinite planets and ourselves no more than a sun beam, or only a speck. If so, let us rejoice! How bright the lights!

11/15: I bought a new phone book this week and threw out the one with a Renaissance map of the world "*ex dono* Sophie Consagra" I got at Christmas 1987 from Maria's mother in Dublin, New Hampshire after *bollito misto* deep in the Monadnock winter. I doubt the hunter green suede model ("#22") will last half so long. In 1987 I was still a bachelor and soon to leave Macmillan as Robert Maxwell looted his London employees' pension funds to take it over after several failed previous raids of US media holdings. I see several Williamstown Theatre Festival friends listed I wish I had kept up with better—Kate Burton, Steve Collins, Ed Herrmann, Kevin Kelley, Connie Ray, Nikos and Jeannie Hackett. Elsewhere, girls I took out or wanted to. Still three years shy of marriage then. I see people I met and wanted to know better. Others who became dear friends: The Groeners, Laurie Kennedy and Keith Mano, Bill and Gena Everett. Some I felt sorry for and others who have passed away.

Cattails on the lawn, blown off the November marsh by whipping winds that reached 60 miles per hour two nights ago, and the golden light highlights the thinning trees.

The last of the hollys were ripped away from Holly House this week as John and Nancy Sipp put their mark on the new house and property. At the Yacht Club small birds frolic in the dunes, and the first sewer line ever nears completion.

Jack Nicholson: "You live on barbed wire and bug juice until you're 28, and there's no price to pay; but after a certain age you pay for everything."

Rhoads was magnificent in his play as Vasco de Gama with beret and robe!

In the dismal gloom of a rainy November, fog shrouds the marshes, and the mornings are filled with mist. The wind roars in the dark before the dawn, rocking our little cottage so that it sways slightly, just as we are all jostled over the course of a long life.

11/22: A Happy Week! Christopher Daniel (for Uncle Dan Monroe, Patsy Emery's father, who gave my Dad a desk at his Wall Street firm when he returned from the war and later took Schuyler on a golf tour to Ireland) MacGuire marries Irina McCreery, a gorgeous, lovely girl (and Chris a very good boy). How in this multi-racial, cultural and etc. age could two NYC Irish-Catholics find one another? The pub network, no doubt, not the dreadful Gothams as of yore. Chris' twin Tim cried and could not finish his toast as he gave Chris the identical silver cigarette box we all gave Schuyler in 1968. Peter McCallum, normally so expansive, choked up as well. The young ladies had no such problems as they embarrassed Rina "totally" with histories of her romances or refusals to discuss same. Good fun and Chris was quite relaxed. He said that he and Tim had roomed together in NYC for eight years. I am getting even older than I thought! Thought it was yesterday . . .

Meanwhile Rhoads draws a picture of the four of us and adds the caption: "Get back together." He gave Lanie a copy as well and told me, "I've done everything I can think of to do." Sweetest little man.

Quiet Thanksgiving with Kevin and Sally in Sally's perfectly kept house. Much of mother's china, candlabra and the Butler Gold Cup on display, as well as many of Sally's family's beautiful things. My kids played football with John and Jay in Texas, and Pierce went to the hospital for stitches in his scalp when he ran into a cow gate!

Governor Howard Dean spent the day in Cedarhurst with his wonderful, though steadfastly Republican, aunts, Sylvia Lynch and Helen Corroon and their broods. Hillary Clinton went to Afghanistan but was trumped by President Bush's surprise visit to Iraq. Leading into the primaries, Dean looks ahead, though his nomination would lead to a lopsided Republican win.

My initiative at the Corporation for Public Broadcasting will develop History and Civics content to create a more civil and civic-minded body politic. The target audience is middle and high school students. Hallmarks would be participatory democracy, public service, corporate conscience and family values, as well as respect for tradition, religion and the virtues. But we must create the content in multiple media to find young people where they are. Not just broadcast television, but video for the classroom, web sites and interactive games across multiple platforms, as well as print of course. It's complicated.

*Master and Commander* was magnificent! I loved taking the children to it and seeing them react to the moral dilemmas and courage displayed.

Michael Garvey tells me that, according to Tony Hillerman, oft-funded by PBS "Mystery" author, the movie version of "Cheyenne Autumn" has real life Navahos yammering in their language obscenely and is thus still a huge hit in Southwestern drive-ins.

*Give Hope . . . A Poem for Christmas, by Christopher Fry (1907–)*
*The darkest time in the year,*
*The poorest place in the town,*
*Cold, and a taste of fear,*
*Man and woman alone,*
*What can we hope for here?*

*More light than we can learn,*
*More strength than we can treasure,*
*More love than we can earn,*
*More peace than we can measure,*
*Because one Child is born. . . .*

12/8: My first and doubtless last Gold Racquets appearance. Fred Heath and I nearly stole our first-round match from three-time national champion and thoroughly nice guy, David Proctor, and his partner, Ted Bruenner. We ran away with the first game. By Rick Shepard's count I hit nine of the first ten shots for winners. They won the second. Freddy was magnificent in the third, and we took that as well. They toughened down in the fourth and fifth, and I tinned out at 14–12 in the last. When I went to pick up Rhoads at the Madsens he was shoveling snow off the back steps with Benton, Lawrence and Christina singing, "We Wish you a Merry Christmas."

12/15: D.C. friendly and slower paced. I called Liz Callan yesterday and, after complaining I had not been in touch for three years (her parents were my godparents), she said, "Well, I'm sure you wouldn't want to do this . . ." and asked me to the NewsHour Christmas party at Jim Lehrer's charming Cleveland Park home. He himself was most gracious, and the rest of the scene like an adult theme park with Kwame Holman opening the door, and Mark Shields giving me a wave as if he had known me forever. Terry Smith and I discuss his Dad, my hero sportswriter Red, and Ray Suarez was wonderfully irreverent off screen. Basement office an *homage* to Lehrer's Oklahoma bus driving father.

Next morn a yellow dawn over F Street from the Marriott window. I like this town . . .

*Christmas 2003:* Rhoads and I trimmed the tree very happily. We went to Christmas Eve Mass and had dinner after at our house. Rhoads embarrassed Pierce by volunteering a solo of "Let it Snow." Julia and Rina were much moved. Up at 7:30 for presents including a flying saucer and hovercraft. Then a very good dinner at Sky and Dean's and a long walk afterwards. Lots of squash and drinks at John and Deborah McWilliams new house on Boxing Day. When I was young it was the Whitney Dall's. Lanie spent an hour with the kids at most and then took off to Russia for two weeks. I took them to the Giants and watched Jim Fassel's last game as coach, Rhoads learning "new words" from the boisterous crowd.

Over New Year's Bob Baldridge asked me over for drinks. He is now squiring Andree Dean, Sylvia Lynch and Helen Corroon's sister, who grew up here but went to Park Avenue and East Hampton with Howard Senior after the War. I tell them the story of the last time I was on the property—when after seeing Secretariat win the Triple Crown by 31 lengths in 1973, I went to two parties in Westchester and a deb party at the Staniford's in the IOW and, driving Peter home, crashed into the LILCO pole outside of Bob's at 4:30 in the morning. He came out and got us into the ambulance. The next day I left for Europe with Pierce, slightly complicated by fact I had been driving his car. But the best part was that Peter later told me that the younger Dean boys approached him at the Beach Club bar that afternoon to say how guilty they felt they had not stopped, but they couldn't because they had ripped off the Staniford's silver punch bowl and were afraid of getting caught by the cops.

12/31: The year is running out. Yesterday I took Rhoads for his ERBs. His proctor said he was "talkative," and he was thrilled by the quesadillas after in the dining hall of Grand Central Terminal, so much so he launched his coke across the room with a well misplaced elbow. The guys next to us were most kind to the friendly mop-haired fellow, and, as he left, Rhoads said, "Thanks for making me feel better."

At home, Pierce and I played squash. Great fun when in this bone lazy, sleep late adolescence stage he rouses himself to try. To bed early and I rose with yellow light limning the trees. Next to me a mop-haired eight-year-old opened his eyes and frowned, then looked at me and broke into the world's most beatific grin.

"Good morning pardner!" he said, and that is what it's all about.

This year ends, everything having gone wrong, nothing material left, and yet I feel incomparably blessed by things unseen and more hopeful and committed than ever for a future of hard work, creation, service to others, and love of God.

The move to DC will be hard in some ways. I will miss the boys terribly but will find the way to care for them. And the New Year is filled with possibility.

Onward. Explore! And "Never Ever Give In!" (Winston Spencer Churchill at Harrow late in life).

## 2004

1/1: New Year's ushered in with a good dinner at Michelle and Fiske Warren's—pate, caviar and salmon. The Lawrences, Thayers and Lengyels. The ladies, Mt. Holyoke alumnae, reminiscing. A gentle night, Fiske and Michelle radiating goodness, and home in time to share the New Year with Pierce and Rhoads, a non-event except for the pleasure it gave them, bound and determined to stay up.

The New Year dawned bright and sunny. Pierce and I went to the Club for New Year's brunch. I have the feeling of doing many things for the last time hereabouts. I call Suzie Gatehouse and DeeDee Baker in their respective hospitals. Then I walked to Crooked Creek, smoking my first ceremonial cigar in months. Rhoads rightly takes credit for this though the new laws of NY State were sufficiently harassing to discourage me as well. Then I found I didn't miss them.

Encountered Patsy Emery along the way, having walked her dog. "The Club lunch wasn't bad, but it was nothing like your mother's," I said, referring to Aunt Marge Monroe's legendary feast, which Mother always recounted in approving detail. "Yes, black-eyed peas for luck and all that," Patsy remarked, "Although the problem was that in those days the Hunt Club tea didn't begin until five and no one would leave until they could get another drink there." So it was. A more bibulous era.

1/6: The last Lord of the Rings, "The Return of the King," a triumph, much beloved by the kids. "The Men of the West" speech reminiscent of St. Crispian's Day, Ian McKellen as Gandolph was superb, the Horrible Orkes and their gargantuan and avian monsters had Rhoads pressing into my side, and the final charge, led by the two Hobbits, brought tears of joy and admiration.

1/7: The MacMillens came in for the last night of Christmas, Epiphany. Funny that we begin and end the Holy Season with my family's most agnostic friend. Bill is 90 and Ba 92 this year. She ran into the dishwasher door when it was down and cut her leg; it ballooned, and they spent six hours at the Emergency Room. He fell down in the bathroom after taking his first medicine in 60 years. Thankfully, he did not crack his skull but only wrenched his neck. Both are fine now, and it could have been much worse.

Pierce woke at five, hormones popping, took a shower and went right back to sleep. I had to wake him for the bus at seven. Ba says he has grown six inches, and I'm sure she's right. They were incredulous when I told them this would be the 10th year since we moved nearby.

1/14: Cold snap. 1 degree. Low hanging clouds on the water and a supernatural mist rising off Reynolds Channel and Crooked Creek, like something out of Jules Verne's "Journey to the Center of the Earth."

Busy week in Washington settling in to CPB, interviewing candidates for staff, and seeing Jim Percoco work his multimedia magic with history students at W. Springfield High School. I finally got home late Friday in the frigid cold to my dear boys.

Our neighbor Sue Gatehouse died this morning. She had been in great pain with cancer, a shut-in all summer and hospitalized since late Fall. A fragile figure, single but stylish, a daily communicant and proud graduate of Sacred Heart, many early beaux and a late friendship with Doc Savage, solidified by AA. She had a childlike zaniness that our kids adored. "Suzie was the sweetest person," Rhoads said with feeling. He and Pierce offered the gifts at her funeral Mass. "OK Babe," were her sign off words to me the last time I called, recalling the swift set of the '60s of which she was the most innocent member.

I drove Pierce down to karate last night after a two-year hiatus. The Israeli instructors act more frenetic than ever, and Pierce was the only participant without a yarmulke. Across the street is the Lawrence-Cedarhurst Fire Department's impressive stone structure. On the third floor is the banquet hall where our beloved cook, Mary Ita O'Connell, married Luigi Benvin, Nick's younger brother, in 1964. A great night with much toasting and dancing, and Peter and I spent some of it tying the shoelaces of an especially drunken uncle of Mary's together under the table. Mary looked beautiful beyond words that day, and my Dad wore his morning suit to take her up the aisle. She bore Luigi two children and died of a punctured lung during a long siege of asthmatic pneumonia at 29.

Luigi was crushed when Mary died but within a few years married again. When I see him at church at Christmas no words are necessary, just a bear hug of loss and remembrance, and out into the twinkling night. To me he will always be young, happy, and unshaven, rubbing his day-old growth against Mary's cheek, she saying, "Ye old fool!" And when I asked her if she were going to marry Luigi, she smiled at me and asked, "What would you think if I did, Jim?"

Of course, we were all thrilled. Those were happy days.

Such are my thoughts as the karate class ends, Pierce and I talk of what exercises transpired therein, his steps toward his next belt, the Iowa caucuses, winter sports and all the other things that concern us as we drive back towards the water, deep in the January night.

2/4: Mark Zuckerberg starts Facebook at Harvard.

2/5: Winter continued cold. Clarissa informs me she's once more "free," an echo of 20 years ago. Framed by Howard Chandler Christy's nymphs at the Café des Artistes and as beautiful as any of them, Mr. Wien approaches our table and asks with well feigned earnestness, "Did you say Dr. Bullitt? But she's only a girl!" Good show.

Back on Long Island I went to Ellie Snyder's funeral. She was a beauty of the '30s, admired by Potter Stewart, John Hersey and Howard Hughes. She tended her husband through 15 years of Alzheimers and then succumbed to it herself. Phil, Rob, Peter and twenty others. The black supply priest at Trinity was very dignified.

The next day Kitty Stankard, who had tended the key desk at the Lawrence Beach Club for 45 summers in addition to teaching during the school year, was sent off as well. A lovely lady, and on a day of freezing rain her extended family turned out and a few die hards in the community, Cornie and Carol Shields, Art Murray, Sylvia Lynch and Judy Conway. No LBC governors, though, which Artie called, "A disgrace." Father Paul related talking to her after she broke her hip at 98. "Just because I'm old they think I don't see them sneaking by the desk without signing in (something I did myself as a young bachelor before Lanie made me join), but I do."

A lovely, gentle demeanor, steady, watery-blue-eyed gazed, but stern enough when she had to be—a full career in the public schools. The prayer she kept at her bedside was that as long as she lived she might give; and that she did, by example *and* spirit.

2/6: John Kerry emerges out of Iowa and comes close to Bush in the polls nationally (46–43). I cannot quite believe he will ignite any fires, but there are many variables and much that could go wrong for both going forward.

Leszek Kolakowski on the Book of Job and the Problem of Evil in *The New Criterion* quotes Augustine that the very fact of evil must be good; suffering is not an evil; it is the human condition for all at some point; but then one is left to ponder in what sense it can be a good?

2/10: To Brooklyn to see Rhoads interview at Packer, much admired and hard to get into, but a dreary physical environment. I walked to 110 Livingston Street to see the ruins of the public-school establishment. For me Brooklyn has always had the shabby quality of dear, dirty Baltimore. I feel very affectionate toward it but do not myself want to live there again.

2/13: The tenth anniversary of Mom's death. She died on Shrove Tuesday after being in a coma for two weeks. The church was packed that morning, and, despite the snowy roads, people came from Baltimore, college friends from Philadelphia, cousins from Easton, Pennsylvania, where my grandfather's company, Treadwell, had its main plant.

Her early life had been in New York City, a city where she could teach her best friend Betty Forker how to drive and parallel park on Madison Avenue (admittedly this may have been because Betty O'Brien, as she was then, was the Mayor's daughter), where the traffic cop at the entrance to Central Park on West 79th Street by their Beresford apartment waved them through on sight, and where another would save them a parking space outside of Saks. Their aunts and uncles lived for close to a century in a house that *their* mother had not wished to move to because it was so far into the countryside—69th Street. On a trip to Coney Island in 1927 my grandfather's chauffeur fought his way through the crowds to find Mom's friends and her with tears running down his cheeks, and cried out, "Miss Joan, Miss Joan, Lindbergh has landed!"

Then came college, and on a weekend visit to her friend Eddie Callan at Yale she met his roommate, and they fell in love. They married in 1941 while Dad was on furlough from the Cavalry and honeymooned in Saratoga Springs. The MacMillens always said they were the most romantic couple they had ever seen. And then the War. My father joined the Air Force and trained as a pilot in Texas before going out to the Pacific. Mother returned to New York, with two sick babies on a crowded train. Just as she felt overwhelmed, a GI standing in the aisle leaned over and asked her if he could hold Schuyler. "I've got one at home I've never seen, and I could use the practice." Fifty years later she still remembered that act of kindness with wonder. Angels walk amongst us.

In 1945 they came to Cedarhurst. My father's family still had racing dates at Jamaica, which was not far away, and Dad knew several people from Yale—Treddy, Tim Carpenter, Court Dixon. Their first house was on White's Lane near the village, now a municipal parking lot. Then the big brick house on Cedarhurst Avenue that could house six boys, a cook and Nanny, and frequent guests. Most of the surrounding lots were empty then, and in the ruins of the stable on Auerbach Lane we could still find horseshoes. Later, Mother built her dream house in the field next door and lived there happily for 20 years. The village became her home, her friends were increasingly here, and she was sought out by many for advice and comfort, which she gladly gave.

For someone so gregarious, however, she had a private side, and one of her solitary excursions was to rise well before dawn each December 13th, my father's birthday, and drive to the cemetery in Westchester where he was buried, a stone's throw from Eastview, Dad's grandfather Butler's farm, where they had courted and spent weekends in the early years of their marriage. And that is where she went 10 years ago today, a reunion she had looked forward to joyously for 20 years, and that but a nanosecond of the reunion in which they both trusted, and which, without doubt, she so triumphantly achieved.

2/21: Nick Hayes, from whom we bought our house on Stable Lane, is in the emergency room with pancreatitis following a liver probe. Groggy and drugged against the pain though he is, he wants me to know that Kathleen McKenna had approached him at Suzie's funeral to ask if she could have his mother's relic of the True Cross for her daughter, suffering from late-stage cancer. Nick is willing to lend it if he can be sure to get it back.

John Conway, a good man, indefatigable marketer of Amex, and with a fiery Irish temper, finally succumbed to Alzheimer's and related illnesses. Al the barber, Bernie Pastor from Pacific Oil, many of the Irish town folk and all the Club employees came. A man much loved in the village. "I'm just a boy from Lowell trying to get along," he'd say in his Harvard-inflected *Bahston* accent without any pretense whatsoever, and people loved him. I especially remember the speech he gave at the party he and Judy hosted for the unveiling of the portrait he commissioned of his Labrador, Charlie, whom he was always yelling at with reddened face as he walked him on his leash, and who in turn adored him totally. Father Paul called John "the last man left on Long Island who dressed for Mass." He was impeccably turned out in tweed jacket, flannels and tie, and was even immaculate in the garden in his khakis and polo shirt. Shame on Long Island!

3/4: A quiet birthday. I woke and cooked for the kids before putting them on the bus. Drove to town. Lunch with Treddy at The Brook with Matt Dick and Ambrose Monell. "Judas" on TV hilariously bad, a lot of gay hippies wandering around earnestly. Spalding Gray is dead at 62. He jumped off the Staten Island ferry and his body washed up eventually at Greenpoint. Son of a suicide. So tough. The monologues were wry, dry and funny, and I loved his low-key stage manager in *Our Town*, though the critics disagreed.

Pierce was turned down at Groton. Poor effort and behavior problems did him in. If he wasn't ready, it's for the best.

3/12: Absence of women a stage I do not especially rejoice in but will endure. The kids must come first, and, as Giulia Patriarca Cruise, in from Rome, said last week, "There's no need to rush into marriage and no need to rush into divorce."

Dinner at Carlos and Lynette Davis's with the very attractive Michelle Coppedge. As usual they overserved us. I may have made a fool of myself when the new Davis puppy started humping Michelle's leg, and I said I was jealous; but when I called her the next day Michelle seemed pleased and agreed to meet me at the Met next Friday evening.

Washington is coming along. Good meetings at National Endowment for the Humanities and with PBS. I like my colleagues and look forward to working more closely with them.

Back in NYC I tour the exhibit at Amber Yard, a great gift to the city by Spain, our suffering friend. Pierce and I win the handicap doubles, beating Tim and Ed Reitler 15–13 in the fifth. Rhoads loudly called out the score, often correctly, and otherwise cheered us on.

4/2: Pierce and Rhoads both have strep and have missed three days of school, in part because Lanie would not bring them to the doctor on Saturday despite their symptoms. On April Fools we played the customary "Pwanks" on each other waiting for the school bus. I sing "April Showers," and Rhoads asks with his shy smile, "If April showers bring May flowers, what do May flowers bring?"

"I dunno."

"Pilgrims!"

Then he scoots to the bus and waves from the window as it rolls up Stable Lane.

Spring has come in wet on Long Island, five or six rainy nights in a row, buds everywhere, but no burst as yet. Last night Rhoads composed and sang me two songs from the bath. "We'll Have a Jolly Old Time," and "I Lost My Little Friend."

Judge Wm. Maher was reminiscing sentimentally on his days at Legal Aid in Brooklyn as he worked his way through law school. "Every once in a while, we'd call in a bomb scare so they'd have to lock the building down for six hours, and we'd go to Coney Island to ride the Cyclone."

And Michelle, after attending our first Holy Week Triduum together, "I don't know which is more surprised, my soul or my poor little vagina."

The kids had gone to Texas after Lanie and I had resolved the remaining points of difference in our separation agreement. Holy Thursday Mass at St. Thomas More with Michelle, Jere Crook and his Aunt Adelaide, down from the Cape. Michelle sings like an angel and looks like one, too, with her blonde-haired, English/Irish/Kiwi/ California combination. Friday, we walked to the conservatory gardens. How many years had it been since I was last there?

The Worst Day. A call came from my old college classmate and racing friend Patrick Smithwick Sunday night.

"Jamie, this is really difficult . . ." My godson, Christopher Elser, 19, had been removed from life support and died. He had been stabbed repeatedly at 6 a.m. Saturday in his Johns Hopkins frat house defending his fraternity brothers from an intruder who had come through a door that someone left open after a party ended at 4 a.m. Christopher himself had his own apartment but had given it to a frat brother to study in and had come to the party and slept in the other guy's room.

"I tried to fight," were his last words as he stumbled into the next room, and he did save the others from the pathetic crack addict or whatever kind of sick monster it was who killed him.

There were 21 in the frat at the time. 911 got him airlifted to University of Maryland Shock/Trauma in 17 minutes. Took 41 shocks to revive him. There was hope for a while, but his brain had been without blood too long and began to swell. 60 or 70 kids stood vigil at the Hospital, and Hopkins President Bill and Mrs. Brody, to their credit, came to the hospital twice, and visited the frat as well. Unimaginable, unbelievable, unreal, and the worst of all nightmares for Kip and Rhetta. And me too, my godson, a sweet, insouciant little boy who grew up a kind but "cool" and bright, hardworking kid.

I drove down to Patrick and Ansley's farm on My Lady's Manor. In Patrick's barn office we hammered out our words. The Elsers arrived, Rhetta and Taylor, Christopher's little sister, especially dear. Tom and Mimi Voss, J.B. Secor and others from the sporting countryside came in. The next day we drove to town. More than six thousand came to the service in the Gilman Quad (Hopkins only has four thousand students). Bill Brody led off, then me, Patrick at his Maryland country finest, and Kip. And then the mike was passed, and the kids astounded us with their eloquence. A boy from Christopher's school in Florida who could hardly get out the words but said he had to try, an old girlfriend, his friend Kyra, the boy who tried to save him, his cousin. John and Lynn Egan came from Louisville, Dan Priest from Lexington, the Bradleys, who lost their son last fall (Christopher went to spend three days with them) from Marblehead, Charlesie Cantey, Janet Eliot, Sally Stoner, Mike Goswell, Warren Dempsey, Charlie Fenwick, Jesse Saunders, Russell Jones . . . and so many others. Henry Elser, the grandpa, looking bewildered and asking, "I'm 81, why couldn't it have been me?"

But why did it have to be anyone, let alone Christopher? The service in South Carolina is Friday, and a convoy of buses is going down from Baltimore. Then the hard part will begin.

4/29: And the wheel turns with the joyous news of Tim MacGuire and Julia Heckler's engagement. He popped the question at the beach. They then cell phoned the immediate world! Wedding next spring in Arizona. Wonderful.

Rhoads turned nine on Wednesday. He led the Pledge of Allegiance at the Spring Play on Friday. He played a hobo in the pageant and sang "Side by Side." Pierce went to Boston on a class trip. He came back and played with Jay Saling on their own initiative in an adult tennis round robin today. Life is moving along.

Margaret Carpenter decides not to run again for Village trustee. She feels cut out of the process by the other, now entirely male, Orthodox trustees. They hold side meetings, come in with a bloc and refuse deliberation. A shame, especially for someone who has done nothing but reach out, on behalf of the Episcopal Church and St. John's Hospital, which serves all members of the community. No one else of Marg's commitment coming along to serve, and that is worrisome.

Brother Philip is experiencing physical, mental and financial difficulties. Brother Pierce says, "Schuyler feels guilty he hasn't helped Kevin; Kevin feels guilty he hasn't done more; and I feel guilty because I don't feel at all guilty."

5/17: Pierce surfed for hours in the still frigid spring water with Jake, Taylor and George Carpenter. Rhoads, Benton and John Sipp formed their own troika. The hamsters, Hemmy and Alexis, escaped twice but were recaptured. The seven babies are to return to the pet shop soon. "Upstairs smells like a zoo," Bibi exclaims. I will stay down!

Swarming, unresolved crises are everywhere. The new job is not finalized, separation complexities, Philip's memory gone, Nick Hayes in danger of death without a new liver. Rhoads is despondent after his Charlie Brown All Stars lose 12–1 and he whiffs twice. Impossible to sleep.

5/20: Flying home from Washington I flew over Sandy Hook and up Manhattan Island. You could see all the way out through Brooklyn and Queens to the Rockaways and every inch was asphalt. No land left! Time to find some?

Pierce and I play tennis and then baseball. He tells me he hates his school. Adolescence! Lanie and his therapist Jeff Lawrence think public school might give him a new opportunity. Maybe. It will certainly give him a break in academic requirements; I am reluctant, but this is not going well. Meanwhile, Rhoads hits well in his game, and his team applauds him. He also catches for the first time, gamely if not perfectly (most balls found their way to the back of the batting cage!). He was pleased by the praise but afterwards in the car asked me, "Dad, can you keep a secret?"

"Sure."

"I was scared."

5/24: Nick Benvin's retirement dinner at the Club after 50 years as manager: A good night with speeches by Bob Hart, Bill Miller, who came up from Florida, and Tom Murray. Kathy Benvin Quinn spoke feelingly about Nick and Maria, recalling his industry, his generosity, and his sense of famiy.

5/31: Cookout at the house Saturday night, Pierce and Rhoads playing baseball with Sky and Pierce. Then Rhoads showed the hamsters. The next night Eileen, in from Dublin, gave a surprise birthday dinner for her husband Dave McGill. Michelle came and we had a good walk on the beach. Rhoads saw us and said with a grin, "Daddy has a girlfriend." He seemed amused. Two flawless, clear, high-skied days.

6/3: Lanie calls at 6:30 a.m., frightened, and says that Pierce went downstairs in the night and drank 8 or 9 beers. Fortunately for him, poor guy, he also ate a large quantity of chocolate chip cookie dough, and the combo made him vomit it all up. When asked by Lanie he said, "I started and couldn't stop." And when pressed, according to Lanie, protested, "But my Dad drinks a bottle of wine a night." (This is an accusation often made by Lanie and occasionally true.) She made Pierce go to school, and he went and put his head in his hands much of the day. Jane Eisenstadt, the middle school director, said he had been doing this for two days and wondered if it was a growth spurt. His shrink was unruffled. He said Pierce always seemed to have to take four or five pieces of gum instead of just one. What I would then tend to ascribe to L.'s obsessive-compulsive behavior coming from Lanie's hardwiring, she calls addictive behavior coming from mine. I wonder if having Michelle at the beach on Sunday had any impact?

I drive to Long Island early. Spring is peaking and the tide is high. I clean out all the liquor and beer in the house as per Lanie's wish. Not a bad idea given his tendencies cited above. Pierce sleeps until supper when I get him up. Then I sit down to work with him. Alarmingly unfocused in French, losing his place, interrupting his questions to ask other questions, and I can see how hard it must be for teachers to deal with him, and how disruptive he must be to others. After two hours he gets an exercise done and I introduce the subject at hand.

"What happened?"
"I had a dream and got really scared and went downstairs and got a beer and then couldn't stop."
"What was the dream?"
"You were driving to Washington DC and . . ." His voice breaks and trembles, and he starts to cry . . .
"And?"
"And you had an accident and died."

By now he is sobbing and embarrassed to be so. I hold him, tell him I have had those dreams too, and there's no way that's going to happen. It's going to be hard, but in some ways it's going to be interesting, and we'll have a good time.

Then more work. Putting both to bed, Rhoads chattering happily about the dog he imagines. "Let's go to sleep."

"I'm too excited. Oh shoot. I forgot to read a chapter of *Charlotte's Web*."
"I can wake you up early."
"No, I can do it at recess. It's my fault, and I'll suffer the consequences."

Pierce gets up twice in the night, and I catch him and put him back. (L. sleeps heavily and he roams at will.) In the morning both are cheery, and Rhoads gets his work done on his own.

6/4: There was a beautiful moment Wednesday amidst the lack of sleep and fear. I jogged at first light. The swans were on the water. I thought I saw something but could not be sure, so I peered through the reeds, and there were 1, 2, 3, 4 little cygnets, shielded by Mama, brown and furry, in the blue water, breeze fresh, sky lit by a golden sun.

6/5: President Reagan has died.

I fly to LA seated behind old Williamstown Theatre Festival buddy and Tony Award winner, Jim Naughton. Quick catch-up after too many years. Then to a KCET briefing. Onward to Bohemian Grove Spring Jinks with Michael McDonnell and our hosts, Nion McEvoy and Joe Tobin. We dine at Poison Oak Camp on lamb chops al fresco. Then the evening show with bandmaster Bobby Vickers and an Afterglow at Hillbilly with Sonny Charles, Sweet Louis, Mickey Hart, Bob Weir and many other fine musicians.

Up in the morning for breakfast and a nature lecture on the Grove. 60 tons of water up and down a redwood every day. Later in the afternoon an inspiring, idealistic talk around the lake by Supreme Court Justice Kennedy on "our most precious possession," the Constitution of the United States. His voice broke and many others were deeply moved. Memorable weekend of camaraderie and good times.

6/8: The transit of Venus.

I spoke to Bob Coonrod, chairman of the Corporation for Public Broadcasting. He makes his offer for CPB, and I will accept after some to and fro. I start July 1st. The kids are apprehensive. I try to tell them it will be an adventure, which I very much believe.

6/11: Rhoads received the Lamp of Learning for the third grade at the Moving Up ceremony today. He then read his poem, "I AM," by Rhoads:

*I am a third grader.*
*I wonder if my Dad will buy me a dog*
*I see Gab looking at my work*
*I want a dog . . .*

*I touch laughter*
*I think anybody can be a friend*
*I cry when people die*
*I understand space*
*I pray for world peace*
*I say everybody should be friends.*

*I am a third grader,*
*But I am looking forward to . . .*
*The fourth grade.*


As Peter Boneparth said, "He stole the show." The audience erupted into cheers, and John Passeggio, there in his grandfatherly function, came up to me and said, "So, are you gonna buy him a dog?"

Jack Bierwirth's 80th a happy occasion at the LBC on a perfect summer night. Family surrounding. His daughter Susan's winery supplied the very potable grape. Jack is hale and hearty.

6/19: At a session with the psychologist who will analyze Pierce for learning disorders Lanie rather disarmingly quotes Rhoads as an example of how he can express feelings whereas Pierce holds them in.

"Mommy, my life is almost perfect. The only thing that isn't perfect is that you and Dad are getting a divorce, and I blame you for that."

And Lanie quotes Pierce when she took him to see the guidance counselor at Lawrence Middle School. The counselor asked whether he preferred teachers who were empathic or strict. "Well, I tend to take advantage of the empathic ones and rebel against the strict ones."

6/28: Henry Kellerman says that Michelle and the ability to have a solid relationship is a big plus. The kids are anxious, he says, because, even if only subconsciously, they know that you have been the rock of consistency and love. Now it's likely to be more chaotic, but they simply need to be reassured that I am only a phone call away, and we will have many good times together in DC. A sweet weekend with them.

6/30: I enjoyed walking the DC streets around the Hotel Madison, the old hotels, the White House. People are smiling in the summer languor. I can't quite believe I'm here, and still living like a Bedouin, of course. We'll see . . .

Fourth of July fireworks with the boys. They now want to sit with their friends away from me, which is quite pleasant! But many memories of younger lap sittings and exclamations. They went with Lanie to Crested Butte the next day, and Michelle came out to Long Island, calm, patient, cheerful and affectionate. Fun at the LBC Luau with many friends around, and at the Thornton's garden party, admiring Jim's amazing hollyhocks.

7/20: On Long Island Tommy Murray was stricken with a massive coronary and went into cardiac arrest in the ambulance. He was saved, but there was some damage. Tommy looks good now and is adjusting his lifestyle. His Dad died the same way at 42, rascally Pawney, always with a twinkle in his eye, so Tom has to be careful.

7/29: Kip Elser and Helen Richards married around the pool at Louis Wylie's 1100 acres in The Plains, a beautiful Virginia holding from the 1730s.

Nick Hayes is off to Mayo Jacksonville for a liver transplant. He is number 11 on the list. And dear Sandy Whitman dead, Treddy's oldest friend.

Sandy, a gentleman of the old school, capacious in mind, very funny in a subtle way, a product of Saint Paul's and Harvard College, worked in the shipping business, but a great example of someone with a 135 or 140 IQ who doubtless worked for higher ups with 120s. The children's tributes at Trinity St. John's were wonderful.

Zander told of how much his father disapproved (hair length, dress code, propriety, etc.) but of how much upon which they agreed—(Loving the Sea, the greatest comic writer of the twentieth century, Guy Gilpatric, Scotch, etc). Having explained karaoke to him Sandy was soon calling it teriyaki . . .

Stephen, my old day camp counselor and a fine junior tennis player (his great Uncle and Sandy's Uncle Mac having been national champ in 1898–1899 and "aught one"):

"He was a man of great integrity whose example has driven and inspired all of his children. He was a man who had a hard time adjusting to the times—because he did not think there was any good reason to adjust. . . . He majored in art history, and he liked to use his mind, but he didn't like to tell anybody—or show it—because he thought that is not what people like him do. With one notable exception. He agreed with Charles Lamb that "a pun was a noble thing per se." His notepaper heading: "List of things I would not have to do if life were fair."

Angelica Harvey ("Pie") reminisced on the last day she spent with Sandy, taking her son Nathaniel and her on the Essex Steam Train: "My father loved to travel and preferred to go by boat if possible. He loved to get up early and wax poetic about the same 'rosy-fingered dawn' Odysseus knew. Returning from Europe by ocean liner he woke me at five so we could go on deck and watch the Statue of Liberty appear out of darkness—and change colors as we sailed into New York Harbor. In younger years he sailed in the Bermuda Races.

"My father loved music. He used to talk about going uptown to Harlem at night as a teenager to hear the music in the clubs. When he worked downtown in New York he would come home from a long day in New York, followed by a stop at Fusco's, have his dinner and start belting out something from *My Fair Lady*. One night when he had stayed in their apartment in New York my mother got an excited call. 'You've got to come in! I'm in a club and I'm singing with Judy Garland.' He would leap at the sound of a regiment of bagpipers and follow their winding parade with tears in his eyes.

"My father had a Navy saying, which usually came after he had worked out in the yard and was about to lie down on the sofa and watch a football game, beer in hand. 'Whitman, take a well-deserved rest!' Duty-bound, he would answer: Aye Aye, sir!
"Whitman, take a well-deserved rest!"

My own memories of Sandy were not so poignant, but he was truly droll and had a wonderfully sly sense of humor. When someone explained that the reason Tim and Mary Grant were moving to Locust Valley was because the Colemans, the Tilghmans, and "all the nice people" had already gone, he affected outrage and snorted, "The Nice People. The Nice People? Those aren't the nice people. The Nice People left in the Twenties."

At Mother's 70th Theresa was invited and proceeded in her way when partying to dominate every conversation and the dance floor simultaneously. A group photo was called for, and she sat on the floor and raised her skirt to show some additional leg. Sandy was sitting next to her and promptly did the same with his gray flannels.

Most of all I remember the first night Lanie and I asked them to drinks on Stable Lane, they having welcomed us back to the community most kindly when we arrived. Sylvia was sick and said that Sandy would probably not come either, but he showed up and said, "I couldn't resist," as he took a glass of champagne. The crowd was growing, and, a bit bashfully, he asked if he could see a then newborn Rhoads, sleeping upstairs. We went up together, and he stood over the crib and looked at that baby for a long time. Then he looked at me. Whatever he was thinking he did not choose to verbalize, and without a word we went downstairs together and back into the scrum, but I always felt close to him after that.

I have many good friends here of my own age and younger, but there is a special sadness as the last of my parents' great friends expire. And yet, it has been a privilege to be with them again in their old age.

8/18: Wonderful time playing in our first Father-Son tourney with Rhoads last weekend, something he has been asking me to do all month. He was two to six years younger than the other boys competing. He hits a moonshot of a serve and, amazingly, some go in. He dives for the ball on every point he can and loves the fun of competition. When he hit me in the back of the head with one shot, and I dropped to the ground as if mortally stricken, he was convulsed for minutes and shook so hard he fell as well. Pierce is 5'11" now and his technique has improved. Growing into himself and fun to watch.

8/24: David Walsh died in his sleep this morning. He was 32 and not expected to survive childhood with muscular dystrophy. A sweet soul, Christ-like really, trapped in his mechanized wheelchair, much beloved by his friends. Hundreds came to the service and Chris and Tim MacGuire's age group crowded John and Mimi's apartment after. Over Labor Day weekend a small shrine was festooned with flowers where he sat on the beach by the volleyball nets, and Rhoads stopped, made the Sign of the Cross, and prayed at it.

The Madsens show the films Phil and Rob Snyder and the rest of us helped make as kids, "War Shorts," "Psycho II," "Mr. Miser," etc. The older crowd—DeeDee Baker (who taught us all Latin before being ordained to the Episcopal priesthood), Bob Hart, Bob Baldridge, the Bierwirths, and MacLeans all fascinated. The movies were hopelessly amateurish but wonderful things for 14-year-olds to do well. My own acting was awful.

The kids run to and hug Kip when they see him in the paddock at Saratoga, and he gives them a long embrace in return. Everyone in the steeplechasing crowd remarks on it, and a lady wipes away a tear. I cannot imagine how difficult living with Christopher's murder must be.

"It must be Hell," I said to him the night before the service at Hopkins. "Jamie, it's Hell." They have a suspect in custody for another crime but not enough evidence to charge him for Christopher's murder.

Pierce was very grown-up walking across the paddock, "I have to go say hello to the MacMillens."

Al Solomon is a month shy of 105, blind, mostly deaf and in bad shape, but clinging to life with terrible tenacity. Birdstone got home in the Travers moments before a calamitous storm broke and washed out the remaining race on the card. A good win for Mary Lou Whitney.

Labor Day weekend, one of my last on Stable Lane, and, sleeping on the narrow day bed downstairs, I listened to the crickets thundering, damp wind blowing easterly as Hurricane Frances bears down on Florida. In the morning there are the cries of strange birds and crows are picking at the remains of the fallen pears. Casey and Clay came for a cookout and have become great beauties. Rina and Julia were also on hand with Chris and Tim and looked lovely. A happy time for the family.

After washing up I checked my messages, and Catherine French had called to say that Al Solomon had died the night before at 104, 11 months, and ten days. Mrs. Burke, the manager of the Reading Room, ceremoniously placed a Maker's Mark and water at his usual table, and a crowd of old friends gathered to celebrate him. And his birthday party will go on regardless, as he had decreed.

And so, the last Labor Day in Lawrence ended, the breeze blowing hard through the window all night, and Rhoads coming down to cuddle at three in the morning. The car cleaned ("The Executive" car wash package for $25 on Rockaway Turnpike) and packed to the brim. Last tennis with Ed Reitler, Larry Phillips and my brother Peter. Last lunch with Treddy. I call the MacMillens to say goodbye. Pierce played with one of the incoming USTA senior grass championship contestants. Rhoads hugged me. I took Lanie from the train, went to the beach on a brilliant blue afternoon for one final glorious ocean swim, and then drove on down to Washington.

9/19: The boys arrived at noon on Friday, taking advantage of their Rosh Hashanah break. Rhoads immediately pronounced Washington as "the best of eighteenth-century history and twenty-first century technology" (he was alluding to the comparatively modern, clean and spacious subway). We walked to the Air and Space Museum, the American History Museum, the Washington Monument being relandscaped and secured, and then the WW II memorial, where we communed with Dad, their other grandfather, Lee Sauder (also a pilot), and Treddy.

And then the final hike to the sublime Lincoln Memorial, along the southern allee and beside the reflecting pool. Pierce was palpably moved. And we passed the Vietnam Veterans Memorial on the way back, searched out George Whitney Carpenter's name, another camp counselor of mine, family friend of all of ours and the uncle of Pierce and Rhoads' buddies, Taylor, George and Timi. By the end of our march the kids' tongues were hanging out on a humid day. But they were troopers and were bought an X-Box as promised.

The next day we went to the Jefferson Memorial and Arlington National Cemetery. Just as we reached the breaking point, we came upon the Changing of the Guard at the Tomb of the Unknowns, and all stood transfixed. Then home again and dinner at our new favorite hangout, "Sorriso," which means smile. Pietro, retired from the World Bank, and his lovely Scottish wife, Rosemary, and two great kids, Isabella and Stefano, run this cozy family Italian spot in Cleveland Park with especially good pizza. Rhoads helps turn the pies in the wood-burning oven. Rosemary admires his curls, and asks, "Can I take him home with me?"

11/2: Bush defeats Gore.

11/5: Fall goes on. The kids came down again and again, and we had great times. Once Rhoads and I walked to Rock Creek Park, and as we sat on a log and skipped stones I asked, "Do you ever think of what you want to do with your life?"

"WHY do people ask me that? I have so many ideas."

"Like what?"

"Well, I'd like to do something to help animals, or be a tennis pro. But I used to want to be a pro baseball player."

Today when I called, Bibi had taken him to Christian doctrine class over his objection that he was too tired, and when he emerged, he exclaimed, "Bibi, talkin' about God makes you feel so good!"

11/22: Work is pleasant but so much slower than in the private sector. Here I am criticized for trying to go too fast! But, much as I enjoy CPB and the History Initiative, my monthly bank statement sings out the need for more income.

Back to NYC for Thanksgiving weekend. It seemed more crowded, narrower, grittier and dirty. Within five minutes of coming through the Holland Tunnel, an aggressive cab driver had knocked my sideview mirror cockeyed. I drove to Long Island the next evening to cook a steak in the rain for Pierce and Rhoads, the charcoal surviving despite all odds.

We had another wonderful Thanksgiving at Sally and Kevin's in Connecticut. Lanie had gone to Paris for the holiday, so I spent the weekend on Stable Lane. On Thanksgiving night, the rain gave way to a new front and wind whipped in, whistling through the roof and rocking and rattling the old house. At one point around 2:30 in the morning a gaggle of geese began honking from far away and passed directly overhead, crying wildly as Rhoads snored beside me. I sensed, as I had on thousands of nights before in this house, that I was on board a ship, the sails hoisted and wind filling them, God steering the tiller, and only He knows where.

I lie awake imagining a few of the possibilities, but there are infinite others beyond my ken, and the Tide has shifted slowly but decisively. At Mass Saturday evening Bob Baldridge sits close by us. He looks thin to me, this veteran of D-Day plus 4 on Omaha Beach who won a battlefield commission and Bronze Star before he was twenty. Within three months he will take Communion at a Saturday evening Mass, go home and die in his living room chair: An enviable end to an honorable life.

On my last night I walked the Isle of Wight at sunset. Sylvia Lynch tells me she can't walk fast anymore. "Your knee?"
"No, that has healed. My emphysema." That won't.

Sylvia says Nancy Sipp lost a baby this fall, poor girl. The Burgstahlers are in residence where Penny and Tony Coe once presided. Cee Cee Belford, the Brooks and Madsens are all remodeling, and the Wadsworths are adding a pool. Treddy cracked up his ancient Oldsmobile into someone's rear end on the FDR Drive. They accused him of inebriation, but he may simply be getting too old to drive to town. There's a beautiful sunset over the Atlantic Beach Bridge. Debbie Drake's studio light is on. She has developed into an artist with a great color sense and has been working on a series of studies of the marsh. I sent her citations of two Heades in the Wilmerding Collection at the National Gallery of the Newberry Marshes at the mouth of the Parker River south of Newburyport from the late nineteenth century, which could be interesting references. Chuck Leonard drove by in his SUV. Earlier in the week he had met with Web Golinkin, up from Houston, who presented his new health testing and treatment company's plan. Victoria and Nick Banks are in residence at the Bulkleys, and Artie Murray, a youthful widower in his early 70s now, waves from his sunporch window, the last before the headland and the now desolate yacht club. I walked to the bank of Crooked Creek and looked over the marshlands, 1700 acres of them, stretching east.

I thought of the harbor seal I had seen "stand up" and peer with its delightful, bewhiskered face and saw the cormorants, as I had often before. I thought of the studies that say the seas are increasing in size as the ice masses of Greenland's glaciers melt. Someday New York City may be another Atlantis—a lost city.

In one cubic foot of water from the sea there are 120 plankton animals, untold millions of smaller microscopic animals, 12.5 million plants, as well as larger plants and animals. The sand itself is a museum of gems, minerals and chemical compounds of all kinds.

There is lots of muck on the banks of Crooked Creek. "Muck" is central to the salt marsh. It is the marsh's main floor, covered with a cushion of bacteria, fungi and algae, organic material thoroughly decomposed and little oxygen.

In 1878 Sidney Lanier wrote, "The sea and the marsh are one." A self-sustaining garden. One acre of salt marsh in Georgia produces ten tons of organic material. On Long Island, due to its winters, the number is between three and seven tons.

The tide is high. I think of the Fen dwelling monster Grendel from "Beowulf," or Bunyan's "The Slough of Despond." Could they be out there somewhere, in this place I have for decades called home?

And there, as I wander in my thoughts, rising in a huge pale-yellow, luminous ball, is the very moon itself, exerting its strange, inexorable pull.

But where will it impress me?

50 Cedarhurst Avenue. The Mother Ship from 1948. Photograph courtesy of the author.

The House at 7 Stable Lane in 1996. That's baby Rhoads playing in the road. Photograph courtesy of the author.

Governor Ritchie of Maryland with great grandfather James Butler at Laurel Park, 1930s.
Photograph courtesy of the author.

Walker Evans Photo "Damaged" with Butler Grocery Store sign in background. A metaphor? Photograph courtesy of the author.

Grandfather Schuyler Casey with daughters Joan and Julia, Jersey Shore,1924. Photograph courtesy of the author.

George Bull and my grandfather, Dr. D. Philip MacGuire at the Saratoga Yearling Sales, 1940s. Photograph courtesy of the author.

My father, Army Air Force Captain Philip F. MacGuire, 1944. Photograph courtesy of the author.

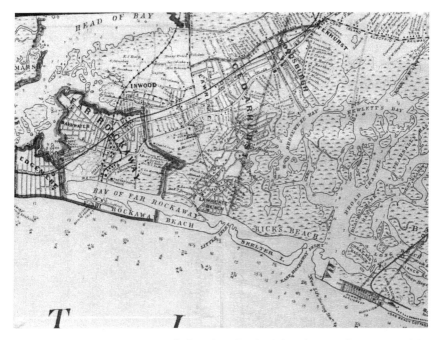

1880s map of the Five Towns, including the Isle of Wight. Photograph courtesy of the author.

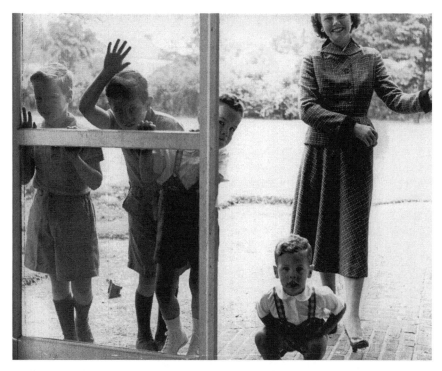

Pierce B. (crouching) with Joan MacGuire on Cedarhurst Avenue in Town & Country, 1951, Schuyler, Philip Jr. and peeking Kevin at left. Photograph courtesy of the author.

Lawrence School in Hewlett Bay Park, Long Island, the former Henry Devereaux Whiton estate, 1930s. Photograph courtesy of the author.

The Rockaway Hunting Club, Long Island's oldest country club, founded 1878. Photograph courtesy of the author.

Joan and Phil MacGuire walking on Worth Avenue in Palm Beach, 1960s. Photograph courtesy of the author.

After Schuyler MacGuire's and Dean Tyndall's wedding, as the groom prepares to leave on his honeymoon: Schuyler, Kevin, the (barely) still standing author, Pierce B., Peter and Philip MacGuire Jr., 1968. Photograph courtesy of the author.

Father Hilary, the "Good Shepherd," on The Farm at Portsmouth Priory, 1950s. Photograph courtesy of the author.

With classmate and Campion co-author Christopher Buckley and former teacher "Uncle Billy" Crimmins at Williamstown Theatre Festival, 1987. Photograph courtesy of the author.

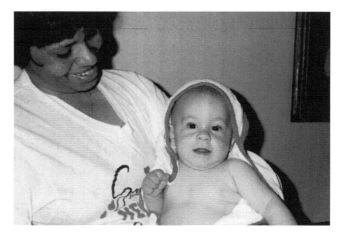

Bibi and baby Pierce P., 1991. Photograph courtesy of the author.

Lawrence Beach Club 4th of July Parade with Uncle Sam, 1961. Photograph courtesy of the author.

Rhoads at the bat on Stable Lane, 1998. Photograph courtesy of the author.

Christmas Photo 1998 with Pierce, the author, Lanie and Rhoads. Photograph courtesy of the author.

Rockaway Hunting Club 125th Anniversary 2003 with Gray Beverly, the Author, President William T. Ketcham and Ray York. Photograph courtesy of the author.

Joan MacGuire with Bill and Barbara MacMillen, 1990s. Photograph courtesy of the author.

Cedarhurst Yacht Club by Lee Stinchcomb Staniford, 2011. Photograph courtesy of the author.

Beloved Isle of Wight Neighbors Ann and Jim Thornton. Photograph courtesy of the author.

The Marsh. Photograph by Courtney Hardart.

Michelle Coppedge and the Author, Hawaii, 2018. Photograph courtesy of the author.

Boarding school roommate and Chronicle Books CEO Nion McEvoy at SPIN magazine party with Author, 2007. Photograph courtesy of the author.

MacGuire Thanksgiving Dinner 2018 at Wee Burn Country Club, Darien, Connecticut. Standing: Casey, Michelle, Chris, Peter, Emily, the Author, Anabel, Alex, Pierce P., Lily, Julia, Tim, Tyler, Rina, Rachel, Ryan and Schuyler. Sitting/ Kneeling: Clay, Dean, Becky, Pierce B., hosts Kevin and Sally, Rhoads. Photograph courtesy of the author.

P.J., Pierce P., Alex, and Walker MacGuire at home in Georgetown, Texas, 2021. Photograph courtesy of the author.

Isabel Keogh and Rhoads MacGuire on the 9-Bar Ranch in Decatur, Texas. They were engaged in May of 2021. Photograph courtesy of the author.

## Chapter 6

# A New Chapter, 2005–2008

### 2005

April 2, 2005 Pope John Paul II dies and is succeeded by Cardinal Joseph Ratzinger, who chooses the name Benedict XVI.

My nephew Tim MacGuire and his beautiful bride Julia had a joyous wedding in Arizona that Spring. Afterwards, Michelle and I had a blissful week in Paris staying with Florence Mauchant near the Bois de Boulogne and in London with Michelle's Kiwi cousin, Brigid Plowman, in her flat on Eaton Square.

By late summer my work at the Corporation for Public Broadcasting was substantially done, much more quickly than anyone thought possible, and I was back in New York.

In July, my brother Peter turned 50, and Michelle gave a festive dinner party at 1170 Fifth Avenue. I read from a letter Peter had scrawled on a Western Airlines cocktail napkin when he and Maitland Horner had gone to Eaton's Ranch unaccompanied at sixteen or so. "I had a great time and was pretty much perpetually drunk . . . started a small forest fire last night."

In other happy news my brother Schuyler and his wife Dean became grandparents on July 17th when Chris and Rina MacGuire welcomed Lily Joan. Rhoads and Pierce went off to Camp Longhorn in Texas and reported on their water slide activities. Tom Russo and I were upset winners of the William F. Talbert Men's Doubles over much younger teams in the semis and finals— Matt Schmeelk and Charlie Leonard, then Chris MacGuire and Greg Gately, both in three long sets on a hot and very humid day.

I had two wonderful weeks with the boys on their return from Colorado in Saratoga, Keene Valley and on the Isle of White. On Long Island the humidity slowly bled as the sun waned and the temperature fell. I woke one morning with Rhoads crushed to my side and giggling as he slept. I giggled back involuntarily, and he woke, asking, "Are you havin' the same dream?"

On September 12th I drove Pierce to his first year at Portsmouth after much last-minute repacking and crying from Lanie and a dear, distraught Bibi.

He was full of humor and Comedy Central one-liners and, once settled into his room and new roommate, soon signaled that my presence was no longer required.

Later in the month Rhoads got braces, did well academically at Lawrence-Woodmere Academy and loved starting football with the Inwood Buccaneers.

Pierce came home for Columbus Day and walked in the surf with his first girlfriend, Michaela Murphy, and her dog Charlie. Rhoads was deliriously happy to have him but downcast at the Yankees loss to Chicago and elimination from the playoffs.

In December I took Rhoads to Confession for Christmas. Unlike me, who burst into tears at my First Confession, he appeared completely comfortable, plopped himself into the chair rather than the kneeler and sang out, "Hi Father Paul." Rhoads played the xylophone at his holiday concert and Pierce enjoyed reading *Beowulf* in his English class at Portsmouth. We had a good week after Christmas skiing in Crested Butte.


## 2006


Nick Hayes, who sold us his mother's house on Stable Lane, died in early January of liver cancer, and I was asked by Lisa to read the Prayers of Intercession at the Mass in Arlington. Only 58 and a dear guy. Another LBC regular of old, Jimmy Thompson, nephew of the CIA and Thai Silk legend Jim Thompson, died at 57 in North Carolina later in the month. He worked at Coliseum Books for many years and was always kind.

Peninsula Library Research while staying with Rhoads:

- "Lawrence by the Sea" was how the Isle of White was often referred in the 1880s. The Isle of Wight was organized by Rufus W. Leavitt, a Flushing lumber merchant named Beck and several investors. They set off by a ditch a 30-acre piece of land that jutted out into the ocean.
- The Cullullo monument at Wood and Keene Lanes (Wood being Samuel Wood the developer of Woodmere and Keene being James R. Keene, the Silver King and father of Foxhall) reads:

"Here lived and died Cullullo Telawana A.D. 1818, the last of the Rockaway Iroquois Indians, who was personally known to me in my boyhood. I, owner of these lands, have erected this monument to him and his tribe."—Abraham Hewlett 1888

- Buckminster Fuller married Ann Hewlett at Rock Hall on July 12, 1917.
- Monroe Hewlett was the director of the American Academy in Rome in 1931. He also designed the magnificent ceiling at Grand Central Terminal. He went broke in 1932 and his beautiful house stood empty for several years until Mr. Bierwirth Sr. bought it in 1940.
- Lawrence School was the Charles Whiton estate.
- The Finlayson House (Stanford White, architect) was owned by Sally Flagg.
- George and Betty Tilghman's on Longwood X was originally a carriage house for a large estate.
- The Polo Inn on Park Row was lived in by a titled hermit before Crowell and Dee Dee Baker bought it. They found oyster shells left over by feasting grooms in the basement.

One morning I woke Rhoads and got him moving for his "boring" field trip to the Brooklyn Museum. "Why is it boring?"
"It's got the word 'museum' in it, doesn't it?"

1/25: Disney buys Pixar from Lucasfilm for $7.4 Billion.
Over Spring break, I took the boys to Hofstra to watch heavily favored Johns Hopkins get upset in lacrosse 15–3, Rhoads looking dubiously at me sideways as the massacre unfolded! Pierce is playing good squash. 55 attended the RHC St. Patrick's dinner, including the Bierwirths and MacMillens but also younger members like the Savins, Belfords, and Morledges. The torch is being passed, and life will go on.
4/6: I sold the lot on Stable Lane I bought from Nick Hayes to John Minnegan, who promises he will build for a member there (Art and Peggy Nicol, as it turns out). I did well, but that was never the point. End of a family compound dream. Onward!
4/10: Rhoads, looking at me, after the account of Christ's Passion from the Gospel of Mark at the Palm Sunday Mass: "Whoa!"
5/10: Rhoads' birthday is a great success. He and three classmates went to *Scary Movie 4*, a flatulence and Viagra-joke-filled flick by the makers of *Airplane* at Green Acres Cinemas. Rhoads called me at recess from the School office to say, "Dad, I'm just calling to confirm you really will take us to *Scary Movie 4* this afternoon." Once we got there, he promptly spilled his 32 oz. drink on the floor upon receiving it from the soda jerk, who cheerfully refilled it gratis. The kids loved the movie. We repaired afterwards to Stable Lane for trampoline acrobatics, pizza and ice cream cake. Lanie called to ask

if he was having a nice day. "I'm having a wonderful day," and that made all the messy details more than worth it.

## Summer

Rhoads went to a pool party in Bellmore at Jakob Cayne's, 28 attending in the postage stamp-sized backyard. Rich Cayne hosted, a friendly guy, covered in tattoos. The next day Rhoads and John Sipp played all day at both houses and at the beach. Pierce is into his exams, but he broke his finger the week before and is in a splint, just to make it interesting.

Pierce was handsome and happy when I collected him from Portsmouth. He loves school and is beloved but needs to go to summer school to make up work. Rhoads is happy to have him home and fielded well in his Little League win last night. The next week he was delighted to win the father-son tennis round robin despite the dearth of opponents.

He was hilarious last night at the Junior Sports Dinner. "What would you do with a $250 gift certificate?" "Send Pierce back to School."

7/5: Lanie and Michelle finally meet at Burtch and Debbie Drake's beautiful Fourth of July garden party on Friday, cordially if a tad awkwardly. It was good of Lanie to make the effort. Rhoads and I romp in the waves, play tennis and golf, and then are off to the fireworks. He and Benton disappear to dig a suitable bunker but return to watch with their parents. The next week Rhoads asks me to take him to confession before he goes off to camp! His first letter reads, "I'm glad you're happy. I love you. Who won Wimbledon?"

7/21: After a year-long decline from unattended skin cancer, Treddy died peacefully at home. The Marine Honor Guard was magnificent in playing "Taps" and folding and presenting the flag at Trinity-St. John's Church in Hewlett. Seth French, Treddy's oldest friend (born in Hewlett on the same day Treddy was born in Cedarhurst), and I were asked to eulogize, and here is what I said.

*William T. Ketcham, Jr. (1919–2006)*

Let's start by remembering how much FUN Treddy was. Patron saint of racquet sports, Rockefeller Republicanism, New Amsterdam ancestries, Hill and Yale, countless clubs, cigars, stingers and rose wine, which he often mixed himself. Breeziest of banterers, perky and chipper, cheerful and optimistic, he could see the humor in the direst of circumstances, loved life's absurdity, and reveled in every social situation.

Events like today's, in fact, were among his favorites. "It's the end of an era!" he'd bark, or, in what was perhaps his favorite phrase, "A GREAT

AMERICAN." Treddy would go along to the service and enjoy it, and then he would proceed to the reception, and REALLY enjoy that. And he would want us to do the same today.

His amiability and remarkable resilience stood him in good stead over his long life, in war time, his grave illness of a decade ago, and especially in the last nine months, when, despite every setback, he kept a positive outlook, planned for the future, maintained his interest in his family and friends, and *never* complained.

I'd like to add a word to all those who went the extra mile for Treddy to lighten his burden in these last months—Hanna and Dennis O'Rourke, Paul and Sara Strader, Margaret and Tim Carpenter, Ray York, Tim Hellmuth, Michael Meehan and Treddy's many friends at The Brook who kept him coming down for lunch and dinner with such frequency and conviviality that on one occasion when he returned to the nursing home near midnight the night manager snarled, "This isn't a hotel, you know." Many others gave of themselves to keep him going in ways large and small, each in its own fashion a perfect example of what Our Lord asks of us in the Gospels. Treddy would want us to SHOW our appreciation, so let's give Hanna and all of them a hand.

Coming to terms with Treddy's life is challenging, in part, because of how very multi-faceted his achievements and interests were, in the foreign service, at Davis Polk and IBM, in the sports at which he excelled and competed so cunningly, and in all the organizations to which he contributed and helped to run.

Seth French spoke movingly about Treddy as a family man. If I may speak personally for a moment, his annual visit was the highlight of our family's Christmas Eve, and in recent years his presence on Christmas Day was as well. His stays at Mom and Dad's house in Saratoga every August were filled with laughter, high-spirited games and even an occasional winner at the track. The friendship he so generously gave us during our parents' lifetimes and after their deaths, here and in town, was a precious gift for which my brothers and I, and all of our families, will always be grateful.

And I know that each of you, from his oldest friends—Seth, Worthy Adams and Henry Mellen—to the youngest person here today—and Treddy had a special gift of friendship for the young, which helped keep *him* young— have similar memories and sentiments. Like Mr. Chips, Treddy had no children and "thousands of 'em."

But to understand what made his life special, what set him apart, we have to look beyond the familiar memories and the fun, to the events that defined Treddy, matured in him a profound seriousness of soul, and of which he almost never spoke. Like Bob Hart, who celebrated his 90th birthday this week, and Tim Carpenter, his fellow Eli, Marine and veteran of Iwo, Treddy went to war, did his job, came home and got on with his life, "Partaking," in the words of his hero's Farewell Address, "In the midst of my fellow citizens the benign influence of good laws under a free Government."

In addition to George Washington, Winston Churchill was another hero of Treddy's, and he met the Great Man several times while working for NATO in London. Treddy agreed wholeheartedly with Churchill's words in his blood, sweat and tears speech: "You ask what is our aim? I can answer in one word: Victory." After all, Treddy had lived by those words.

A company commander of Company One, Third Battalion, in the 24th Regiment, on February 19, 1945, Captain Ketcham landed with his company of 230 men on Iwo Jima. The beach was already littered with corpses when they landed late in the day. After a month of fighting, they had advanced only a quarter of a mile and remained pinned down. Just nineteen of his original men survived.

What happened next, as Tim Carpenter has pointed out, was something company commanders normally delegated and were not expected to do themselves.

From the citation sent by Secretary of the Navy John L. Sullivan to the President of the United States:

"With complete disregard for his own safety, Captain Ketcham moved alone over some two hundred yards of exposed terrain to a rocky crest. In spite of heavy mortar and small arms fire aimed at him, he directed accurate 60mm. mortar and artillery fire on four pillboxes. After destroying these fortifications, he led his company forward in another assault. The position was taken after bitter hand-to-hand combat. Although very weakened from his wounds, Ketcham personally directed a speedy reorganization of his company to successfully repulse a counterattack. His skill, initiative, and courageous devotion to duty in the face of enemy fire are in the highest tradition of the United States Naval Services."

Here I should point out that Treddy always considered himself a Marine, and there is a story told about his mother being seated next to a previous Secretary of the Navy, James Forrestal, at a War Bonds lunch. "What branch of the service is your son in?" he asked by way of breaking the ice, and, in her timid way, Mrs. Ketcham replied, "The Marines. That's the fighting branch of the Navy, you know."

Treddy's actions and those of other valorous Americans helped break through the Japanese lines and led to victory on Iwo Jima and the indelible image of Marines raising the Stars and Stripes on the peak of Mount Suribachi, which Treddy witnessed. Victories such as this, earlier in the Pacific campaign at Guadalcanal, and later, on Okinawa, were the crucial building blocks to total victory and VJ Day in August 1945.

This is traditionally a month for patriotic speeches, and Treddy would endorse Daniel Webster's words from his Bunker Hill oration of 1825, on the

50th anniversary of the shots heard 'round the world: "Let our object be our country, our whole country and nothing but our country."

In his Funeral Oration for the Athenian Dead, Pericles declared, "It is greatness of soul alone that never grows old, nor is it wealth that delights in the latter stage of life, as some give out, so much as Honor." How better to describe Treddy?

Finally, at Gettysburg Abraham Lincoln exhorted "us the living" to be dedicated to the great tasks laying before us, but in so doing urged that we must build on the lessons and examples left by those who have gone before.

Though characteristically he deflected attention from himself in this regard, Treddy was a man of faith, *semper fidelis*, as Dee Dee Baker has so eloquently described in her homily. For decades he ushered here at the Christmas morning service so that Dads could play Santa at home.

At his brother's service in March, he read the *Prayer of Saint Francis* which you will also hear today, and I would have loved to get a rise out of Treddy by complimenting him on the journey toward Rome that such a selection implied, but that conversation will have to wait; and in any case, when he chose to be serious about it, Treddy believed we were intended, in the words of Saint Paul, to try to overcome our divisions and, "Be One in Christ Jesus."

If ever there was a man over whom Death had no Dominion, it was Treddy. He had seen too much of it, laughed in its face, and gone about doing what he thought was right, his spirit inextinguishable. And so, it will always remain.

Not long ago we were talking about the hymns we had enjoyed at a friend's funeral, and Treddy suddenly said with feeling, "I want the *Battle Hymn of the Republic* played at my service," and expressed his dismay that this magnificent, stirring, and profoundly spiritual anthem of the Union and anti-slavery cause had been deleted out of the most recent edition of the Hymnal.

We will sing the *Battle Hymn* today, and as we depart we will hear the *Marine Hymn* as well, on a day when the Corps has once more been summoned to the shores of Tripoli, thanking God as we do for a loving Uncle, a wonderful and often very funny friend, a *bon vivant*, a public-spirited citizen, a philanthropist, a champion and sportsman, a warrior and hero, a leader, an exemplar, a patriot, a man of honor, a Christian gentleman, or shall we say: "A Great American?"

There was a huge turnout locally and from town, and afterward hundreds gathered at the Hunt Club for a joyous reception, though I am not sure Treddy would have approved of the sushi bar his nieces arranged!

### September

9/8: International Lawn Tennis Club Day with Broward Craig, Les Nicholson and others. Good fun and dinner after with Ralph and Julie Earle. But the heart of the day was throwing footballs on the beach with Rhoads, practicing plays, swimming in the sea, and racing laps in the pool. It was a pretty, quiet September day, reminiscent of another, even stiller one five years ago, when I got home in time to tear then 10-year-old Pierce away from the TV and its catastrophic images and take him to the beach as well.

Rhoads and I talk a long time, and he says, "You know Dad, it's not very often that the best athlete and the best student is also the class clown." Just as it should be!

Watching Monarch butterflies fly across the dunes and throwing balls to an 11-year-old who loves to fly through the air catching them, remembering that feeling of freedom and communion with the soft sand.

10/9: Pierce is home with a fine new Spanish friend, Jaime, and Rhoads has become a statistics-spewing, ESPN Sports Zone obsessed, football maniac.

11/1: I drive out to play ball, cook dinner and spend the night with Rhoads. At bedtime he asks to sleep with me, presses his increasingly unmanageable mane of mop-haired brown curls into one's side, spouts a steady stream of Giants stats and what ifs, recites his prayers with fluency, asks a parting question, and shares a final triumph from that morning's recess touch football game. Then he is gone, clutching my side tightly and breathing deeply.

When my arm falls asleep, I turn to face the other wall, and within moments he has clambered up on my back, hugging it, though still fast asleep. Occasionally a word or phrase pops out, or even a delighted giggle, but then he nestles in deeper, this 11-year-old, so quick to show his wiseness of the world, machismo and command of street talk when awake, but now betraying the deep tenderness, affection and profound sweetness of his being.

At four I rise and stumble towards the loo. Coming back, I look out one window to check the moon and the stars; another window to look across the marsh and Reynolds Channel to the Atlantic Beach Bridge; out the last to gaze into dear neighbor Madsen's deep, windswept field. And then I go back, my side of the bed now nearly annexed by 106 pounds of future football talent. I re-assert my rights as best I can, pushing him back across the mattress to his side, but as if by a yoyo he winds back to envelop as much of me as he can. I think of all the nights his mother and I spent like this and let that bittersweet thought drift on. Tomorrow is full of challenges and choices, but the choice I made to keep this boy and his brother close to me has repaid itself a zillion times, already.

A happy Thanksgiving at Kevin and Sally's and the next day the boys and I went to *Borat*, a work of subversive genius and high hilarity. It offset Rhoads' dismay at the Aggies upset of the Longhorns.

## Mid-December

Court Dixon and Huschi Denson are both gone. Huschi's mother was a princess and she herself a countess, then became a housewife and all-around good egg on Long Island. But she never lost her sense of self. I remember her wringing the neck of a wounded goose who could barely walk on the golf course several years ago. As her own disease advanced, she knew when it was her time to go.

Rhoads loses half his vision in left eye for thirty minutes at school. Highly unusual and scary. Transient lemianopsis. He needs to see a pediatric neurologist. An ocular migraine ("without aura"). I spend the night with him when Lanie goes off to the opera.

These last months, Jim Higgins and I have tried to create a Convenient Care franchise plan with Web Golinkin. It hasn't worked. Portsmouth has asked if I would help them with their capital campaign, based in NYC but up in Rhode Island as often as necessary. With Pierce not doing well it could be a good move, and so, after Christmas, I began.


## 2007

1/5: Nancy Pelosi is elected first lady Speaker of the House.

1/9: Steve Jobs introduces the iPhone at Macworld.

In my first squash tourney of 2007 I ruptured my Achilles while leading Jamie Minnis 14–11 in the first game of the finals, and things got complicated. I had it repaired, but the doctor gave me too much of a pain killer and, somehow, I tore it again. Then I got a staph infection on the second surgery and ended up having 70 percent of the tendon removed, with a gaping hole in my leg. I was in bed three months on a vac machine to close the wound, sweetly and patiently nursed by Michelle.

Sylvia Lynch died after struggling with emphysema, perhaps Mom's best friend the last 10 years of her life. She was always wonderful to Dad too, whom she sat with every Monday for an hour when he was depressed and could not tolerate anyone else.

Rhoads visits me in the hospital and at Michelle's on weekends but otherwise we talk on the phone. Basketball is a new enthusiasm. He wants to play at Portsmouth. "I'm planning ahead." I ask him where he wants to live when he grows up. "It depends on who drafts me." He and Lanie are off to Club Med. "Everything legal in *Mehico!*"

## Spring

By late April, after multiple surgeries, I had healed enough to get back out to Stable Lane. Bill MacMillen was alone in his house, sounding depressed, Ba having gone into a nursing home (He soon followed her). It was a weird feeling, being back after four months away, and with so much change. It's up to our own generation now, but even there, there is flux with Burtch Drake retiring and Artie Nicol, long a successful trader, leaving his job. I need to hang on and get Rhoads through the last two years of grade school.

I watched a lot of Little League this spring, mostly from the car.


## Summer

Now on vacation, Pierce hooks up the house for wireless, Bibi's brothers build new doors, the boys submit to haircuts, and Rhoads and I play basketball, his second scrimmage of the day. In the evening we grill burgers. Rhoads retains about 70 percent of the ones he flips. The Yankees win again, and I go to bed before my sons. "Dad, you always talk to us." What a lovely life, if I can only keep it going a few years more . . .

At Dartmouth football camp in July, Rhoads has a Rudi moment, when he's matched against a much bigger kid in a tackling drill. "MacGuire, get out of there, we're putting someone else in."

"No way, I'm taking him down!" He did, and the coaches loved it.

Summer in the Thornton's Garden, serene and green, the asters and the orchids rise beyond the stream, a magnolia blooms on the far bank, brought from Virginia wrapped in newspaper in Ann's handbag a decade back. Snapdragons and lilies waft in the light breeze. Blue hydrangeas line the southern border. Jim speaks slowly in his North Carolina drawl. Four duckling chicks scramble up from the brook, their legs pedaling furiously, their mama with the deformed leg waddling behind them. She's been here 10 years now. Shy at first, the Thorntons threw breadcrumbs on the grass, then pieces of Entemann's coffee cake. Now she comes up onto the porch, and the chicks use the dogs' water bowl to swim in! The pleasant evening of a cool day with high clouds and old friends.

8/4: Both boys enjoyed the pig roast at Bill and Jenny Dobbs. Pierce is playing a little tennis but going with the Skakels to a concert in Hartford and then hanging out with them in Watch Hill. Bobby Quinn, the ever-enthusiastic Club tennis pro, made Rhoads buy new sneakers, and he told Bobby he wanted to donate his old, broken ones to the Hall of Fame. Rhoads wins one junior tournament and is the finalist in another. He enjoyed the beach overnight with the Sipps, and both boys became friendly with Augustus, Joshua and Elektra Northrop.

Over Labor Day Rhoads and I won the Parent-Child Round Robin, which he much enjoyed.

In other news Killer Kowalski has gone from us as well. One of wrestling's True Immortals in the days when Big Pierce would watch the matches from Sunnyside Gardens on TV!

In September Rhoads joined the Inwood Buccaneers football squad again, and they had several early wins.

10/9: Pleasant weekend with the boys going to Rhoads' Pass, Punt and Kick contest and then having pizza. Two friends of Pierce's got kicked out of school and a third, Dan Flanigan, was suspended. Too close for comfort, especially given Pierce's grades.

10/ 22: Pierce was dismissed from Portsmouth this week for smoking pot and not much work. We look at Lawrence Woodmere, Salisbury and figure Hyde in Bath, Maine, is the best bet. He goes down to the family's 9-Bar Ranch outside of Decatur, Texas to work for Jim Bob for a month, digging fence post holes and branding cattle.

### November

Serene November Sunday, leaves golden or red, falling off the trees. Rhoads is leaning into me on the sofa this afternoon until we play catch out back, trying to forget Eli Manning's five interceptions in the Giants loss to the Vikings. Jack Bulkley has three grandchildren under three to contend with, the Madsens shot skeet, Pierce calls from the Ranch, working hard and happily. All is reasonably well.

### 2008

That winter Rhoads did well at school as Pierce turned himself around at Hyde. Michelle and I went to New Zealand for her cousin Nicholas Plowman's wedding in Hawkes Bay, and I had ongoing business in Manila and Hong Kong.

In March, rising prices led to food riots throughout the Third World.

Rhoads and I resumed our ball throwing. My old Latin teacher turned Episcopalian priest Dee Dee Baker died of emphysema. I smoked a Cohiba in her memory on the IOW ballfield watching the Lawrence-Cedarhurst Fire Department practice drills on the surrounding roads.

On Cinqo de Mayo Rhoads became my second teenager. I drove out early to watch his third baseball game in three days. He made two good plays at second base, had two hits, scored twice and had an RBI in a last-minute win over Lutheran. Many congratulations from teachers and friends, a hug from Bibi, and afterwards swordfish on the grill as requested, with ice cream cake to follow on a lovely Spring evening with the marsh flooded at high tide. A growing boy full of bright ideas and good humor.

*My brother Pierce is my best friend*
*He throws me ten feet but others even farther*
*We laugh together even when we're apart*
*Every morning I put on Old Spice and remember him*
*Listening to the Grateful Dead reminds me how much he loves them*
*The best on earth is Pierce.*

5/12: A disturbing day for Rhoads as his classmate Chancellor, twice his size, socks him in the nuts when he thinks no one can see him, possibly after a smartass remark by Rhoads. It doesn't help that Chancellor is Black, alas, and was already under suspension, meaning he was supposed to be constantly supervised. Rhoads was very upset, but the pediatrician says no damage was done. The Headmaster and I try to figure out a way for Chancellor to stay in school, but his mostly absent, angry Dad gives Alan Bernstein no choice. Sad.

5/20: Several days later Rhoads is revitalized and in high hilarity. He had a swarm of 13-year-olds overrunning the Club for his birthday and all enjoyed themselves. Rhoads was ecstatic and gleeful throughout.

Cool and breezy night in the last half of May, the trees bursting forth. Buds blooming into leaves, and the calling of songbirds settling in. Sweet fragrance from the olive trees walking outside Jack and Diane Bulkley's, a new walk by the children's playground at the Yacht Club, and a full moon rising between the bending branches of the old wild cherry tree.

Then a cloudy May dawn, the sun bubbling up to the cloud cover but not breaking through enough to dry green lawns covered with fresh dew.

## Summer

In June Ray York and I won a handicap tennis tournament for the last time. He has been a wonderful, trash-talking tennis partner and friend over the decades. Then, of course, Rhoads had to be played, and he has improved his backhand and serve after only one week in the sports program. Good for Tonny! And that night a 13-year-old boy with dreams of becoming the next Rafa Nadal stuck his snout into my neck and brooded over a baseball feud he was conducting with his best friend.

6/29: Wonderful MacGuire, McCarty, Roach reunion with supper for sixty at RHC. Uncle Tim Carpenter spoke beautifully, called Mom Aunt Kitty's best friend, spoke of his friendship for Dad and admiration for how he faced up to what "was not the fairest deal life ever offered."

Jack McCarthy, Mom's childhood friend and IOW neighbor of ours, is dead after a long illness. Great guy and a good father to Sheila's kids, whom he adopted. Sylvia Choate Whitman died this week as well, another giant of our childhood (She offered Pierce and me the princely sum of $2 per hour when we cleared her basement when we were young—a real Yankee) after a long neurological decline.

Rob and Caroline Williamson give a wonderful housewarming to their beautiful new home with decks and roof tops overlooking the yacht club and marsh. Gorgeous.

I got to the finals of the men's singles at my advanced age and after last year's injury, beating two tough opponents and good friends, Sandy Severino and Ed Reitler, for what would prove to be the last time; but then I was mowed down by my nephew Christopher MacGuire in straight sets, 4 and 3, the first member of the latest generation to win the MacGuire Cup. "Thank you for saving us the psychiatric bills we would have had to pay if he had lost," Chris' wife Rina sweetly said as she gave me a consolation kiss!

8/1: Eleven mountaineers have died on K-2.

Casey and Clay are heading to the Cedarhurst Yacht Club after dinner for some summer brews, and I thought Life is Long. All of you are only doing what we did too. We come and, after a while we go, just as the box turtles make their confused progress out of the salt marsh only to be disturbed by encroaching golfers on their nesting grounds.

## Chapter 7

# Passages

July 2008: The Cedarhurst Yacht Club Centennial was a festive dinner dance for over 200 at the Rockaway Hunt Club with Tommy Murray presiding in fine fettle.

Originally, the Yacht Club's site was the Cedarhurst Bathing Pavilion, the precursor to the Lawrence Beach Club, but when the channel between Long Beach and Atlantic Beach that had allowed the ocean to flow there filled in, the Beach Club moved to its present sire in 1920. The Cedarhurst Yacht Club was incorporated in 1909, and one of its incorporators, William S. Whitehead, became the first Commodore. Raters, "O" boats and Sneakboxes were early boat classes. Until the Atlantic Beach Bridge was built in 1928 there was little building on the beaches, and the CYC boats had the Reynolds Channel waters mostly to themselves. Zephyrs, Lightnings and Comets came in the late 1930s. Tea was served after the races every Saturday and Sunday, and the cost of the annual dinner dance was $2.00 (65 cents being the charge for the dance portion!). The War years were hard on the Club. Afterwards the younger members sailed Tech Dinghys, Sunfish and Sailfish, and in 1955 Dick Koehne started a Junior Yacht Club program that is still thriving today. In the mid-1980s two-man 420s and Optimists became the favored boats. In the last quarter century Commodores have included Arthur Murray, John Passeggio, Jeff Nelson, Seton Ijams, Tom Morrissey, Joe Vencil, Corky Boyd, Tom Murray, Stephen B. Owen and Michael Donovan. The clubhouse burned when two non-members set it on fire in 1998, but out of crisis came opportunity, and a lovely new clubhouse with enlarged deck rose in its place. Thus, after over 110 years, having resisted adverse wind, water, flame, and seductive siren, the Club looks forward to new centuries.

9/12: Pierce and Rhoads are off to good starts at school. Rhoads has developed a very funny take on the universe while retaining an essential sweetness and spirituality. Pierce's new-found commitment to do his best is impressive.

The hurricane passed, humidity was down, the sun shone, and the sky was a stone-like blue as we rallied in the beauty of a September evening. Rhoads hits his top spin forehand with the fury of Nadal and rushes the net like Kramer. The next morning as the stars shone and the first birdsongs and crickets rose, I heard the grale screech and crow oppose him as the dawn approached and tomorrow's champion slept, full of dreams.

The financial crash came later in September, triggered by the failure of Lehman Brothers.

10/ 11: Pretty Columbus Day, sun trying to shine through. I emptied out the bath house at the beach. Rhoads enjoyed his play date with Benny and Noah and spends a joyous day at the Lawrence Woodmere Academy Homecoming Fair.

11/26: Wednesday before Thanksgiving, I am back from my first trip to Asia for Portsmouth, much of the country still celebrating President Obama's historic election.

Lanie is off to Paris. I came out yesterday for Rhoads' parent conference and first confirmation class, played squash with Pierce and shared pizza before dropping off to sleep. To Darien in the morning, Rhoads with football in hand. Peter Gogolak, ex-Giants kicker, is part of this year's enlarged feasting group. "Trivia question," he asks Rhoads with his broad, open face and trace of a Hungarian accent, "Who is the Giants leading all-time scorer?" Rhoads, hesitates, grins, and answers, "You are."

12/27: The boys seem well after Christmas in Texas. They played in the Ketcham Junior Squash yesterday, and Rhoads was kind to the younger boys. Gonny (Grandmother Sauder) gave them tickets to the Giants-Carolina game, and guess who is taking them? 17 degrees! It went into overtime, and they were overjoyed by the Giants' win. Rhoads photographs the scene on his iphone and high fived all around including the guy naked from the waist up and the slightly scary character in a Santa costume. We had a freezing ride home to LI, and, knowing my Manhattan garage would not open until six a.m., I reclined with cocoa on the living room couch. I rose at 5 and had a sweet, slow drive down 5th Avenue past Rockefeller Center and the tree, and then to Mom's old haunts, Blessed Sacrament Church, the Meehan house on W. 69th Street, the Beresford, and across the park in light traffic. Serene, mostly silent and beautiful.

## 2009

1/5: Rhoads was in the *Nassau Herald* playing the cymbals at his school concert and looking forward to the Fiesta Bowl. He is rightly pleased with his test scores.

Last night I wandered, cigar in hand, poking around the Little Beach and other assorted backwaters of the IOW, wondering how much time could go by, so many years flow on, and now we are in the last full year of Rhoads' grade school before it all ends. It was comparatively mild for January, the moon tried to break through, two hot rodders careened in and out. The boys were thrilled at the Longhorns last minute win over OSU.

Then, this morning, as we came out to get in the car and go to school, I looked up at the wild cherry beside the courtyard and on an upper branch saw a large bird, sitting serenely. At first, I thought it must be an owl, but Rhoads came out and said, "Eagle." And so, it was.

1/9: Bill MacMillen died last night, and the family asked me to speak at his memorial:

## William C. MacMillen Jr.

It's only a minute or two past eleven but I can already see the frown turning into a scowl on his face. He considered lack of punctuality a serious dereliction—"stealing other people's time"—in Graham Greene's memorable phrase, so let's get started.

I hardly need to say what an honor it is to talk to you briefly this morning about Mr. MacMillen, as I nearly always called him, or Bill or Mac, or Doll, or Dad, or Gramps, as you may have done. "You've known him so long," Ann McLeod's and my friend Jeanne Jones asked me once, "Why do you call him Mr. MacMillen and not Bill?" And I answered, "I know him much too well for that."

That my brothers and I knew him at all was, of course, a function of his and Barbara's wonderful friendship with my mother and father, dating back to before World War II in Saratoga, and then as neighbors on Cedarhurst Avenue once the MacMillens moved in across the empty field between us on Long Island in the early 1950s.

My own first memory of Mac was wandering across that field, aged three or four, on a Saturday afternoon, briefly escaping from Theresa, doubtless to cadge a cookie from Mrs. MacMillen or Mary Comer, their housekeeper, and encountering him digging his spade furiously into the vegetable garden he kept so well. He greeted me and patiently explained what he was about. I'll miss those tomatoes, and, later, the rose bushes and hundreds of daffodils that so beautifully carpeted their garden on Victoria Place.

Then there were the famous sports figures—Bud Palmer, the Knicks star and CBS Sports announcer, or Davis Cup captain Billy Talbert—that Mr. MacMillen brought into our lives. And later, we laughed at Mother telling stories of the great jazz parties at the MacMillens, and how Mac, always adhering to the strictest self-discipline, had gone to bed early but then could not restrain himself from coming down to sing along with one last set, in his boxers.

There were Christmas Day touch football games, Derby parties and many other occasions that our two families shared. One of the gentle ironies about Mac was that for one who prided himself on being analytical, contrarian and completely unsentimental, he was in fact one of the most fiercely loyal friends anyone could ever have, as well as one of the most modest.

I saw this side of Mr. MacMillen in many settings. For a couple of years in the early 1980s I spent time each month moonlighting from Time Inc. to write a newsletter for the New York chapter of the HBPA—the Horsemen's Benevolent and Protective Association—that was then inserted into *The Horseman's Journal*. Mac had taken on the presidency of that organization as a retirement project and transformed it into an exemplary operation that achieved enormous efficiencies and improved agreements with NYRA and the State. When after seven or eight years he felt he had done what he could and resigned, the owners and trainers whose situation Mr. MacMillen had so greatly improved wanted to honor him with a dinner. Of course, our friend immediately put the kibosh on that, saying to me, "If I can leave knowing that I've made some improvements and done as much as I could to try to make others, that's all the credit I want."

But it wasn't all the credit he got. In recognition of his extraordinary service to racing, Mr. MacMillen was elected to the Jockey Club.

A final example of his innate modesty occurred on our way into the very last Giants game Mac took me to. I asked him if he wanted me to drive, and, somewhat to my surprise, Mr. MacMillen said yes. This proved to be a mixed blessing, because we had barely gotten out of the Isle of Wight before Mac was telling me which lane to drive in, to go faster, what level of the George Washington Bridge to take etc., until we were entering the Meadowlands complex, and he said, "And now we're going to run into a very unpleasant man who's going to tell us we can't go any farther but have to go back to an outer parking lot, which makes for a much longer walk."

Indeed, a not very welcoming attendant was manning the barrier, and he looked decidedly irked when I rolled down the window and gestured to him. "Yeah?"

"Excuse me," I said, "But my friend is 90 years old this year, and I was hoping we could get a little closer to the stadium."

The attendant peered into the car for a moment, managed a disarmingly genuine grin and said, "Of course! Enjoy the game, sir!" and let us through right away. After an awkward moment of silence Mac quietly said, "Thank you." Despite being season's ticket holders for half a century and a minority owner of the Cleveland Browns, it had never occurred to Mr. and Mrs. MacMillen to ask any concession at all to their advancing years. The Greatest Generation.

Now, of course, there was just a *slightly* contentious side to Mac. He loved a spirited debate and enjoyed getting in the last word. I can remember him finishing an exchange on the squash court over what *may* have been a let with his friend, Payson Coleman, then the managing partner of Davis Polk and the mildest of gentleman, by saying, "I don't make the rules; I just play by them."

Or with Treddy Ketcham, the friend whom Mac loved to wrangle with most. During Mr. MacMillen's years as squash chairman at the Rockaway Hunt Club, Treddy would come up to him before Gold Racquets and say, "Mac, you haven't invited thus and so to Gold Racquets this year. They've been coming for years, they're some of our oldest friends from our sister clubs in Boston or Philadelphia or Baltimore. . . . you have to have them." And Mac would answer, "I'm sorry, Treddy, I invited the top ranked sixteen teams in the country. My job is to put on the best possible tournament, not to guarantee that you get to go to other people's squash weekends all winter."

A philosophy major, Mac favored Aristotle over Plato, but his outlook was ultimately Stoical, and he agreed with Epictetus, "To the rational being only the irrational is unendurable, but the rational is endurable," and, again by the same thinker, and so characteristic of Mr. MacMillen, "First say to yourself what you would be; and then do what you have to do."

There are many other memories, great games of squash and tennis, stirring afternoons at the track, countless convivial and often challenging talks by the fire or on the terrace ("contemplating the Infinite" as he liked to say quoting an old Williams prof) over a Maker's Mark or two, delicious meals, Mac sometimes grilling the meat in winter in that same fire and Barbara cooking countless other delicacies. I was delighted to hear, in fact, that one of those—corn pudding—was on the lunch menu today.

Most of all, I remember, amid all the banter, laughter and the love of friends, how strongly and completely Mr. MacMillen loved Barbara and all of his family, even if he didn't always show this in the way they might have liked. But Mac was always toughest on himself, as anyone who ever saw him throw his squash racquet to the floor after putting an easy reverse corner winner into the middle of the tin can attest.

In a few minutes Ray Bird will speak for the MacMillen family, but if I may say a word on behalf of our family, a great gift of more recent years was being able to re-encounter the MacMillens as neighbors after Lanie and

I moved out to Lawrence in the mid-1990s, and they embraced and enjoyed not only us but also young Pierce and Rhoads, part of the fourth generation of MacGuires they had befriended. Pierce and Rhoads are at school today, but Lanie has stories she can share about those times. One of mine is that the first evening the MacMillens were coming over for supper I came down the stairs at Stable Lane, and then four-year-old Pierce looked up from his Game Boy and said to his normally slovenly father, "Dad, why are you dressed up?"

"The MacMillens are coming over tonight," I answered, "And I always wear a jacket and tie when I'm with them at night."

"Then I want to wear a jacket, too," Pierce exclaimed and ran to the front hall closet to put on his ski parka, which he proudly exhibited to them when, impeccably dressed as always, they arrived a few minutes later.

Mr. and Mrs. MacMillen have always raised our standards.

I'll close with a few lines from Rainer Maria Rilke, the first word of which our agnostic friend might frown again at, but he would approve the overall sense

*Lord, it is time now,*
*For the summer has gone on and gone on.*
*Lay your shadow along the sundials and in the field.*
*Let the great wind blow free.*
*Command the last fruit be ripe.*

## Racquet and Tennis Club, January 14, 2009

1/20: Barack Obama is sworn in as the first Black president of the United States.

Pierce sounds a bit glum at Hyde, but he has to get through this term, and it will get better. I drove to pick up Rhoads at Josh Torres' house in Valley Stream during the storm. Icy and treacherous and my new brake assembly groaned, but we made it, and in the morning the roseate sun came up as in Prague, snow and ice adhering to the tree branches.

1/25: Rhoads' classmate, Tristan Rubin-Diaz, lost his mother to cancer yesterday. When I asked Rhoads last night if he wanted to attend the funeral, he said no. Then, at nine, he asked me if he could go. Benny and Noah's mom, herself a widow, sweetly offered to take him. When I asked him why he had changed his mind he said, "He's my best friend, and I love him." Today he looked marvelous in his blue suit, but he's outgrown his dress shoes!

Rhoads had another ocular migraine and lost peripheral vision temporarily. Testing is normal. Clear, sunny, first of February Super Bowl Sunday, mild enough to walk to the yacht club in just a sweater. Jim Thornton is clipping vines and clearing up the underbrush on Eliza Chauncey's "other" house, on which he has taken an option and hopes to renovate and sell. He wants to know if I'm interested.

A pleasing prospect. If I had the right NYC job, maybe. But I may be at Portsmouth five more years and then at 62? And no one knows how much worse the financial morass may get. Walking home I look around. The Madsen's house construction project is in its fourth year with several architects. Greg Gately is asking $1.5 million for his house. Joy and Charlie McClendon have sadly separated, and their place is on the market. Rumor has it our lovely neighbors, the Diemars, who bought Sue Gatehouse's house, are putting their house on the market as well. And behind us, the Passeggios have now bought a house in Beaufort SC, and the one here might be too much to keep up. The Heaney house is also for sale, but the Vencils have sold their townhouse and moved out here full time.

3/5: Meanwhile, Rhoads' unalloyed sense of joy is a delight to observe. He's a second or third stringer in basketball, but once he gets on the court he positively beams, happy to be out there, doing his best. An enviable disposition and one that will serve him well. I played in the Mixed Member-Guest Squash with Margaret Hartigan. After sitting with her at lunch, Rhoads says, "She's nice."

I am 57 today and after a busy day drove out to be with Rhoads on his Science Fair Night. Can Handwriting Predict Gender? Apparently so.

4/18: Rhoads has grown four inches and covers court like a madman. His shoe size has expanded, and his voice is down an octave. He enjoys taking the affectionate piss out of dear old Dad. Soon to be 14.

5/6: Rhoads had 20 friends to his birthday party, four boys spent the night, and in the morning, he walked them all two miles to the Village and bought them video games! Later in the month he did a good job serving Fr. Luke's Mass in my brother Philip's memory and enjoyed the laugh-filled dinner afterwards. That Sunday he was confirmed by Bishop Libasci, one of nine, about half as many *confirmandi* as were in my class if I remember correctly. He is his own man. When I asked if he would like to join Casey at Johns Hopkins (where his Uncle Peter and I went) he says, "I will not be attending." When I ask him if he thinks he might have a vocation to the priesthood, he says, "I will be having a family."

6/4: Pierce and Rhoads are overjoyed to be reunited after Pierce completes another successful year at Hyde. He is off to the Rome pilgrimage and the Salamanca Spanish program, before returning to Portsmouth for his final year.

6/7: When I take Pierce to RI for the Rome trip Bill Crimmins, gently and firmly, urges Pierce to keep his act together. No longer "Disciplina" (imposed from without, "as it had to be on you") but "Severitas," imposed from within, "as you now have to do yourself."

7/18: A pleasant summer evening with Rhoads, who engages Peter DuBois on baseball and Ralph Earle on the Eagles at the Hunt Club Thursday buffet. We had a great trip to Wimbledon and then toured Ireland. Mary Alice Sherrill says that when he went to dinner there the other night, he complained of having always been seated where he had to make the toast!

Delicious salmon at the Burgers with Van, Mina and Fred Alexandre. Mina is still steaming that at the last yacht club dinghy dinner when she asked Howard Johnson if Van and she could join their table, he said, "Absolutely not," and stuck out his arms, "The whole table's taken," quite sternly (surprising if true, since Howard in my experience has always been one of the world's nicest guys). "Imagine Howard Johnson having the nerve to speak to me like that," she exclaimed, "His grandfather sold ice cream out of a truck, and my grandfather was the Shah of Iran."

A tragedy this weekend as a 41-year-old Dad and his five-year-old son crash their ski jet into the Sylvester's dock on Crooked Creek. It was clearly marked as a 5-mile MPH speed limit area, but people have to show off their motors and their cahones, even in shallow mudflats, which the Creek is at low tide. The poor man was wedged between the jet and dock until extricated, lifeless. The Carpenter boys and Jay Saling came by and went on to the yacht club to get help. Tom Murray and Paul Strader brought a hook and did what they could, but in the end a police helicopter and squad cars arrived. The little boy died of internal injuries the next morning. Terrible.

In today's social news, Page 6 reports that John Jeffords, whose parents Walter and Kay used to live here in the 1950s, is selling his Wyoming ranch, transgendering as Elizabeth and moving to a community of eunuchs in India. And so, it goes . . .

## August

Parties for Lawrence Woodmere Academy and at the Sipp's lovely new house. I left at four in the morning to drive to Rhode Island after rising at three to make sure Rhoads was home. He was, asleep in front of the TV! He had played in the McCallum Cup and gone on to the Dobbs' pig roast, then partied on at Robbie Wilson's. Pierce is down at the Ranch enjoying his work with Jim Bob.

## End of Summer

A small brown marsh wren flew in advance of the approaching hurricane, heading out to sea when she might have huddled in the reeds as I rounded the corner on Edward Bentley Road with the moon high. Then something moved and I could scarcely glean two white rabbits, doubtless left here in winter to die but surprisingly spry, sipping rainwater and then hopping back toward their marsh abode.

8/26: Rhoads had a melt down after losing in the Rees Cup to Will Burke in a third set tie breaker. When I congratulated both players, he said, "No," and hit me with his racquet. I walked off to watch Chris MacGuire play in the doubles tournament final. About 7:30 that evening the apology call came. The next morning, very unusually, he called at nine to ask if I was coming back out. Given the hurricane, I wasn't, but the next day I did. He had updated his Facebook page to list me as his father and added "Christian-Catholic" as his religion. We had a good tennis game, a good swim, a good steak and visit to the ophthalmologist. He was pelting me with family and sports questions the entire time. Passionate, funny, sweet little boy!

Ed Reitler beat Chris MacGuire in the finals of the MacGuire Cup singles, a great win for Ed who has improved his game steadily over two decades.

Labor Day doubles between Chris and Rhoads and Pierce and me in what I hope will become a family tradition. Michelle told Chris how kind he was to Rhoads, and Chris replied, "I was just doing what Jamie always did coaching Tim and me."

Today Pierce and Rhoads left early for pre-season football at Portsmouth. I am overjoyed they can be together this year, and I can be with them some of the time. Lanie says Bibi came by early to say goodbye and was sobbing uncontrollably. She has given her life to those boys, and it must be hard, but they love her back and always will.

September: At his express wish brother Philip's ashes were spread by Schuyler in the Atlantic Ocean just off the Lawrence Beach, though doubtless he would have preferred, the Bath & Tennis, Bailey's Beach or the Southampton Bathing Corporation. He was lucky not to have drifted into El Patio's (today The Sands) waters!

Charlie Sullivan and Bob Hart both died this week. Charlie was 92, married to one of Mom's best friends. Bob was 93 and much diminished by Parkinson's in recent years but a giant in every way. Mother called him and Uncle Tim Carpenter the two best dancers on Long Island!

I loved playing in the USTA Grass 55s this week and reveled in the glorious sight of 100 players in whites on RHC's green grass courts, lit by the golden September sun.

## 2010

The boys had happy terms at school, a good Christmas in Texas, after which we skied in Colorado and returned to Long Island for a couple of days. Pierce was one of only five Caucasian attendees at his party in Montclair one night

and had a great time. Rhoads is perfecting falling to sleep in front of the TV
. . .

2/13: Yesterday the piano movers took my Grandfather MacGuire's 1923
Steinway from Stable Lane to make way for Lanie's new interior decoration.
It's old, the case is scratched, and the keys and soundboard need substantial
renovation. I tried to give it away to Lawrence-Woodmere Academy, but it's
too far gone.

## Spring

4/20: The Deepwater Horizon drilling platform exploded, the worst oil spill
in history.

Pierce and Rhoads ended School well, Pierce roaring up and down the
lacrosse field and Rhoads playing varsity tennis. "The great secret of Rhoads
MacGuire," writes Nick Micheletti in his report card, "Is that behind the mask
of relaxed tomfoolery lies one of the sharpest minds in his Form."

6/21: Pierce and Rhoads are back from a post-Graduation cruise to Haiti
and Mexico. We stay in the RHC Annex since the house, which has been
undergoing a facelift (after appearing as a bedraggled across the railroad
tracks Hamptons cottage in "The Affair"!), is not yet ready. Somehow Van
Burger and I won the senior doubles versus John Lindenthal/ David Delaney,
coming back from 2–5 and love–30 in the third set. Rhoads commented on
his salmonella attack that had him in the Infirmary at the end of the year: "For
three days I lived like you, going to bed at ten thirty and waking up at five,
and it was terrible!"

Sam Williams is dead after a rapid onset cancer at 73. A sweet, gentle
soul and good father to Edward. His family's business, Ichabod T. Williams,
was the oldest in New York for many years, importers of exotic woods. His
grandfather, Resolved "Res" Williams, would drive in from Cedarhurst in
his old car, careen through the Brooklyn Battery Tunnel and park over at
the company plant on their Hudson River wharves. According to Tony Peck,
Sam's roommate for many years until he married Susan, the one time he rode
in with Mr. Williams he broke into such a sweat from the driving he had to
go uptown and take a shower!

Louis Auchincloss is gone as well. He lived on upper Park Avenue and for
many years summered in Bedford. Little known, however, is that he was born
on the South Shore of Long Island in Cedarhurst, just down the road from
the Isle of Wight, which for a period of time from the 1880s was the original
summer resort on Long Island. As he wrote to me in 2003:

> "My parents lived in summer in a large white house called 'The Bray' (as it once
> had stables) at the very end of Breezy Way which was a one-way street. I was

born in the 'little red' house across the way from it, in 1917, as my grandmother Stanton then occupied The Bray into which we moved when she died. Also on Breezy Way were my mother's cousin, Courtland Dixon and his family, and the Dunstans, Works and Batesons. In 1927 we moved to the north shore; my parents built a summer house in Locust Valley. In the winter we were on East 91st Street in town. As a boy I loved the marshes, and we went daily to the Atlantic Beach Club."

The occasion of our correspondence was my discovery in his collection *Manhattan Monologues* of the short story "Collaboration," a story of selfless heroism during World War II that has its origins in the friendship between a young narrator (Auchincloss, of course) and the protagonist, Arthur Slocum, who in the 1930s find each other's company birdwatching on long walks in the marshes at the back of Cedarhurst preferable to polo and other country club pursuits. Though much of the world has changed, and Cedarhurst most certainly has (it is now more commonly called Lawrence), the cedars of Cedarhurst—*juniper virginiosa*—are still abundant, and the marshes are teeming with osprey, eagle, swan, duck, geese, heron and many other sea birds.

Auchincloss used this setting to meditate on what is real beauty—nature or art made in its image—as a means of leading up to his story's message, which is that real virtue and real honor are often concealed from, or misunderstood by, the world.

It is a powerful and uplifting tale by a master of discrimination in its highest sense.

July: Summer heat and the fan whirs violently in the un-air-conditioned house. At 3:30 a.m. comes a most hideous screech as some poor bird is hunted down by a feral cat which has it in its clutches.

7/25: Wiki Leaks release 90,000 confidential U.S. Government reports on Afghanistan.

Bob Hart's memorial service was dignified and moving. Monsignor Rahilly told of him coming to confession one day and saying he wasn't sure he had the strength to face his inevitable decline due to Parkinson's and prayed that God would give him that Grace, which the Good Lord most assuredly did.

RHC former Governors' dinner: Jack Bierwirth, ex-CEO of Grumman, says he could have bought the Mets for $23 million from Mrs. Payson's estate, but since Grumman was emerging from bankruptcy at the time with Federal aid, he thought it was inappropriate. He also recalled the consortium that bought the Burton estate for $3K apiece (Herrick, Hart, etc.). "When I had to pay $6K for my piece I felt robbed." Worth a million today! "Carlie Timpson held back from building until George Jackson did. One night Carlie came out of a huge cocktail party at your parents' big house on Cedarhurst Avenue. He'd taken too much to drink, as he so often did, and he slammed his foot on the accelerator and couldn't get it off. His car went into and up the back of the car in front of it time and again. I'll never forget it."

Michelle's 60th birthday dinner at the LBC was a rousing success. Her sister Kelly, brother Tim and other New York friends remarked on how beautiful the setting is, something we too often forget. Walter Chatham said, "Michelle, all your friends commented on how 'moral' you are. I just think you're hot."

Pierce's College Essay:

Sitting on a horse in an open field, I look straight ahead at the challenge waiting for me and four other men to meet. The hundred or so Water Buffalo staring back at me cannot possibly be that different than Cattle, and those are easy to drive. Slowly we approach them, timidly hollering in a vain attempt to make them move. They have other ideas. A bull makes a bluff charge at us, he comes about 30 feet and turns back. I am legitimately scared but, of course, we are not ready to quit just yet. We keep moving forward; the same Bull charges again and turns back yet again. "Next time he won't stop," says Jim Bob, the ranch foreman. We ride even closer, the Buffalo still show no sign of moving, and the bull looks more and more threatening with each step. Suddenly, the bull goes into a full charge, but surely, I though, he was bluffing. He was 40 feet away, 30 feet away, 20 feet, and looking right at me. "Get out! Get out! Get the hell out!" shouts Jim Bob. I jerk the reins on Sarley, an eight-year-old mare who before this experience was not known for her speed. She turns and nearly throws me off as she bolts into a full gallop. On top of being considerably meaner than cattle, Water Buffalo are also about three times as fast. I chanced a look back; the buffalo was within five feet and had lowered his head revealing its threatening horns. I had the reins up to Sarley's ears, it was just a matter of which animal would give up first. Luckily, the Buffalo got tired quickly and turned to rejoin his herd, snarling the whole way. Sarley slowed down a few seconds later, and as the adrenaline slowly left my veins, I relaxed and gave her a well-deserved pat on the neck. Of course, now that the danger had passed, my fellow ranchers began howling with laughter. "Boy you should have seen your face, like something was after you!" said Jim Bob. I smiled and lowered my head, it seemed that what for me was the most terrifying experience of my life was for them just another day at the office.

I have been working at the 9-Bar ranch every summer for two to three weeks since I was fourteen. Growing up in a Long Island suburb, it was certainly unlike anything I had experienced in my life. Waking up at 6 and working until 8 p.m. on a ranch was something nothing in my life had prepared me for, and. at first. I would count the days until I went back to the comfortable life of tennis and videogames that awaited me at home. With time however, I developed a strong bond with the place, and the people.

Building a nearly twenty-mile-long wire fence along Highway 380 was the most physically taxing and mentally challenging thing I have ever done. My third summer, when I was sixteen, it took the whole three weeks I was there. I drove T-posts into the ground, carried heavy metal braces and tied wire to the T-posts over and over again in 100-degree heat. As I watched my co-workers counting the seconds until the sun went down, I realized there is a certain attitude that these men have, a special one, no matter how impossible a task seems, no matter how long it takes, they will get it done. Slowly over the 3-week project, I developed it too. This is the most important lesson I have learned, and one that I could not have learned anywhere else. I probably will not grow up to be a rancher, but I could not be more grateful for those men, and for what they have taught me.

8/6: It's Pierce's final weekend before heading off to college in Texas. We had good tennis and a final MacGuire family dinner at the CYC on a pretty night with a breeze blowing.

8/10: Pierce likes his roommate, who brought a wide screen TV, whereas Pierce contributed an Xbox. No doubt they will create a monastic scriptorium of their room.

Rhoads, meanwhile, beat Christian Tomasson in the Men's "B" division singles final as darkness fell, 6–2 in the third set; Grange Johnson in three sets with a withering forehand at the last; Stuart Foster 6–1, 7–5 in the semis and put up a good fight in the finals, losing to 18-year-old Frankie Porcelli 6–4, 6–3. It was a year of generational change as James Heaney won the "A" championship over Chris MacGuire.

Summer ended, the grass burned, fescue flowered, the osprey nest was dismantled. In the super clarity of the post-Hurricane light, my brother Schuyler, won his 6th RHC golf championship over Mike Grady, 30 years younger. There were late season parties at the Sherrills and for Dede Brooks' 60th at the CYC. Cormorants on the dock, clouds studding, stars shining.

With both boys away I spent much less time on Long Island, but Pierce came home for Columbus Day with Tessa Condon, and we picnicked at the beach on a cloudless October day, sand pipers skittering, geese migrating, monarch butterflies fluttering, and a few dogs romping on the sand.

Barbara MacMillen is gone at 96, a good long life!

12/30: Christmas was a delight with the boys. We enjoyed *The King's Speech*, a beef dinner at Michelle's on Christmas Eve, and the traditional lunch at Sky and Dean's with cigar and a walk across the golf course bridge afterwards. When we started Pierce and Casey were just two. Now they are twenty and greet each other with genuine affection. Rhoads plays the Bad Boy Peck to Clay, who swats him down!

The year ends with a huge snowstorm. Pierce is off to see Tessa in London, and Rhoads and I enjoy a weekday jaunt to the Oyster Bar and the Last Supper installation at the Armory.

# 2011

### Barbara MacMillen (1913–2010)

Her maiden name was Barbara Greenwood Christy.

I first knew her at the age of three or four from tramping across the overgrown field on Cedarhurst Avenue that separated our houses, doubtless trying to cadge a cookie. She was always poised and dignified, gracious and kind, never in a hurry, never cross. She let Mac take center stage in social settings but had a way of managing him quietly. Not much escaped her, and a glance or sometimes even a word *unsaid* was all that was necessary to restore order.

It was a great love affair. They shared so much together—sports (I wouldn't dare say so if he were here, but she was the better athlete), travel, racing, friends, generations of family, whom she dearly loved, and food. I will NOT go into rhapsodies about the cold cucumber soup, the chicken on the grill, the homemade pizza. NO, I will NOT salivate about the Thanksgiving goose, the steak from the German butcher in New York that Mac cooked in the fireplace on winter nights, the ham biscuits on Derby Day, the ham steaks and sausage from Saratoga and the fresh corn followed a day later by the corn pudding, the plump tomatoes from the patch beside the kitchen, the Rumanian salad, the cherry pies, NO, I will NOT be reminiscing about any of that!

You can see in the old photos that used to hang in Mac's study how glamorous and fashionable Barbara was. She was never loquacious, but after her strokes she became more economical with her words, yet she always got her point across. When the time came to give up tennis and golf, she never complained but carried on gardening wonderfully, reading, keeping her impeccably beautiful house here and in Saratoga, and traveling for as long as she and Mac could. It was a blessing to have the years we did with them when we moved to the Isle of Wight, and I can still hear Barbara's delighted laughter when Pierce and Rhoads would offer an impromptu concert or performance before dinner on the porch in Stable Lane. They went on and on, and despite her own increasing frailty, Ba kept Mac going. "She's almost entirely spirit," Lanie would marvel, but what a spirit it was.

After dinner one night in early 2006, Mrs. MacMillen took me aside and gave me the article from the New York Times I'm holding here now. It is the story of a trip that Times writer David Carr took with Pulitzer Prize winning historian David McCullough to Green-Wood Cemetery in December of 2005, and I'm going to read you four short paragraphs from it.

"At the cemetery he led me to the statue of Minerva commemorating the Battle of Brooklyn, a horrific and demoralizing loss for the Americans, who had followed the British down to New York after brilliantly maneuvering them out of Boston. 'Here and along the slopes of Greenwood hills,' the inscription below Minerva reads, 'our patriots for the first time faced their foe in open field; and we stood the test.'

"Mr. McCullough is driven from book to book, he explained . . . by basic questions: 'Who the hell are we? Where did we come from? And how did we get where we are today?'

"He took my arm and walked me along the path at the top of the hill. Washington may have ridden his horse along this ridge, he said in hushed tones, taking in the woeful conditions of the makeshift American army and surveying the might of the 400 British ships in the harbor. 'It must have been breathtaking.'

"Written after the 9/11 attacks, (McCullough's book) *1776* seems intended as a reminder of Americans' ability to face down and triumph over unspeakable challenges. It leans hard on the journals of the farmers, fishermen and tinkers who fought the war . . . One of the more compelling journals was kept by John Greenwood, a 16-year-old who walked from Maine to Boston to join the fight as a fifer, playing at taverns along the way. 'They used to ask me where I came from and where I was going to, and when I told them I was going to fight for my country, they were astonished such a little boy, and alone, should have such courage,' . . .

"Jeffrey I. Richman, the historian of Green-Wood cemetery, who was along on our walk, mentioned that John Greenwood . . . was buried just down the hill, and Mr. McCullough had trouble containing himself. 'This is so exciting,' he said and was off with a gallop to the car to drive down for a look. (As it turned out, Greenwood became a dentist and made teeth for George Washington.) It is this kind of serendipity, Mr. McCullough said, a kind of magical realism full of small world moments, which keeps him wading into the past."

On the last page of the article she gave me that wintry night in early 2006, Mrs. MacMillen wrote in her still strong, clear hand, "My maiden name was Barbara Greenwood Christy. John Greenwood was my great, great, great, great, great grandfather."

Think of it! Just seven generations from 1776 all the way to 2010—234 years.

Of course, Barbara wouldn't tell me that, but, ever modest, she slipped the papers into an envelope and gave them to me, at the end of yet another magnificent meal in Mac's and her marvelous company.

To answer David McCullough's question, that's who we are, or at any rate, who *she* was; and our lives were ennobled by knowing her.

## Rockaway Hunting Club, January 8, 2011

1/12: And now Uncle Tim Carpenter is gone as well (1919–2011). A full house at Trinity-St. John's for a gallant life. Carolyn helps a momentarily shaken Jake read.

2/7: Steve Finch RIP. One of Dad's best friends. Peggy writes remembering the day Dad came to drive him to Highwatch Farm. "'Peggy, your father is never going to drink again.' I cried. I was 12. And he didn't, thanks to your father."

2/11: President Mubarak of Egypt resigns under pressure.

3/15: Rhoads is home and plays much indoor tennis with Tonny at Point-Set in East Rockaway. A happy boy.

4/25: Our Stable Lane neighbor Tyler Mullally was found dead at home after failing for the last year. She never stopped smoking and in recent months gave up the ghost. She was a good neighbor and loved the boys, living her final 20 years largely alone, after three husbands.

Lanie and Pierce are off to Jay Sauder's wedding in Austin. "I don't think there's a happier boy in America than Pierce!" Lanie exclaims. What a sweet thing to say! "And Rhoads (laughter), he's a good time Charlie." He had called her for a deposit on his Prom tux, having been invited by a Vth Former!

5/1: Osama bin Ladin is killed by American SEALS in his Pakistani hideout.

6/20: Rhoads goes to Rome with the Portsmouth group. A good Father's Day with Pierce and Michelle at LBC after tennis with Ray York, sporting a new set of false teeth. We had a dinner with the Whales, a great Transatlantic club including old friends Robin Frost, over from England, Mark Hinckley and Mark Donovan.

I take great joy in watching Pierce mature. He is now a man, self-possessed, witty and warm. He and Rhoads are winning rave reviews as Junior Sports counselors in what remains a special summer place. Bobby Quinn says of this year's most challenging camper, Gregory Reitler, "A few years ago I had one just like him, but he now works for me, so I just said, 'Rhoads, you're in charge of Greg,' and he's handled him fine."

July: LBC's 125th celebration was an excruciatingly hot dinner dance for 500; Michelle had to take three showers getting dressed, and we cooled off at 2 a.m. with Rebecca and Steve in the Madsen's pool after.

August: Hilarious story of Ann Thornton putting her cat statue outside the house next door they just bought from Mrs. Chauncey's estate. One day it went missing, and several weeks later Jim was driving on Stable Lane and saw it outside Tyler Mullaly's house. Ann didn't want Jim to say anything and eventually she brought a cake she had baked to Tyler and enquired, "Tyler, where did you get that cat? It looks just like mine."

"I stole it. It was outside the house next to you, and I love cats, so I had Amanda help me take it."

"Actually, that house is Jim's and mine now. We bought it when Mrs. Chauncey died."

"I didn't know it was your house!"

At her yacht club memorial, former Commodore Seton Ijams remembered her mantra, "Setsie, get me one more little drink, and then I'll start cooking dinner."

8/28: Serious storm on IOW; not too much damage: but a harbinger.

Ed Reitler's birthday party. Of my many friends in Lawrence none has been more steadfast since I steered him to buying the Pardee's Red House. We and our families went through good times, and times that were anything but, and through it all Ed always put the welfare of others first. He deserves his happiness with Joyce.

Rhoads is off to early football. There's a prairie dog on the golf course!

10/10: Lovely Columbus Day weekend in the 80s, Rhoads has Charlie Ramsden, Chris Soriano, Zack Pray and Gabe Miller down to Lawrence, getting into as much trouble as they can without going too far.

## October 15, Dario's Party

Nearly 600 people attended the celebration of Dario Muskardin's 50th anniversary at the Hunt Club on Saturday, October 15th. An excellent meal including brief presentations was followed by dancing until midnight and a large number of revelers who stayed much later on the Terrace. I was the Master of Ceremonies:

"Good evening and welcome to the celebration of *Dario: The First 50 Years*. Please take your seats and let's start by introducing our honoree, Mr. Dario Muskardin! (Theme Song from *Rocky*). Dario has spent half a century being the Club's leading Ambassador to the world at large and the Members' best friend, with a photographic memory and desire to do everything possible to make our lives easier. Dario and Lily are surrounded by family tonight. Let's give them a warm welcome as well . . .

"I'd like to start by telling you a little bit about Dario's early years.

"Born in 1939 on the island of Cres in what had in his father's time been part of the Austro-Hungarian Empire, was then Italy, became Yugoslavia after

WWII and is now southern Croatia, Dario grew up on a farm with sheep and a vineyard. He was the 9th of 11 children, ten of whom survive today, and we are delighted to have many of Dario's nieces and nephews with us here tonight.

"After graduating from high school Dario went to Italy to work before emigrating to the US in January of 1961. His brother Joey, picked him up at Idewild Airport, not Kennedy Airport at that time, although President John F. Kennedy was inaugurated that very month. Joey brought Dario here, and he started work on February 24, 1961.

"The Nobel Prize in Literature was won by Yugoslavian author Ivo Andric in that year. Dario assures me that had he stayed home the outcome would have been very different. Roy Emerson won the U.S. Tennis Championship at Forest Hills that year, Gene Littler won the Golf Open, and closer to home, Ralph Howe was our Gold Racquet Champion. Dario filed the first of many formal protests that he was unfairly excluded from the tournament.

"When Dario started at the Hunt Club he learned from a master, Nick Benvin, our manager for over 50 years. Nick, take a bow! That is to say, like Nick he did *everything.* The first job he remembers outside the Club was washing windows at the Maitland house, and it's good to see that family so fully represented here tonight. He has known every President since General George Wickersham, and starting under Eddie Wardwell, he has now worked for (or should I say outlasted) nine of them, and Art Nicol will be the tenth.

"My first memory of Dario is at age nine when Lars Potter and I sought sanctuary in the dining room at Sunday lunch during a blizzard as my brother Kevin and his friend Freddy Herrick were pounding us with snowballs outside. No sooner had we run in in our snow suits than a particularly hard packed ice ball cracked into the wall above where Ogilvy & Mather original Mad Man and Club Vice President Shelby Page was nursing a hangover and his second martini. When everyone looked at us as if *we* had done it, we did the sensible thing and lit out for the territories, Joey, Dario and Nick in hot pursuit. Eventually we hid in lockers in the locker room until Potter, who was genetically incapable of silence, could not contain his giggles, and then we learned firsthand what strong leadership the Rockaway Hunting Club possessed. Most strong I assure you.

"It's impossible for me to look out over this sea of faces without thinking of the hundreds of people Dario has befriended and helped over the decades, many of them the parents, grandparents and even great grandparents of members here tonight.

"The truth of the matter, as the attendance of over 500 of you tonight eloquently attests, is that for half a century, like Joseph Conrad's *Nostromo,* Dario has been the essential man in the Club's operations, and an irreplaceable presence in all of our lives, a reality well illustrated by Dario's memory of asking Treddy Ketcham what his title was, and Treddy answering, 'Dario, you can make up *your own title.*'

"And, of course, behind every great man is a great woman, and none greater than Dario's wonderful wife, Lily. Lily, please come up here.

"I'd like to close this part of the evening with a word about character. Eight summers ago, we had our 125th Anniversary celebration. We had a new manager, a brand-new chef, and an absolutely tremendous response from the membership. I know this will come as a great shock to Father Owen and Monsignor Paul, but there are times when not even a membership as stellar as ours acts as if it belonged to that greater Club—the Communion of Saints. But amidst all the jockeying for position, the occasional squabbling and intense anxiety over how many we could accommodate, Dario carried the day by pleading, 'Let them ALL come, sir. WE CAN DO IT!'

"And he and the entire staff did do it magnificently, and the result was the most memorable occasion in the Club's history, until tonight!

"Let's enjoy our main course and then we will conclude the evening's program."

(Later)

"Good evening and welcome once again to the celebration of *Dario: The First 50 Years.* I am delighted to announce that this saga is soon to become a major motion picture produced by Liz Gateley with the somewhat altered but I'm sure you will agree arresting title of *A Legend in His Own Mind.*

"Turning now to another dimension of Dario's life at Rockaway, in the 1980s he was encouraged by our then President Blair Gammon (here with us tonight!) and Millard Atherton (stand up please both of you) to take up squash, and since that time he has become a holy terror on the squash courts, taking on all comers at all hours. In fact, in Nick Benvin's later years at the Club when anyone asked, 'Where's Dario?' Nick would answer, 'In his office.'

"When we sat down to prepare for tonight, Dario in his most modest and gracious manner, smirked, 'I remember beating you, the week after you won the Club championship.' So, he has an indirect claim to the Club championship.

"We should mention a couple of hallmarks of Dario's approach to squash. One of which is scoring. In Dario's system—let's call it the Croation New Math—whenever he wins a point it's worth two or even three; and whenever his opponent wins a point it counts as minus one.

"Then there's the matter of lets. If one is trying to get to a ball and, finding himself tripped by Dario, who also has an elbow jamming his ribs, if when this happens one is so foolish as to call, 'LET,' the response is shocked indignation and a defiant, 'That's no let!'

"On the other hand, if one has lobbed over Dario's head and he goes to the back wall and makes a weak, two wall return before falling down in a heap by the door and you drop shot for a clear winner, the call comes forth in stentorian tones, 'That's a let!'

'*Why* is that a let, Dario?'
'Because I fell down.'
'I had nothing to do with you falling down.'
'It's still a let.'
'The last time you clearly blocked and tripped me, and I fell down, you said it wasn't a let.'
'That's right.'
'Well, why wasn't that a let, and this is?'
'What are you, *stupido*? It's because that was you and this is me!'

"Aha, I'm beginning to understand. And then there's the interesting phenomenon of how, on those occasions when Dario is victorious, the entire Clubouse offers his hapless victim condolences as soon as he is out of the shower and has learned each and every detail of Dario's latest triumph. But when the result goes the other way, for some reason Dario has been rendered mute. A rare and mysterious medical condition. Dr. Mina Burger has dubbed it *Dariomania,* and I'm pleased to announce that Dario has donated his brain to the National Institutes of Health for further study, although that process will not be completed until after brunch tomorrow.

"We have another special and deeply touching message from Dario's homeland tonight—a telegram from the Croatian Squash Federation: It reads, 'Dear Mr. Muskardin, many congratulations on this auspicious occasion. Our emotions remain *high* at the memory of your last squash tour of Croatia, and we wish to express the hope that the honors you receive tonight will keep you in America for many years to come.'

"President Nicol will now make the final presentation. Artie, the floor is yours!"

*Art Nicol:*

"Dario, I'm something of a newcomer by comparison to you, but in the 33 years I have been a member here I've had the privilege of watching you perform every conceivable task at the Club and around the community and perform them well. In the early years I remember you bringing beers over to the Sunday afternoon softball games we used to have behind the old golf house and then serving more drinks and hors d'oeuvres on the terrace until after darkness fell, although sometimes the players fell first. I've heard you and Lilly sing at parties, and maybe later tonight we'll persuade you to give us an encore. I've had the somewhat dubious pleasure of playing dice with you on late nights in the winter bar, and I can confirm Jamie's report of your highly original counting system.

"Most importantly, I've seen you perform countless acts, not just of service but of true friendship to countless members over the past decades, and I know I speak for everyone here when I say we can never fully express our gratitude for everything you have given us.

"When it came time to decide to what a fitting tribute to Dario would be tonight, the decision was really very easy, so it gives me great pleasure tonight to announce that what Nick Benvin calls his 'office,' Dario's favorite squash court, the one on the left as you head out to the paddle courts, will henceforth be called DARIO'S COURT, and the plaque Frank is holding here will be placed outside it, which reads:

DARIO'S COURT
Dedicated to Dario Muskardin
In Honor of His First Fifty Years of Devoted Service
With Affection and Gratitude
The Members and Children of The Rockaway Hunting Club
October 15, 2011"


*Dario:*

(Holding the plaque on high, to sustained standing applause): "NOW I AM IMMORTAL!"

12/31: Quiet end of year with little time on Long Island but both boys well.

# Chapter 8

# Superstorm Sandy

## 2012

The boys loved their visit to London with the Northrops. Hilary was a fantastic hostess.

1/30: Rhoads is home from Portsmouth with his buddy, Aidan O'Farrell, Noreen Drexel's grandson.

2/21: Greece is bailed out again by the Eurozone.

5/1: There was a huge turnout at Heavenly Rest after Robert Williamson's tragic drowning. Caroline and the children are amazingly strong.

5/2: A pastel version of Munch's "Scream" sells for $120 million.

5/14: Pierce is home from college; Rhoads is finishing up the year well.

6/12: Michelle gives me a beautiful 60th birthday party in NYC on Florence Mauchant's gorgeous terrace on Carnegie Hill. Pierce and Rhoads were thrilled Lanie came and had a good time. They eventually got home to LI (sans Pierce's wallet!).

6/20: Tyler and Rachel MacGuire's wedding was a triumph in Denver. Uncle Peter chaperoned the younger generation into the wee hours most conscientiously!

7/4: CERN reports a new particle consistent with Higgs Boson.

8/4: Lovely parties for Mare Hart's 90th and Emma Miller's 80th. "I am most grateful for my Catholic Faith," a now foggy Emma said in her remarks, and her brothers David and John Gillespie added, "And for your annulment!"

8/13: Pierce obtains his visa for his semester abroad in Spain. Lots of late season tennis.

8/22: Fluffy Lynch's memorial. She was 92 and had lived upstate since leaving Holly House.

8/27: Rhoads wins a third set tiebreaker over Marco Vonderheide in the Rees Cup final, the Club's 21 and under championship.

9/3: Summer's end. Pierce is safely in Barcelona for his semester abroad. Rhoads is packed and relaxing at Russell's before driving up to Portsmouth with me tomorrow morning for his final year at boarding school.

## STORM / SURGE: A Sandy Diary

10/29: On the upper east side an eerie calm descended early on Monday, October 29th, the day that Super Storm Sandy hit. Kids abandoned their games on the Asphalt Green, and a bit after 4 p.m. the wind began to rise off the East River and rattle the windows (several in building lobbies on York Avenue broke altogether). Nonetheless, life went on a little and friends came to supper. The great storm broke over us a couple of hours later, our dinner guests were rescued by friends evacuating downtown, and in the long night that followed, leaves, branches, then trees, lights, gas lines and even buildings began to break apart. There was flooding at York and 92nd Street and elsewhere nearby, but nothing compared to the devastation downtown and in the outer boroughs.

Nonetheless, the streets above 39th Street were mostly navigable by late the next morning. Their electricity out, people from downtown streamed up by the thousands, filled the midtown streets and took shelter in hotels or with family and friends. By Wednesday some buses were running free of charge and filled to the brim. It was then that the scale of the catastrophe and the longevity of its effects began to become apparent.

11/2: All Souls. We took Lanie out to see the house on Friday. She was understandably anxious and late to arrive at the garage since there was no electricity in her building, necessitating much running up and down the stairs.

There were no lights on Rockaway Turnpike, trees were down everywhere, and the Isle of Wight was a chilly Purgatory. The house on Stable Lane got a foot of water, enough to ruin carpets and furniture, but perhaps only the first four feet of wall will have to be replaced rather than the entire first story as with most of our neighbors closer to sea level (our house is nine feet above).

The houses on Albert Place are all a mess. Mark and Tibby Hinckley thought they could ride it out with furniture on sawhorses, then waited too long to leave. "We saw a huge wave break over the dike coming towards us with something really big riding on it." It was a dock from the Yacht Club.

Jim and Ann Thornton were flooded and will have to rebuild from the studs once they clear out the muck.

Ed Reitler stayed as well, fearing the car might stall out with kids in it. He did get a car to high ground at the Ogden's on Ocean Avenue and then had to swim back to his house. Later he went to check on bed-ridden Carol

Lawrence, dying from cancer, in her bedroom with no oxygen after the power went. Climbing up the stairs he heard her call out, "Ed Reitler, if you're dragging mud onto my good rug, I'll kill you!"

Price and Nancy Blackford's house is OK except for water in the porch and the basement. He says that Edward Bentley built it right after the hurricane of '38 and must have measured the highwater mark.

Don Wilson owns three houses on the Isle of Wight (causing Jim Thornton, who only has two, to refer to him as "Don Zeckendorf Wilson"), and he came to them to ride out the storm. The Bulkleys arrived from Arizona soon after.

Many, many cars are lost. The Heaneys and Gateleys say their homes are tear downs. Docks and other debris washed up on Helen Corroon's and the other houses along Reymolds Channel. Thanks to Art Nicol, Dario came and pumped out our crawl space. Art and Peggy built their new house to flood specifications and only lost a car. Art hired security for the Isle of Wight, and the first night confronted a flatbed truck that was shining a light at the Madsen's house. Mexicans are walking in the neighborhood as well. Looking for work?

Michelle and I walked the golf course. Trees were down, the skeet and trap ranges and skeet house destroyed. Turkey Point is devastated. Dick Aldrich lost the most trees, but the Mullen's driveway was completely impassable, filled with marsh debris. A boat came to rest in the right hand rough of the fifteenth hole! 100 yards from the nearest estuary. The storm surge was over 9 feet at its highest. Nick Brodziak and Ernie were patiently cleaning up, raking away at the accumulated debris washed up from the marsh, looking for all the world like escapees from a Thomas Hardy novel. Indeed, over pumpkin soup and tuna fish sandwiches at the Club, longtime neighbors spoke stoically of it being like living back in the nineteenth century again, houses dank and without heat or hot water for the foreseeable future. It made for a melancholy journey and, despite our damage being comparatively slight, we left filled with pity for dear friends and concerns about the future.

In the Rockaways, a resident said, "We're living like cavemen here." Poor Breezy Point burned, and 120 houses were lost. But the New Jersey shore was hit hardest of all.

I can imagine everyone rebuilding this time if they get their insurance, but what if it happens again in another five or ten years?

11/6: Obama defeats Romney and is re-elected to his second term.

11/21: Rhoads is home for Thanksgiving, reverent at Mass and stayed to Michelle's flank steak supper. Quite chatty on the School. He and Chris Soriano have become critical of Israel. Isabel Keogh has invited him to the semi-formal in December in this a Sadie Hawkins year. The girls ask early which the boys never would! Rhoads is off to Paris with Lanie and Pierce for Thanksgiving.

Much talk of "IOW Radicals" threatening to sue the Village for not maintaining the dike properly, cleaning up fast enough, etc. in accord with our 1972 agreement. That could be counter-productive and Margaret Carpenter counsels a more conciliatory approach. People are understandably stressed and frayed, and doubtless property values have been hurt. If the dike is not repaired until Spring it may discourage many from rebuilding in such vulnerable conditions.

John McEvoy always warned of a "100-year storm" until his mother Frances died and he hied off to Lynbrook with his lady friend. Good timing.

12/8 I tour the IOW after squash. The dike is being strengthened and reinforced. Ruined furniture, carpets, clothes and other junk continue to pour out of the flooded houses. Bibi has been heroic mopping and cleaning up the house. And a single bloom on the rose bush I planted 20 years ago brightens the lawn amidst the surrounding muck and rubble.

12/14: The Sandy Hook shooting kills 28.

A happy Christmas for the boys and their new iPads in Wichita Falls. Rhoads and Lanie are driving a new car back to replace the one ruined in the storm via Memphis (Graceland) and Cleveland, including a detour to Frank Lloyd Wright's Falling Water in Pennsylvania. Pierce is staying down in Texas until school resumes. Only a year and half of college left. Where did the time go?


### 2013


Rhoads' college application essay:


## THE GAME


Effort is a great indicator. From the tennis court to the classroom, determination makes you more valuable. My Dad always told me that running down an extra ball in a tennis point was important, "One more shot back is one more your opponent can miss," was his mantra for me. This always spanned beyond tennis in my mind. Going the extra mile, whether you are trying to help someone or just giving a project a little extra pizzazz will never be something you regret. It does not matter whether it is actually effective. It is just having that sense of pride knowing that you did everything you possibly could.

When I was six years old my father put a tennis racquet in my hand for the first time, and we played a match, which for the sake of my scrawny legs was only a few games. My parents had separated a few months prior, and these matches with my Dad provided a bond I still share with him today. We both love playing tennis. My Dad taught me more lessons on a tennis court than I can count, and he reinforced them by letting me win when I played with a level head and complete determination. The actual lessons he taught me helped me not only to become a better tennis player but also to advance as a young man.

My father has always been considered by others and myself as a consummate gentleman. I recall a match with my father when I was twelve where I threw my racquet one too many times and he stopped playing and left the court. When I troubled him for an explanation on why he no longer wanted to play he said that I needed to conduct myself more appropriately, because others can only judge you by your actions. This always stays with me because, no matter how you view yourself, other people's perception of what you do forms their opinions of you.

Dad and I loved to trade quotes on this subject. He would cite the famous sportswriter Grantland Rice, "When the One Great Scorer comes to mark against your name, he counts not whether you won or lost, but how you played the Game." I would respond by quoting Hall of Fame coach Vince Lombardi, "Winning isn't the only thing, it's *everything*." (Ed. Note: Eventually we found a middle ground. We went to Wimbledon for Rhoads' eighth-grade graduation present, and one of my old Cambridge teammates brought us into the Members' Enclosure. At the Players' Entrance to Centre Court hangs a sign emblazoned with the following lines from Rudyard Kipling's poem, *If*: "If you can meet with triumph and disaster, and treat those two imposters just the same.")

Conducting oneself properly and demonstrating grace under pressure is important whether on the tennis court, in a job interview, in our working lives and during personal crises. The most important thing my Dad wanted me to carry away from the court was to stay mentally stable, competitively agile, and to conduct myself like a gentleman. I like to think I have taken my Dad's advice to heart on and off the court. With his help I have become the varsity football quarterback, tennis captain and someone who has earned admiration from his peers and his adversaries. I am glad I will have my father's counsel for the next big step in my life—in college.

February: The rebuilding  house on the Isle of Wight began. Inevitably, some residents began to feel frustration as contractors, some of whom had overbooked themselves, began to fall behind. There is a hearty weekend squash group, and Michelle and I enjoy lunch and a walk after. It will take time, but things will get back to normal in a year or two.

2/28: Pope Benedict resigns.

March: Rhoads is home for Spring break after a triumphant visit to his cousin Casey at Johns Hopkins. He's uproariously ebullient and looking ahead!

4/3: Pope Francis is elected.

4/15: Boston Marathon bombing by two Chechnya-born Islamists.

Over Easter I saw Marion Bierwirth walking on Ocean Avenue and commiserated that Jack was having such a hard time. "The whole family's having a hard time," she answered and gave my arm a sympathetic squeeze.

Later in May I walked into the Club just as Dario was putting the notice of Jack's death from congestive heart failure up on the announcement board. My last letter to him had arrived two days before he went. The family was strong, and he was memorialized in the press as a good leader of Grumman, Long Island's largest employer.

## June

Rhoads finished up his prep school years very well, with many celebrations and fond farewells. He went off to the Philippines with his posse to visit the Sorianos and sends me Father's Day greetings "from the other side of the world."

6/15: "Dad, I wrote this short poem about our summer tennis seasons. Many of my fondest memories. Happy Father's Day, Dad. I love you. Love, Pierce."

*In seeming perpetuity*
*I am defeated by the mental acuity*
*Of a man I call Dad*
*Surely at this point I am stronger*
*My reach is longer*
*I even teach the damn sport to toddlers*
*Alas he cannot be broken*
*But still stays mostly soft spoken*
*Aside from the occasional thunderous laugh*
*Often after a jest some might call crass*
*These mostly after he demonstrates mastery of his craft . . .*
*But the young challenger must say his greatest pleasure*
*Is when father and son play together*
*He will always remember their happy summer days*
*And wants to wish you a happy Father's Day!*

July: Later in the summer, I'm happy to have both boys home. Pierce enjoys his construction work in Texas. After a steamy tennis match Rhoads and I drove into town for his graduation dinner, and he entertained Rob Barnes, Michelle and me at "21" with his theories on physics, thoughts on new methods of influencing the subconscious, new business ideas and comments on literature. He has a creative and confident mind.

8/15: Rhoads had his Portsmouth buddies Charlie Ramsden, Michael Stark and Gabe Miller down for his last weekend—a reggae concert in Brooklyn and many barbeques. He defended his Rees Cup championship over Marco Vonderheide 6–4, 6–4, and Bobby Quinn gave him an extra racquet to take to college as a thank you for teaching in the Junior Sports Program this summer. He is off to Southwestern University with Pierce in Georgetown, Texas, another step on life's road.

End of summer family gatherings at the Madsens and Blackfords. My mother prized family above all else and would have loved it!

A funny lunch with Carol Lynch Brackenbridge (Fluffy's daughter and one of Cedarhurst's greatest beauties in her day). She recalled Billy Parkhurst's Corvair and surfing with him one day when he went white when he saw fins behind her. They began paddling furiously to get away from the sharks and Carol lost her board beneath her. When it popped up it clunked her upside the head. The sharks turned out to be dolphins.

"My mother was this great squash and tennis player, and there were trophies all over the house. She finally asked me to play in a tournament, and I thought now I'll have a trophy of my own. We played and won, but that year the prize was a fruitcake!"

## Chapter 9

# Lanie, 2013–2015

August 29, 2013: Oh no! Lanie's dear friend Jane Moos called. Poor Lanie has been diagnosed with bladder cancer at Memorial Sloan-Kettering. She fell from her bike and thought she had cracked a rib, but the MRI showed a spot. Evaluation is ongoing, but they think it has metastasized. She was to have left for Venice today but was told not to go. She has had some discomfort in the past several weeks and told the boys in Texas last week there might be an issue. Pierce sounded strong and optimistic at first, then not so much. He says Rhoads has made a great start at SU and doesn't want to burden him with the full story. Terrible.

8/30: I wrote Lanie a note assuring her we would do everything we could. Then, on Friday, I dropped off flowers and a card in the boys' names. She thanked me via text and asked if I could take her home Sunday, which, of course, I will. Chemo will start soon. Bibi is understandably distraught. She says Lanie told her she hoped for five years so she could see Rhoads graduate. Dear Lord!

9/2: We celebrated Schuyler's 70th last night at the Hunt Club. Annabel and Lily MacGuire were adorable with Casey. I toasted the transition from patriarchy to matriarchy in the new generation.

10/11: The boys came home to see their Mom, and we had lots of good tennis, a last picnic on the beach, and dinner at the Club with twelve MacGuires.

11/29: A good Thanksgiving, little Emily stealing the show, the younger generation now ten strong! What a world they are walking into. Lanie has finished chemo, and we all pray it has gone well. The boys had supper with Lanie and Bibi on Stable Lane last night. Pierce has made the Dean's List and Rhoads has an unusually high GPA for a Freshman, 3.25.

Christmas: Michelle and I exchanged gifts with Lanie, Pierce and Rhoads. Lanie looked pale but well, though Michelle said she felt "bone-thin" when

217

she hugged her. Lanie came to lunch at Schuyler's in high spirits, wearing a high-belted skirt and long boots and looked chic. Rhoads said Grace, and, perhaps stimulated by the champagne, held forth loudly on many fronts. Lanie was toasted for her pecan pies. A couple of days later she came to dinner and then wrote a heart-rending thank you note: "The atmosphere was warm and welcoming, the pasta was delicious, and I'm sending you my pecan pie recipe unbidden, because the MacGuires really seem to like it, and I'm not sure how long I'll be able . . ."

Yegods. But by mid-January she was in partial remission and "apparently" cancer-free.


## 2014

Since I was running media programs at IESE Business School and working many weekends in town, we got to the Isle of Wight infrequently.


### Winter

2/22: The Ukrainian revolution begins.

Rhoads reported that his induction celebration into Kappa Alpha at Southwestern was "somewhere between lunch at The Brook and 'The Wolf of Wall Street'." Pierce took his law boards and described them as "an out of body experience." But in March he was accepted into Baylor, a top fifty law school.


### Spring

We gave a fun dinner party grilling veggies and butterflied lamb for the Thorntons, Hastys, Sylvesters, Dean and Sky.


### Summer

In late June the boys came home, and the house was filled with Donovans and Burkes, Casey and Clay, watching FIFA. One night we went to the Hunt Club buffet, and Steve Madsen toasted Capt. Jonathan Leathers, still in dress uniform after returning safely from Afghanistan. (I remember young Steve and Jonathan being disciplined by Steve Sr. for trying to cadge drinks from the bar of our cocktail party when they were 12!) Deo gratias.


### July

Kvitova beat Bouchard and Djokovich won a stirring five set finals over Federer at Wimbledon. Meanwhile, L.J. Morledge and I won a really important tournament, the Jimmy Burns Handicap Doubles. It was my first win in that event, though I clearly remember playing in it at 14 with Bill MacMillen and beating Uncle Tim Carpenter and Steve Owen Sr. 8–6, 6–8, 12–10 in the first round in the pre-tiebreaker era.

Our IOW neighbor Alistair Hanna has died, a good man, brilliant physicist and microelectronics consultant. 1200 came to St. Bart's where his wife, the Reverend Nancy, presides. He was only 69 but had battled cancer for four years.

7/8: Poor Lanie. She had been doing well in her remission but lost her speech in a therapy session with a client last night. Her client walked her down to Sloan-Kettering and, after much testing, they determined that the cancer had spread to her brain. She had hoped to join the boys on a Kenyan safari but will now begin radiation immediately. She is adamant that the boys go on without her, hopeful for a complete cure, but also at peace. "I'm satisfied with what I've accomplished." Kerry is choked up, and Bibi is keening.

8/1: The boys got back happily from Africa, and Lanie's treatment went along as well as it could. We went to a drinks party celebrating the Lalor boys' membership at the Beach Club, and Peter Lalor confessed to me that when we were young, he had crushes on Mimi Hart and Clay Brooks, the sexiest kitten of her day out here, who at 16 went to a concert of the Dave Clark Five and ended up having an affair with the drummer.

8/8: Pierce is off to Law School, and Lanie insists on going down to Waco to help him move in. So brave. Rhoads is slugging it out on the Har-Tru with James Heaney and then heading to Ultimate Frisbee and the Apple Store in New York. I swim in the ocean and see Putnam MacLean, a childhood friend down from Boston to visit his parents, looking well. Margaret Carpenter, her daughter Posie, and her partner Maureen were swimming laps in the pool. Tom Keating, Woody Kerr, Joe McCarthy and Steve Shiels were having lunch with Pierce the Elder. Then Van Burger, Pierce and I had a glorious round of afternoon golf as the north wind blew, the tide rose, and the world was basked in evening's glow.

At the Hunt Club buffet dinner that night were Jack and Kate Oliver, Marie and Bill May, Price and Nancy Blackford, Tony and Siri Mortimer, the Stanifords with Tonchie Vest up from Charlottesville, the Reitlers, Madsens, Yuns, Susan Williams, Monsignor Rahilly, pretty Harper Robinson with Holly, Marc and Helen, the Nicols, Bulkleys, Wadsworths and Nancy Hanna. Good to see her out! I bunked down in Pierce's room after and had a beautiful swim in the crystal-clear ocean the next day. Then I had breakfast with Rhoads who has become the Mayor of the Lawrence young set. The very cute Maria Elena Ubina, national junior champion in squash and playing for Princeton, Elizabeth Nerich and others sit with us. We will have a couple of more sublime days and games before Rhoads is off back to college.

8/9: Michael Brown was shot and killed by a cop after Brown attacked him in his squad car in Ferguson, MO.

9/2: Last outing to the US Open with Ray York, lame and limping. Old tennis buddies Charlie Jones and John McLean joined us, as boon companions as ever. We have been doing this for 30 years.

10/12: Brother Pierce is 66, Helen Corroon 87, Honor MacLean ditto, Anne Thornton 77, and Jim 82. We have a dinner party for the Thorntons, Madsens, Keatings and Burgers. Pierce and Rhoads joined us on their weekend home to see Lanie. She has felt understandable stress and pain and suffered a seizure two weeks ago that left her temporarily unresponsive. Better now, and the official line is still that a complete recovery is possible. She insists on riding her bike against doctor's orders and resists having someone with her at all times. Dangerous. Kerry Graham was up as well to tend to house renovation issues.

10/31: House sitting at the Hinckleys, who have, very sadly for us, put their house on the market. The sudden death of Mark's brother, two months shy of retirement, was the final blow. They want to be closer to family. The house has simple, elegant lines and an American aesthetic with a glorious view overlooking the marsh and lambent Autumn light. The Thorntons, Sky, Dean and Pierce Sr. joined us for swordfish, late corn, tomatos and apple crisp. Then the trick or treaters descended, Burgers, Simonds, Klausners, Lily MacGuire and many others, a whole new generation of adorably spooky spirits.

Lanie and the boys went to the Ranch for Thanksgiving. We were at Sally and Kevin's as always. Then we enjoyed a wonderful night at the Opera with IOW neighbors Nell and Robert Kleinschmidt.

12/18: The boys are up and enjoy yoga with Uncle Pierce at the Racquet Club and a delicious quail and wild rice lunch at The Brook. We have good squash, a gala Christmas Eve cooked by Michelle, and a happy Christmas Day at Dean and Schuyler's but for the fact that Lanie felt too poorly to come. Pierce was visibly upset.

## 2015

New Year's squash and lunch at the RHC. Caroline Stewart cooked gumbo and mixed Manhattans on Stable Lane. Good of her to come out for Lanie and the boys.

1/5: The news from Sloan-Kettering was not good, and Lanie has entered her final decline. Pierce called to give me the news, his voice emotional but completely manly.

1/7: Boko Haram massacres over 200 in Nigeria.

1/31: Rhoads decided to take a leave of absence from college for them both, since Pierce cannot do so from law school. He came up and was offered an internship by our neighbors, Jim Thornton and Robert Kleinschmidt, at Tocqueville Asset Management, so he had a place to go and learn during the day. His buddy Russell Aldrich was awaiting his call from the Coast Guard and proved a loyal companion with his dogs when they were out in Lawrence.

## February

By mid-February Lanie, still walking until then and getting to the Opera, realized it was time to move into her NYC pad full time and accept home hospice care. She had emailed me "to take care of the boys" and now called me, speaking a bit tentatively and mixing up words, to let me know what a great job Rhoads was doing for her. Sweet. She is now in a wheelchair. I am still in shock that Lanie could be dying. That vibrant, beautiful, high-spirited girl!

Her best childhood friends, Jennifer Estes and Joannie Payne, flew up to become the corps of a group of "angels" to support her. Rhoads cuddles close to her when he is there, recalling the story book we used to read the boys when young: "I'll love you forever, I'll like you for always. For as long as you're living, my baby you'll be." But on the last page, it's the now middle-aged former infant holding her aged mother, and the last line changes to "My mommy you'll be."

## March

Lanie died on Sunday, March 1st at about 7:45 p.m. We were just leaving Alice Tully Hall after a Chamber Music Society concert and dinner with the Kleinschmidts when the call came from Caroline. Michelle and I rushed over to the apartment on East 66th Street. Pierce was devastated but with friends at the Baylor Law School Library. Rhoads had been advised to leave by Caroline because "She doesn't want to die when you are here with her." He went out to Stable Lane, and Bibi drove over to be with him, Russell and Russell's dogs.

Our Isle of Wight neighbor, Quinn Barton, took him to dinner the next night, and in the next month Ed Reitler gave Nolan Crawford and Rhoads summer internships at the venture arm of his law firm.

There was a burial service the following week at the cemetery next to the Ranch in Decatur, Texas, and a lovely memorial later in the month presided over by Bishop Andrew at the Little Church Around the Corner on 29th Street. Both boys spoke memorably.

**Eulogy for Lanie by Pierce**

About two months ago Mom and I were discussing her post-departure plans. She mentioned that she did not want to have a funeral. I asked her why on earth not? She said she was afraid no one would come. I told her that that was ridiculous, that we would most certainly be having a funeral, and that it would be well attended by the people that loved and admired her. I hope she can see this from where she is, because for once I was right.

I was in the law school parking lot about to drive home when I got the call that Mom had passed away. That night was difficult, but the most amazing thing happened. As I was drifting off to sleep, I heard my Mother. I do not know precisely what she said, but it was to the effect that she was well, and that Rhoads and I should not worry about her because she was happy where she was.

I woke up and debated whether or not this had actually happened or if my brain had invented it as a coping mechanism. After deep reflection, I am firmly of the belief that my Mother communicated with me that night.

As if this was not extraordinary enough, my dream that night was the most vivid and memorable that I have ever had. I dreamt that Gabriel and Michael were holding Mom by the arms and ascending towards heaven. Mom, however, was not being co-operative. She was continuously insisting to the two archangels that she had to tell her boys that she was happy and safe, and that if they would not let her do so, she would not accompany them to heaven. The angels tried to explain to her that that is simply not how it works, but Mom kept insisting. My dream did not last to the resolution of this dispute but based on my earlier experience I think I know who won.

I tell you this because I believe it happened, but also because it illustrates Mom's most enduring and powerful trait: her indomitable will. Her power could not be stifled. She searched and searched for a proper medium to share her gifts with the world. First it was business school, then social work and then she finally found her true calling as an analyst. Few people could reinvent themselves in the drastic ways that my Mother did over her career, but she had something to give, and she refused to quit until she found a way to do so.

Her will also served her passion for art, health, and bodily well-being. People often tell me I walk too fast. They were never a 12-year-old boy trying to keep up with my mother on a walk to the Met. Her love of riding her bike in tandem with her ravenous consumption of the arts and her professional pursuits made her one of the sharpest people I have known.

Even cancer, that most cowardly of diseases, could not overcome her will to learn, to teach, to experience, and to explore. Here is just a sampling of things my Mom did with cancer: she hiked a five-mile ocean-side pass in

Hawaii, she toured Europe, she moved me into my Waco apartment, and she wrote her book on the persona. What will stick with me most though, and what I am most proud of, is the lecture she gave to her fellow analysts only weeks before her death. By the time she was due to give this speech, the insidious cancer had begun to diminish her ability to speak.

I remember sitting with her in New York only about a month ago, the day before her big speech. We were rehearsing, and it was not going well. She was stumbling over every other word and getting quite frustrated. At several points, she said she did not know if she could give the speech, and, frankly, I had my doubts as well.

We came up with a solution though. We decided that she would give the speech, but I would stand at the podium with her . . . ready to finish tricky sentences or clarify an ambiguity.

Finally, it came time to give the speech. Watching Mom speak to her fellow analysts was the most glorious and beautiful struggle I have ever witnessed. Struggle is not a misnomer. It was not easy, and it took a long time to finish even with my help, but the analysts all listened, fascinated by the subject matter of Mom's speech. They asked wonderful questions and congratulated her endlessly afterwards. It will always be one of my most cherished memories.

"Beating Cancer" seems to be defined as surviving it. Well, I believe my Mother and the countless others who refuse to yield their way of life to cancer have expanded the definition. My Mother, just as much as anyone else, beat cancer.

Death is a truly ironic thing because it is the ultimate separation, but also a great unifier. That my Mother has died is a paradigm shifting reality that is difficult to accept or even comprehend at this point. Yet, at the same time, death can serve as a great unifier of those left behind. I am so glad that you could all be here today to celebrate Alane's life with us. She was a truly special woman and her impact on her world will not soon be forgotten. Amen.

### Eulogy for Lanie by Rhoads

It has been 27 days since my mother passed away and I know that for many of you, like myself, it has been four difficult weeks of grieving. The mourning is far from over, but we have not gathered here today to mourn. Instead, we are here as friends and families to celebrate the life of an extraordinary woman. I believe that's the way she would have wanted it.

My mother had many amazing characteristics that she developed to squeeze every last drop out of life. Her passion for her work, appreciation for the arts and her loving care as a mother were all unmatched. She was also an incredibly humble person. You would never know when she entered a room, with that wonderful smile, that she was almost definitely the most intelligent person there. One of the few things she loved to boast about, though, was hiring Bibi. She loved to tell the story of interviewing Bibi when the young Pierce MacGuire began to cry in the next room. Without being asked Bibi immediately jumped up and went into the next room to change him. "But you haven't got a changing cloth," she said to Mom in mild reproach. I think my Mother knew right then she not only had a babysitter but someone who would be a dear friend.

The reason I tell you all this is because it shows one of Mom's traits which I have become most grateful for, her ability to surround herself with wonderful people. From the first diagnosis, my mother's friends formed a powerful and loving network of friends behind her. At first, my mother's strength and courage powered this group. Her refusal to give up her practice and her lunch break trips to the Met even through radiation and chemo, was a true inspiration

As time went on though and the cancer spread to her brain and then liver, it became apparent that my mother was terminal. My mother was still as brave as she could be, but her strength began to deteriorate, and it became obvious she could no longer live alone. I know this was huge blow for her and that she was somewhat embarrassed to not be able take care of herself. Luckily, though, my mother had some wonderful friends who were more than willing to drop their own schedules to come spend time with my mom, and I am grateful today to thank Bibi Moonsamy, Caroline Stewart, Gay Wally, Jane Cohen, Jennifer Estes, Joanie Payne and Sherri Salman, by whom my mom was loved and supported throughout the last weeks of her life. Whether it was one of those final few walks through the park, drinking Manhattans and eating *foie gras* at The Modern or simply sharing secrets and walnut toast by her bedside, these people allowed my Mom to take what pleasures she could out of the toughest time in her life. These women showed me the importance of loving someone in their time of need. They wanted her to go through the final stage of her life as comfortably as possible, and I am profoundly grateful for having had them so close to Mom, Pierce and me in such a challenging time.

I believe it is such a testament to my Mom, the type of selfless person that she was, that her friends here wanted to love and care for her the way they did when she was in such a vulnerable state. My mother was an incredibly generous and loving person, and it is a tragedy that she is no longer with us. But let us be thankful today that we all have had an opportunity to know such a beautiful lady inside and out.

# Chapter 10

# Renewal, 2016

May 8, 2016: Spring is finally taking hold on Long Island, with many memories of Lanie and the boys growing up on Stable Lane. The grass is green and flowers are blooming everywhere. Rhoads has been down to Johns Hopkins to visit Casey and Clay and appears well but confesses to anxiety and unspecified anger. He broke his brother's tennis racquet playing tennis tonight and says, "I know I'm a little crazy." What he needs is time, and love.

We have his buddies to dinner with him often and more than once Chris Donovan decides to sleep over. Just as it should be. When Pierce gets home later in the month they come into lunch at Michael's and enjoy the scene—Patricia Hearst Shaw, Tom Brokaw, and Allen & Co. honcho, Stan Shuman, who asks to meet Rhoads. We had many good times over the summer, both boys had their wisdom teeth removed at last, various neighbors like the Lindenthals, and our attractive young ones, Sumner and Renee Anderson and Charlie and Lindsay Higgins, came in. The Andersons have two beautiful girls—Stella and Abigail, and the Higgins three—Martha, Ann and Kate. Pierce's girlfriend Alex Rodriguez came up, and they enjoyed the Met and *The King and I*. She is a very beautiful girl, inside and out.

The Northrops and Smiths came in for dinner one night and the Donovan boys to celebrate Josh Northrop's last's night another, to such good effect that Bull and Toad both slept over. Superstorm Sandy seems to have wiped out the feral cats, crows and many raccoons, but bunnies and bird life have roared back in this green summer. Pierce beat Filippo Arcieri to win the "B" singles and Rhoads beat Tom Russo in three long sets in the "As" before losing to longtime rival Marco Vonderheide. Becky, Peter and Casey came for Saturday steak, twice baked potatoes, garlic bread, prosciutto and melon, Saratoga tomatoes, cake and ice cream. The boys are healthy and happy, surrounded by friends, family, laughter and love, and can now move on.

There was a quiet IOW Association meeting in which the big news was that the roads would be paved this Fall (in fact, it happened the following Spring!). The plumber came to fix the shower thermostat and stem a leak in the sink faucet. The electrician came as well to rewire a dead outlet and install dimmers. The chimney sweep came in and found a large brick blocking the smoke as it tried to rise. Working on a house never ends.

Monsignor Paul Rahilly is retiring at St. Joachim's, and we joined about forty for dinner at the Club to thank him. I was baptized and had my First Communion there, continued with Catechism under Sister Mary Albert's iron hand. Soon thereafter I was riding my bike down Cedarhurst Avenue in the pre-dawn dark to serve the 6:30 Mass in Latin. Sister Mary Albert could put the fear of God in all of them and us too, but I do remember one occasion when even she cracked a smile. My brother Peter and his buddy Maitland Horner were playing basketball with the other school kids before catechism, when she blew her whistle and commanded, "Public school children get on-line for Catechism!" Almost everyone complied, except Peter and Maitland, dressed in madras jackets and neckties. "Why aren't you boys getting on-line?"

"Because," my eight-year-old brother answered, "We go to private school."

When the nuns died out and the convent closed, she wrote a beautiful reflection, "What has been achieved."

And Monsignor Rahilly achieved a great deal in his 20 years as well, negotiating the various elements of the community and defending the dwindling Catholic Christian presence in an ever more Orthodox Jewish world. He recalled Bishop McGann calling him to give him the assignment. "Where is Cedarhurst? I'm very happy here at Deer Park."

"Don't you ever question your vow of obedience! Renew it over and over, and it will liberate you."

"And he was right. This has become my home. I love it and never want to leave, but now I have to."

We sat with Fiske and Michelle Warren, Dan and Lee Klausner and Scott and Lynn LaRue. Michelle enjoyed learning that all of the ladies were Sacred Heart graduates like herself, Lynn's daughter even having gone to the same school in Atherton. The LeRues later hosted a festive Mexican night at their new house on Turkey Point, owned by Miss Timpson, Carlie's sister, when I was a boy.


## September

Time slows down after Labor Day and one can be more present with others. An old acquaintance, Ira Freedman, called out, "Jamie?" from his bike the other day. His daughter, Rebecca, and Pierce were pals in Kindergarten at

Lawrence-Woodmere Academy. She works in PR at Edelman now. Ira and Mara still live in Hewlett Bay Park, and Ira is the oldest employee at Topps, the baseball card company, now 80 percent digital.

I visit the boys in Austin, and we have a hot day on the golf course. Rhoads: "Golf sweat is different than tennis. It *cakes*." We attend a Southwestern U. Friday Night Lights game, and they know many friends in the crowd.

11/2: Mild weather. Frank Bocci felled the nearly-dead from Sandy wild cherry trees at the back of the garden and opened up a splendid view of the large beech tree behind it on the Anderson's lawn, where the birds love to roost in the mornings. The other trees and bushes have all been trimmed up, the driveway has been re-graveled, and things are looking ship shape as we head into winter.

11/26: Rhoads came home for Thanksgiving and had a great time with us and Isabel. Pierce elected to go to a bachelor party on an Indian Reservation in Oklahoma. Our parish of St. Joachim has now been consolidated with St. Joseph's in Hewlett and Our Lady of Good Counsel in Inwood, where I go to Mass at 4 p.m. on St. Andrew's Day.

Inwood is, as ever, the poorest of the Five Towns, and Church Street is a narrow lane of small, often jury-rigged houses with many gardening trucks parked along it. A remnant of the old clam digger and Italian families like the Cappobiancos remain, but many black and Hispanic families live there nowadays as well. Fr. Eric Fasano, originally from North Merrick, is in residence and a judicial vicar for the diocese of Rockville Center. He is dignified and eloquent, and I also enjoy spying the stained-glass window given in 1902 "from the chauffeurs and house maids of Lawrence." Those were the days.

I picked Michelle up from JFK where she had nursed her Dad through the holidays. At 92, Dick is feeling his age for the first time. Woody and C.J. Kerr had a warm-hearted family party—Paynes, Sipps, Porcellis, Warrens, Blackfords, Andersons, Higgins. We went onto dinner with the Thorntons at the Club, a good crowd in the dining room and over 40 at the paddle party in the bar. Schuyler mentioned that a neighbor told him all three of our largely Jewish clubs locally are in trouble. The Woodmere Club is down to 35 members, Inwood has a $16 million note coming due next year, and Seawane is in dire straits as well.

12/21: Michelle decorated the house beautifully for Christmas, and we picked up Rhoads at the airport. Isabel came down from Boston as well, and we had evenings of chili and hamburgers. We drove back out from town on the 23rd heavily laden with food and presents, cooked steaks that rainy night, and Pierce revealed the happy news that he would ask Alex to marry him while they skied in Crested Butte next week. A great joy. Johnnie Marie says she looks like Lanie, a dark-haired beauty, and it's true.

On a mild Christmas Eve, the boys went off to golf with Uncle Pierce. I helped Michelle around the house, and we welcomed the Nicols, Madsens, Aldriches and Reitlers as well as family—24 in all, around a beautiful fire. The next day we enjoyed Schuyler and Dean's festive lunch with the beautiful grand nieces, and Russell came back for dinner that night by the fire. On St. Stephen's night we did chili for the Kerrs, Thorntons, Hinckleys, Higgins, Paynes, Warrens, Burgers and Mullens (the Stanifords forgot and apologized profusely the next day!). Peggy Nicol came up to Michelle to say how touched she was to see Pierce hug her on Christmas Eve and say, "Thank you for doing this. You've done so much this past year." When Michelle tried to demur Peggy said, "No, I've seen everything you've done, and those boys are so lucky to have you." At the newsstand the next morning she was still effusive, "You made me feel like family."

"Peggy, after 63 years and all our families went through together, you *are* family."

12/31: After a quiet week in town, a walk on the beach, Michelle's delicious leek and potato soup and a Harry & David's pear, I was reading on the sun porch when a text came through, "I tricked her into it."

Pierce had proposed, and Alex accepted, receiving the ring my mother gave me to give to Lanie. "I was going to do it when we came off the mountain, but I decided I didn't want a thousand Oklahomans looking on, so I waited till we got back to the condo, turned around, got down on my knees, and she said yes."

Lucky boy, lucky girl, and a lovely chat with Tony and Becky Rodriguez, who sound like sweet folks. Calls to Johnnie Marie and John and Cheryl Sauder. Much joy.

## 2016

Winter weekends of squash, dinners with the Blackfords and Hinckleys and lunches with Sarah Nash. The light is coming back slowly, the horizon ringed rose by 6:30 a.m. Shotguns popping as hunters on the marsh go for largely inedible brant. I did see a pair of swan nudging up Crooked Creek toward the Channel. Price Blackford says they instinctively stay just out of a bird dog's reach until the dog exhausts itself, and then they push it down under. The Gateley's house foundation is in, and the second story of the house is being framed this weekend. I played doubles with Dozier Hasty, the fearless Melissa Murray and Russell Aldrich, who tells me he came past the Madsens to park his car in our driveway during the storm because he was having dinner with J.J. Lindenthal and thought that would be safer, but in the end he got stuck in the three foot high tide turning the Causeway corner into Stable Lane and stalled out. The car is ruined from saltwater damage.

2/16: Pierce Patterson MacGuire is 25 today. What a sea of memories and ocean of hopes! He ran a half marathon in Austin on Sunday. A long happy life ahead, or so I pray.

3/17: Shocking news from Florida. Mina Burger died after a full day of the tennis and golf she so loved. Severe abdominal pains led Van to get her to the hospital, where they discovered a large mass. She then had a heart attack, but was revived, whereupon doctors diagnosed severe brain damage, so Van let her go. She had only retired last year, and they were loving Florida. Van wrote, "Mina was the definition of life."

3/25: We had Peter and Jane Keegan for dinner for Michelle's Paschal lamb and pot au crème with pistachio topping. Jane is shy but lovely and had good pointers on gardens. Peter was as serious, concerned and kind as ever. As I drove to Mass the next morning Woody Kerr was walking his dog, "He is Risen," quoth he. "Indeed, He is Risen, alleluia."

Schuyler was in the church, along with Art and Judy Murray, Johnny and Theresa Zorovich, Dario standing in back, and Jimmy, the retired cop and taxi driver who sometimes golfs with Peter Kniffin. So many early Monday mornings he drove me to LaGuardia at 4:30 a.m. so I could get to Orlando. He asked after the boys, and I mentioned they had lost their mother just a year ago. "I know."

Everyone knows everything here! When I was running Catholic Relief Services in Burundi in the late 1970s there was an expression, "When you walk out of your house in Bujumbura, the first person you meet on the street tells you what you dreamed last night." Our little corner of Long Island is a lot like that.

5/23: Sweet symphonies on the 4:30 a.m. lawn, the world aglow in new light. Up at 5:10, out of the house by 5:40, reminding me of my days working as a boilermaker on the Con Edison plant in Astoria in 1972. Beautiful new early light out of the Stable Lane master bedroom window now, and yesterday's walk to the yacht club was fragrant with lilac, dogwood, apple and cherry blossoms, the rabbits running riot in and out of the reeds. Michelle opens a window in Rhoads' bedroom to let in air not realizing it has no screen, and the house becomes an insect nature preserve!

## Chapter 11

# Pierce and Alex

June, 20 2016: Pierce and Alex originally planned to marry after he passed the Texas Bar in the summer of 2017 but have now moved it up to December of 2016. A lot of work to do!

From their wedding website:

> Pierce and Alex first met in the fall of 2011 when Alex transferred to Southwestern. Pierce did not think much about Alex initially, outside of agreeing with the general consensus of his fraternity brothers that she was "hot." Alex likewise did not think too much about Pierce outside of agreeing with the general consensus of her sorority sisters that he was "loud" . . .
>     And so, it began . . .

6/28: Pierce and Alex are here soaking up the sun and decompressing after a long law school year. They have moved into a two-bedroom apartment in Waco, their first home. The holiday weekend went well with the usual celebrations. Rhoads arrived home in time for the Williamson birthday party. He and Pierce stayed up all night and played tennis at dawn. We grilled sausages and vegetables for the extended family one night, and young Anabel and Emily were stars, but the loveliest of all was the dark eyed beauty Alex, now fully bonded with Casey and Clay, our most recent graduate (from Johns Hopkins).

7/11: The boys have gone back to Texas, and we miss them. Good tennis and dinner at the Burgers with Sanford and Beth Jewett up to console Van, their longtime Keene Valley friend. Jovial chat with St. George's alumnus Tucker Carlson on the Hunt Club terrace one evening, where I went to shine my shoes before dinner at the Burgers. "Your Dad and I were friends when

I was at the Corporation for Public Broadcasting in DC. I hear he's lost 80 pounds."

"Yes, he did, and now he's gained it all back."

7/25: More summer nights with Patrick and Michelle Bernuth, recollecting his long-ago Iran adventures over a delicious steak, grilled asparagus and summer pudding. Saturday was the 100th anniversary of the Rockaway Hunt-Seabright tennis match, the country's oldest inter-club match. Sunday a cygnet, brown and awkward, broke loose from its swan family on the pond and sat in a puddle on the Causeway until neighbors drove it back towards its home with paddles, calling it "a problem child."

The worst seaweed I can remember wraps around and trails me as I climbed out of the water like some 1950s B horror movie. A marine centipede adhered to my skin "like a particularly tenacious abalone." The next morning Michelle giggled as I headed for the shower and said, "Jamie, you still have seaweed on your bottom."

8/15: Five days of horrible heat in spite of which Michelle cooked a fajita feast for Rhoads' farewell, the Ubinas, Northrops, Donovans, Neriches, Burkes, Thorntons, John Walsh, and many MacGuires attending to send him off.

8/20: Lovely 75th Birthday party for Burtch Drake at the CYC, with a great rock band playing golden oldies. Friday, we went to a fascinating Garden Club presentation on pollinators. A lovely little world out here.

9/29: Ten degrees cooler this morning. The breeze is blowing through the thinning leaves. The sky is high and deeply blue. Birds begin to chirp, and a large gaggle of geese fly low over the housetop in their gregarious way. Still and serene this Sunday morning.

10/28: A thank you dinner for Art Nicol's many years of service to the Club tonight. Well-deserved. First fire of the fall this weekend and Sunday afternoon I went back out onto the links for a late season, sun swept nine holes. In due course a long line of clouds advanced from the north slowly and inexorably, the storm clouds within showing their sparks, and then the rain hit, a sprinkle at first and then a wonderfully wet wall of rain and wailing winds.

11/2: The Cubs won their first World Series since 1908.

11/8: Donald Trump is elected president over the heavily favored Hillary Clinton.

11/20: The cygnets maturing on the pond have taken to munching on the Madsen Meadow, rooting around Woody and C.J. Kerr's garden, and ambling down the Causeway. One was waddling in the middle of it 300 yards away when he saw me driving slowly towards him and decided to take flight. It was an awesome display of aereonautical ineptitude, but after much flapping he did manage to get airborne and slowly rose, clearing my windshield by no more than a couple of feet magnificently.

11/26: A long, emotional chat with Bibi, who is coming to the wedding in Austin, even though "It will be very hard for me." She still misses Lanie.

## THE WEDDING

Two thousand sixteen ended gloriously with Pierce and Alex's wedding in Austin the weekend before Christmas. Pierce's aunt and uncle, Cheryl and John Sauder, gave a beautiful opening night party for out of towners at the attractively understated Tarry House, we gave the rehearsal brunch on Saturday, there was much music making and listening that night, and the big event was Sunday evening in a party hall downtown. The temporarily Reverend Frankie Pagliaro presided with a beautifully written and delivered service filled with Scripture, and at the reception after Rhoads gave a marvelous toast as best man:

> "Almost a year ago Pierce asked me to be his best man, and I was honored to accept not only as his brother and his best friend, but as someone who has watched him grow throughout his life. If we looked at Pierce just 10 years ago we would see an immature jerk whose bullying escapades included hanging me on a jungle gym by my underwear . . . Over the past few years, though, Pierce has become a much more mature jerk . . .
>
> "I am incredibly thankful for you, Alex, because I know Pierce is in good hands. It has been an extraordinarily happy experience to watch the love you two have for each other grow . . . If I have any advice for you guys going forward it is simply to continue loving each other in the way you already do."

And a joyous Christmas afterwards in California.

## Chapter 12

# Twenty-five Years and Moving On

### 2017

March 5, 2017: A cozy night in front of the fire with the Hinckleys and Blackfords, veal and sausage ragu, salad and cheese and a yummy chocolate birthday cake with vanilla frosting.

3/14: Pierce and Alex sweetly came up for the book launch of *Real Lace Revisited*. Michelle gave a beautiful party at the American Irish Historical Society mansion on Fifth Avenue, and Rob Barnes and Chris Coy hosted us all for dinner at Orsay after. On the weekend Michelle cooked the Grand Hotel roast beef dinner on Stable Lane, and Rhoads arrived as well.

Helen DuBois writes to say she is the longest living resident of the IOW, she and Peter having been here since the Sixties. Chuck and Ilze Leonard have been here 40 years since they moved from Park Row, and persevered, after the Lawrence School in Hewlett Bay Park closed, commuting Alexandra and Charlie to school in New York City every day.

4/16: A quiet Easter with Michelle in California and the boys in Texas. RHC has been asked to join a group of "Founding Clubs" at the International Tennis Hall of Fame.

4/25: Fruit trees are bursting forth.

5/25: Ascension Thursday, raining hard, and tide high on the IOW, running well past the driveway on Stable Lane. A pair of egret peck at Quinn Barton's lawn, whereas we have robins and rabbits. A cat or a coon crawls alongside the Anderson house, stalking. Good tennis one day, Anuj Sahai and I beating Ed Reitler and Maccabiah Games champ Mike Wise. Michelle has joined the Garden Club. A good turnout for my book talk at the Hunt Club, and on into summer.

6/23: Both boys are home, and life is sweet. Pierce, Alex and their dog, Jensen Mae, rolled in Thursday afternoon, having accelerated their last leg of the long drive from Texas, to make the first Thursday night buffet at the Club. They picked Rhoads up at the airport about 1 and were champing at the bit to get to the terrace for cocktails by 6:30. We sat with the Nicols, Paynes and Hinckleys, and Peggy, my old school bus monitor, put the boys on either side of her. The other diners included the Heaneys, Schmeelks, Sylvesters, Hellmuths, Tony Peck, Van Burger, Lori Laub, Sky and Dean, Dean's brother Bobby Tyndall, Helen Corroon, Honor and Malcolm MacLean, and Francine Rowley. Both boys are well and impressively smart. The dinner discussion on AI and driverless cars was like a seminar.

Later in their visit we cooked out many nights, enjoyed the Garden Club tour of Don and Lynn Wilson's several gardens, and the boys took me to a Yankees game where they beat the Nationals 6–3. We sat close to Judge in right field, who earned widespread adulation. A bit more expensive than the $1.50 center field bleacher seats where I started to watch Mickey Mantle!

7/12 : Wonderful three weeks of fun, family and endless laughter, but Pierce and Alex left at 5 a.m. this morning and got to west of Nashville by night, a good stretch of road. When I spoke to Rhoads, he was sitting on his new South Austin terrace overlooking the city. "It's 95 but feels like 105, so I don't think I've acclimatized."

7/23: Heat Wave. 97 degrees in town and hot here too.

8/12: Extreme Right protesters in Charlottesvills incite violence and one counter protester is run over and killed. Shameful.

8/20: A sand bar has formed at the beach, and a shoal of skate are swimming around in the shallow water by the shore. On 8/22 the eclipse passed uneventfully. Tim and Julia brought the adorable Anabel and Emily to dinner. Anabel hears Dean mention Casey's romance and asks if they are "dating."

8/25: Heavenly boat ride with the Sylvesters down to Point Lookout from their Crooked Creek dock. A clear night and calm water, several duck shacks rebuilt since Sandy.

9/9: I took Michelle to DeSetta's Nursery so she could commune with David and Mary on next steps for her garden. A cheery and beautifully designed tennis dinner was given by Gordon and Serena Ogden for the pro staff and committees. The party game is to tell a secret no one has ever heard about before, so Margaret Carpenter and I confess to our long-ago affair, causing consternation among the younger ladies, who, at least briefly, think I'm serious.

9/13: Mother would be 100 today, and it would be Mom and Dad's 75th Anniversary. What would they think? I know I must have disappointed them in some ways, but how she would have rejoiced at Pierce and Rhoads! And we're still here, stumbling along. Tomorrow night we go to Katherine and

David McCallum's 50th Anniversary. Mom and Dad gave their rehearsal dinner in 1967. It will be a sweet night.

9/15: Beautiful sight on the ocean last weekend of the Woodmere Bay Yacht Club's annual 9/11 Regatta in memory of Patrick O'Keefe, 20 sloops under full sail visible from the beach. Beautiful warm water for late season swimming as well.

The world is so beautiful—climbing roses, soaring stars, brilliant birdsongs in the early morning sun, the perfume of love in an upstairs bedroom, photos of beloved ancestors and children around the house and water seeping out of the marsh. Each moment is a universe all its own. A swan strolled down Stable Lane this late September morning, first time ever!

I brought Michelle's maple syrup pie to John and Patsy Emery on Polo Lane, who are leaving for assisted living outside Philadelphia after 52 years. Patsy was emotional, showing me Mr. Hentzel's dining room table and the étagère he and Uncle Dan, Patsy's woodworking Dad, fashioned from Mr. Monroe's leftover wood when he was diagnosed with terminal cancer. Much joy and sorrow over the years. "I love you," I said as I left. "I know you do," she replied as we embraced, "And you always have . . ." through good times and bad. Leaving much unsaid that didn't need to be said at all.

Then a bourbon with Jim and Anne Thornton as we looked over their marsh view with the sun setting, the hawks and planes flying.

Malcolm MacLean buried a dead swan at sea yesterday. "Duck don't like swan. There used to be so many duck on the pond Hallie Dixon complained we were corning it. What Eddie Lynch did was to wait until we were all in our places in the marsh and then throw a firecracker into the pond where the duck were, and all hell broke loose."

10/15: Helen Corroon's 90th Birthday and a sweet sit down with Andree, Maitland and Tracy Horner, Bob Miller, George Baker and his daughter Sandy, who looks a lot like her late mother of the same name. Tish Claiborne, Jimmy Dean, Hilary Northrop, Prissy Smith, the Kerins and O'Rourkes. Andree spoke of her mother's gifts, especially her faith, and young Harper, heading to medical school, spoke well too.

10/24: Weirdly warm end of October. Michelle lovingly tends her new garden, helpfully coached by Daphne Hellmuth.

11/1: All Saints: LBC picnic on a Kiwi clouded day. About 60 trick or treaters came by last night, then a chummy dinner at the Blackfords, with the Hinckleys, Keatings, Paynes, Sky and Dean.

Pierce has passed the Texas Bar amid much jubilation. And the world has begun to fall asleep. Leaves fell and with them twigs and branches. A bloodied robin lay at the garage door, doubtless a victim of the white cat we see hunting about, but the roses still bloomed in the mild air, and the grass remained a deep, emerald green. The swans departed, and the mallards came back.

Mike Davy took a picture of "Cedarhurst," the B&B in Ballybunion our cook Myra started when she returned to Ireland, and got the card of Alex Quane, the present owner. I emailed her and learned that Myra and Brendan sold it in 2002 and moved to a nearby village. She got dementia and died in 2009, and Brendan followed in 2014.

When she left Cedarhurst Avenue to go home to Ireland, she did it before dawn because she couldn't bear to say goodbye to us. She had caught the mumps from someone in her years with us and could not have children. When they bought their little house, she insisted on calling it Cedarhurst Lodge. She spoiled Pierce and me when we visited in 1973, drinks at the pub with Brendan, great meals, Aran Island sweaters, and hot water bottles. They lived quietly and had people in for checkers once a week. When Mom got sick and was dying, she wrote a long letter and then called on Christmas Eve, endlessly generous to the last.

11/11: After squash with Jim Ryan, John McKay and Sky, I brought in the mums and geraniums ahead of the early oncoming freeze. Dinner last night was in front of the fire. This morning light glistened on the green grass, pale sun breaking through clouds. The Reitler and Ryan kids were playing on the ball field, just as Pierce and Rhoads did, and in fact, just as I once did as well.

Thanksgiving: Wonderful to have Pierce, Alex and Rhoads home for another day at Kevin and Sally's, and a Grand Hotel dinner Friday night on Stable Lane with Casey and Clay, before they all went off to resume their busy lives.

2018 New Years: Cold! Down to 6 degrees. Pleasant New Year's Eve with Peggy Nicol, Liz Mullen (still working 60-hour weeks), the Gilgans, etc. There are snow drifts everywhere.

## 2018

1/20: The Thaw finally came, the house warmed, the sun lit the porch, geese, duck and sea gulls went on the wing happily.

Jennifer Egan's new book, *Manhattan Beach*, has segments at the RHC with the "Old Stoves," and a couple of historical inaccuracies—black tie dinner dances in January and walks to Crooked Creek, which would have been a bit muddy! We will get her to speak here. Apparently, she wrote to ask if she could visit when researching the book, and the Board said no. Perhaps they feared exposure of our lack of transgender members? Hilarious!

2/10: Dean and Schuyler were married 50 years ago today, and oh the stories I could tell. I had brought home my first A in an English essay, but, before I could show it to my father, I had thrown up all over it after dancing with as many of Dean's bridesmaids as would let me. When I woke up the next morning, I asked Peter, "Do you think anyone noticed?" Philip was best man and had to eject Uncle John, who had passed out in the limo, so that Sky and Dean could proceed on their honeymoon.

2/11: Ann McGowan gives a great mid-winter at home for the squash crowd. She and Bebe Morrissey are the leaders of a new generation. Why not start a Ladies Singles division of Gold Racquets? The golf course is yellow and brown, and water is rising on the road.

3/27: Quiet weekend with Michelle, still snow on the ground, but geese, mallard and swan are beginning to nest, and cardinals flit in and out of the marsh reeds. Snow drops sprouting and daffodils pushing up, cormorants on top of the dock poles at the yacht club, an osprey back in residence on his tower, but the snow geese have headed north.

April Fools: Dinner at the Hastys, a house I had not been in since Treddy made Jane Rice Coleman Peck give a cocktail party to reintroduce her daughter Beazie to the Governors 20 years ago. Several years of work have transformed it. Great salmon and fun conversation.

5/15: Rhoads is 23 today. Both Isabel and Pierce send affectionate grams. Izzie: "Happy birthday to the most wonderful boy in the world."

Pierce's was: "Happy birthday to my best man, my arch nemesis, and the second biggest Giants fan in the world. We've been through just about everything together, and the future looks even brighter."

Just so, and my joy is unbounded, though there is a slight pang that henceforth they will be ever more independent, as they should be.

5/14: Oil change and tires rotated today. My local expert, John Walson, who owns the garage, tells me Seawane Country Club is going under, like Woodmere, where two Orthodox developers are planning to build over two hundred houses on its golf course. The third local, mostly Jewish, country club, Inwood, home to the 1923 U.S. Open but increasingly in the shadow of JFK airport, is also suffering and "owes $23 million to the Vatican," the landowner, one presumes. Lawrence-Woodmere Academy's auditorium is being used as a shul by an Orthodox congregation on Saturdays, and a girl's soccer field along Broadway has been sold for development. "The few Reform Jews left are fleeing." And yet, so says John, all the Orthodox are broke. "Think about it, if you had six kids and were paying yeshiva tuitions, you would be too." More and more of the houses are being designed with prayer rooms, so the owners can claim 50 percent tax abatement.

Apparently Seawane had many Madoff victims. Morty Davis of Lawrence Park on Rock Hall Rd. pressed him on many of his relatives, now all defrauded.

5/19: Rosa rugosa, lilac and lavender blooming and fragrant after four days of rain. Opening party at the Club and dinner after with Clay, Rina MacGuire,

Sarina Ogden, and Theresa Minson. Pierce is interviewing with a firm in Austin. A hummingbird cheers me as it flitters on the lawn. Michelle plants butterfly bushes, Russian sage, lambs ear, various perennials, geraniums, a fig tree and yarrow in her courtyard garden

5/31: I grilled swordfish in the courtyard and was watching the French Open on TV when Pierce texts, "I have something to tell you." He has taken the job in Austin and starts in late June. AND Alex is pregnant! She sounded radiant and thrilled, and I'm sure Becky and Tony Rodriguez are over the moon as well. Late January is the date.

First ocean swim after steamy tennis is bliss at 58 degrees.

6/21: The eternal cycle. Malcom MacLean died at 90. As Pierce and Alex prepare to welcome new life, Jim Thornton's body is failing, and what may have been several mini-strokes are beginning to affect his memory. And Sonny Staniford is struggling, on oxygen part of the day. Rhoads is happy with Rafa's win in the French, and Pierce and Alex have bought a starter house in the Mueller neighborhood of Austin.

6/25: Pleasant weekend with Jimmy and Eve Wallace, houseguests from Geraldine, New Zealand. The Burgers, Hinckleys and Sylvesters came in for crab cakes and good craic.

7/8: A blissful week with Rhoads home, making friends and connections everywhere he goes. He took in a Yankees game with Bull Donovan, Russell Aldrich and their ladies, visited his old mentor Jim Thornton, had Clay and Casey for overnights and stayed out late at the LaRue, Williamson, Carpenter and Aldrich houses (thank goodness for Uber), whupped me in tennis, lectured Michelle and me on Bitcoin and his favorite virtual currencies, block chain theory and other aspects of data science, all the while following the World Cup with intense interest.

7/11: The hydrangeas are swelling. New IOW families include the Chachas in what was the Savin house and the Sherrills, who have taken over the Wadsworth compound after 40 years. Michelle's courtyard is a riot of color and lovely breezes waft floral scents into the house. The Yale-Harvard tennis team came to play and stayed for dinner before flying to England on their Prentice Cup tour. A good group including ladies now. One, Courtney, is a Seabright member and one of Artie Minson's employees at We Work.

7/15: A beautiful cruise on the Sylvesters boat on a rising tide to see the Russian McMansions in Hewlett Neck, hilarious mega-sized confections.

7/24: Pleasant day playing the Seabright Legends in Rumson with Tom Russo. We won our match against their president, Peter Dickson, and my old Portsmouth teammate Don MacDonald, now an eminent ophthalmologist with a *pro bono* clinic in northern Ghana. A pleasant LBC lunch the following day with Chris and Deb Low and David and Anna Rich talking of Walker Percy.

7/25: Pierce alerted the family to Alex's delicate condition today, a more public announcement to follow soon. Joy all around.

8/11: Pleasant IOW parties at the Gateleys and Andersons before the Jersey Boys night at the CYC.

9/1: Lily MacGuire won the Margaret Carpenter Sportsmanship Award at the Junior Sports Dinner, and Anabel won the David Walsh Surfing Award at the LBC. The Matriarchy is on the move in the new generation!

9/9: The heat finally broke, and I got in a last swim on Friday before melon and prosciutto, fresh corn and cheese for supper.

9/16: A drink with Ann and Jim Thornton before they move south to Virginia for the winter. They have sold their big house to Charlotte Hall Wilbur and will move next door to the "Chauncey" house after adding a new kitchen over the winter.

Afterwards, walking into the Hunt Club dining room for dinner with Dean and Schuyler, Margie Carpenter jumps up and embraces me. "Evey died an hour ago." Evelyn Bates Owen was married to Margaret's brother Steve. Evey and her twin sister, Patsy (Johnson), were debs of the year and on the cover of *Life* magazine in what, 1952? Their Dad, Ted Bates, must have had a hand in getting them on the Clairol Ad, "Does she, or doesn't she? Only her hairdresser knows for sure." Steve had not left her side in three years as she fought cancer quietly but valiantly.

But the next day, when I swam another last, last swim after sweaty tennis, who was coming out of the water but Steve himself? We shook hands, no words were necessary, but he said, "My first swim in three years." Young Steve was still in the water and gave me a hug, his voice choked. Four generations of family friendship.

The cicadas are sounding. The songbirds are gone, but the Monarch butterflies soar and dip on the breeze as they head south.

Pierce and Alex are expecting a boy! I would have loved a little girl, too, but this is a cause for rejoicing. Pierce wrote on Instagram, "Eli Manning MacGuire . . . is unfortunately NOT my son's name (@Alex.MacGuire is so unreasonable) so we went with Patterson James MacGuire ("PJ"). See you in a few months, Buddy!"

9/30: Bluefish for dinner and too much of the disturbing Kavanagh hearings. When has our politics ever been so ugly? My former Portsmouth Prefect and great friend Rob Barnes has died while working out at his NYC gym, and the service will be in East Hampton on Saturday. Michelle and I are desolate.

Wiping mold from the baseboard, doors and walls for hours after this damp, rainy, humid end-of-summer. Too many funerals this Fall but delightful trips to Chicago and Charleston to speak to the Irish Georgians.

11/25: And a beautiful Thanksgiving it really was. Pierce loves his new job, and Rhoads is enjoying his python coding course. Lots of squash and feasting, pasta and pecan pie, steak and chocolate whiskey cake, a heart-warming Thanksgiving with Kevin and Sally on a freezing 18-degree day.

## 2019

2/10: Christmas in Texas with the boys, and then back there again after Alex delivered PJ on January 18, 7'3" and healthy, a little cherub. The Mullens and Sylvesters came to dinner for Michelle's lamb stew, the garlic in which finally cured my three week-long cold!

2/14: Clear and breezy, and I walked the golf course for the first time this year. Amazon has walked out of Queens, costing 30,000 jobs. Thank you, politicians. PJ is four weeks old and thriving. Pierce took his first deposition. Rhoads is now embarked on a data science course that will give him a job in the burgeoning tech center Austin has become. The only sadness is that their trips home will become less frequent. Is it, perhaps, time to consider us going to them?

3/5: Snow this morning on a quiet winter weekend, with squash and work outs. The power failed for several hours. In the future I would rather spend most of the winter in the southern hemisphere or with grandkids, but we shall see.

3/11: Dean called with the terrible news that Ann Thornton has been diagnosed with colon cancer that has spread. She was sick with pneumonia much of last summer and never really recovered, caring as she was constantly for Jim in his own decline. Such wonderful friends from our first day here on.

3/18: PJ is now two months old! Squirming, kicking, yawning and beginning to smile.

Endless car repairs—cylinder coils and brake caliper—but always instructive chatter with John Walson.

Neil Coughlan and Carol Bryce-Buchanan came for St. Patrick's Day, and we drove into the Rockaways to see the house on Beach 113th Street where his family rented a room in summers (his father was a transit worker and moonlighted at the 92nd Street Y, so he could only come on the weekend). Neal teared up listening to the Irish tenors in the car, and we had a fine corned beef dinner and whiskey cake by the fire. Charlie Higgins, a Scots-Irishman from North Carolina who lives across the lane, came in for a drink.

3/30: At a birthday dinner for Michael Sylvester, Katherine McCallum recalled how Mike Nichols once offered to cast her in *The Graduate*. "As Mrs. Robinson?" Michael Sylvester asks. "Michael!" Katherine responds sharply, "I was 20."

Easter: A little golf on Good Friday, pleasant workouts, Mass at St. Joachim and a congenial lunch with the Aldriches. Ricky's wife Bailey and her friend Lexie are most attractive. A whole new generation coming along hunting the Easter eggs!

After sweeping out the annual Mayfly hatch from the TV room, I walked out at dusk and had a good chat with neighbor Madsen at the end of his driveway.

Michelle returns from Easter in California. Her 2019 garden includes black-eyed Susans, a happy reminder of my college years in Maryland, white roses, cone flowers, obedien, ladies' mantle, day lilies, and salvia.

We have a new neighbor. Liz Eielson, a hedge fund trader and longtime leading lady golfer at RHC, has bought Quinn Barton's house. Great news.

4/5: Kerry Graham, Pierce and Rhoads' trustee, has decided that the time has come to put the Stable Lane house on the market, and the decision makes complete sense. They are both settled in Austin and will be up less and less. Michelle and I will miss having it for weekends, of course, but it's a good spur for us to make our own plans going forward rather than house sitting theirs.

5/20: The lovely Jennifer Egan came to talk on her book *Manhattan Beach* which has various scenes set at the Hunt Club in the 1940s. I gave her the tour of the Club and community that the RHC board discouraged when she wrote during her research. She was radiant and interested in everything. She heads the American PEN, a very good work.

5/24: The garden coming alive and glorious golf with Pierce on a wind-swept day. He had me convulsed recalling when "Lady Margaret" Dall, florid and always wearing a white headband, and stick-skinny Betsy Heath could not open the door to the squash singles court one winter day, and no one responded to their cries for help. When Lady M failed to lift Betsy into the gallery above, Betsy final succeeded in lifting Mrs. Dall, a considerable feat given her girth. "Betsy always walked a bit crooked after that."

6/12: I gashed myself shaving with a new blade this morning, when it ran over the remnants of stitches I got when I was three and Schuyler playfully tripped me with a cane at 50 Cedarhurst Avenue. Amazing that 64 years later there could still be such a gusher.

6/15: Summer is iccummen in, and Michelle's courtyard garden and indeed all of Lawrence is ablaze. Lockwood Sloan gave a drinks party for his and his mother's respective birthdays. He wore his late father's lime green jacket with a fading needlepoint RHC insignia on the breast pocket.

6/27: In town we went to see Rebecca Madsen at the Bitter End close her set with "Do You Want Somebody to Love?" 50 summers after I heard Grace Slick sing it with the Jefferson Airplane at the Fillmore in San Francisco.

7/1: Patterson James arrived triumphantly for his visit on Stable Lane, Pierce, Alex, and Alex's parents, Becky and Tony Rodriguez, in tow. We walked down to the Yacht Club where Charlie Leonard's and Lindsay's engagement party was under way. Later we cooked burgers (I graciously deferred to Tony as grill master) and sat on the sun porch, which they loved. Rhoads arrived late, but was happy and well.

Sunday there was much party preparation and Michelle worked her usual miracles. Lots of MacGuires, Donovans, Russell Aldrich and Claire. Hilary Northrop joined the group, and, best of all, Bibi not only came to visit but stayed throughout the evening, taking charge of PJ! When I asked her if I could get her a drink she said, "I can do it, Jamie. It's my house you know." And as she left, to Pierce: "Pierce, if you need me, I'm coming to Texas!" A very festive night.

7/7: After they had explored the city, Michelle and I drove Becky and Tony to JFK on July 3rd so that Pierce, Alex and P.J. could enjoy the fireworks with the Northrops at the CYC. The next day we enjoyed the most beautiful swim of the summer to date as Pierce and Alex marched P.J. around the pool following Uncle Sam. The band from Our Lady of Good Counsel band played Sousa marches as they have since 1938. Topside, we shared a drink afterwards with the former Uncle Sams, including David McCallum, now 85 and still working as Ducky on *NCIS*. Friday Bibi came again so Pierce and Alex could have some time off, we played the Jimmy Burns doubles and enjoyed Scott and Lynn LaRue's drinks party. And then, after driving them to the airport, both boys were safely home in Texas.

7/14: The ladies of the Lawrence Garden Club put on a grand tour of the Madsen Meadow. Good for Steve and Rebecca.

7/18: Klausner Corners on the IOW sold pink lemonade and brownies, sweet little girls of Leigh and Dan, reminding me of Peter and me doing the same, using the Coca Cola inventory on Cedarhurst Avenue.

7/20: Drinks at the "Chauncey House" with a cheerful Ann Thornton and her boys, Helen DuBois as well, "Paella Night" at the CYC, a Springsteen cover band at LBC, the summer in full flower. My old Portsmouth teammate, Don Macdonald, helmed his 32-foot fishing boat up from Seabright with their tennis team, just as Dad's great friend Steve Owen had the other way with the *Sachem* in the 1950s. We won narrowly.

7/28: Cleaning out the house, I left Pierce and Rhoads' bats, balls and gloves on the IOW playing field, and they were soon carried off to a new home.

7/31: We took the bounty of Saratoga (crab cake, tomato bruschetta, melon, and green beans) to Katherine and David McCallum's on Atlantic Beach for a wonderful dinner with them and Carolyn and Andrew Wright.

8/4: Fun chat with David Sherrill on writing his backgammon book before the RHC buffet. Chip Burke left his keys in his Dodge Thursday night and had it stolen out of his IOW driveway, just as Robert Kleinschmidt's son had done a year ago. A lesson still to be learned . . .

8/17: Progressive cocktail party at the Gateleys, Liz Eielson's, the Andersons and Sherrills. Lots of nice new neighbors to carry the IOW forward.

8/28: We looked at Jack and Diane Bulkley's lovely house as we had at the Vencils. Much to ponder.

Pleasant last Thursday buffet honoring outgoing squash chair Anil Sahai. Sudha sits next to me, beautiful as always, and tells me she, too, grew up at a club in Delhi, probably one far posher than ours! Anil sits next to me and describes Michelle, in Newport Beach for Dick's 95th, as "regal."

Labor Day Sunday Steve Madsen's Sundance band played a bravura performance at the CYC. I was a dancing fool with Evey Tomasson, Cecilia Owen, Hilary Northrop, and Andree Corroon, among others. Madsen said the high point for him was the slow dance between former RHC prez Artie Nicol and the current *jefe*, Woody Kerr, "bringing our little world into the twenty-first century," though I remember doing the same with David McCallum 15 years ago at the Beach to a rather less enthusiastic reception.

9/15: Lorraine Heath ingested a yellow jacket at RHC yesterday and was bitten internally, but Eunice saved the day with her Epipen. Beautiful last swims, farewells to Frank McDonough and others clearing out their lockers, drinks with Susan Wald and Phil Douglas, and a cozy dinner with Sky and Dean. Invited to join lunch with Sonny and Lee Staniford, Andree and Helen Corroon the next day, lots of hearing aid failure but infinite good will!

Columbus Day: John and Mary Louise Lindenthal have sold their house to the young Peter Brooks, who sweetened the deal by offering them six weeks rent free for the next three summers when the Lindenthals return from Arizona. Peter grew up opposite 7 Stable Lane in Peter Sr.'s and Ince's house, now the Gateleys. A happy homecoming.

Later in October Charlie Higgins bought Nancy Hanna's house and Frank Argento rented the John Minnegan house opposite us, which the Higgins had vacated. Also, Amanda and Ned Oakley bought the Bulkley's lot and plan to build there, and the Hardarts bought the Bulkley house, so a new generation is settling in.

Houses have their auras, even a little Cape Cod cottage by the sea like ours. I always wondered whether ours might have a curse, since the original owner, Mr. McLean, fell down the stairs not long after inhabiting it and died of his injuries. Fifteen years later his son Harry met a violent death as well, crashing into a tree trunk on the Lawrence Village golf course on his way back from a party on Atlantic Beach. I wondered about that when in our first days in the house in 1994 then three-year-old Pierce careened down the stairs noisily and came to rest with an ominous silence in the front hall as Lanie and I rushed from the dinner table. He was spared, as were all others in our quarter century here, and may whomever comes after us enjoy similar good fortune.

November 2019: And then, in a blink of an eye, it was 25 years later . . .

There was a hilarious email colloquy when Jack Bulkley proposed a Thanksgiving Saturday afternoon touch football game on the ball field, and John Sipp responded that the last time he played in one he broke two ribs trying to block David Sherrill, who did not feel anything. Mary Alice Sherrill then sweetly chimed in, "Not to worry, John, we'll be in San Francisco that week." Finally, eminent endocrinologist Michelle Warren wrote to assure the entire Isle of Wight that there would be orthopedic surgeons and a psychiatrist available (Fiske and their son, Matt) at 268 Victoria Place if need be. It reminded me of long-ago holiday games on Cedarhurst Avenue in the 1960s when the MacMillens and their guests would traipse across the empty field between us after dinner to compete against our tribe on the side lawn.

It was, however, in several respects a sad month in that Anil Sahai, loveliest of gentlemen, died while on vacation in his New Delhi hotel room of a seizure, possibly connected to the horrendous pollution that shrouds that city. He was only 71 but had longstanding heart issues. Then, even more shockingly, Jake Carpenter, just 66, emailed that his cancer had returned, and he would seek treatment, but there was a valedictory quality to his message, and he told another friend, "See you on the other side." He died of a blood infection three weeks later. He was named for Howse Burton, whose family came here in the 1890s, owned Turkey Point and much else. Jake was my brother Peter's best friend and a hilariously mischievous little boy who went on to be a major part of snowboarding's development. And finally, Sonny Staniford had a stroke in Florida, refused rehab and passed peacefully at year's end, soon followed by Jim Hellmuth. A bad run of luck for our little world.

I am struck reading these entries by how many people are no longer with us but heartened by the steady stream of newcomers who find the Isle of Wight as beautiful and congenial a place to live as we always have.

And whatever the sadness, there is always new life, as I was thrilled to discover at Christmas in Austin when Pierce and Alex announced on Christmas Eve that eleven-month-old PJ would become an older brother in the summer of 2020 to Walker Anthony MacGuire.

Joy to the World indeed!

# Chapter 13

# Envoi

Two thousand twenty started slowly and mildly with lots of weekend squash and the occasional winter dinner party, including a fabulous Coq au Vin Michelle cooked for Sarah Nash and assorted friends including the Mullens, Blackfords and Hinckleys on the Causeway over Presidents Day weekend.

Ann Thornton died in February, the slightly daffy, infinitely kind den mother of the entire Isle of Wight. She was at her Virginia home, Beaumont, in Gordonsville, just outside of Charlottesville, where Jim is also ailing. It's hard to believe that Ann will not be enlivening this Spring's fragrant mornings with her walks down Stable Lane, Boo prancing ahead of her on his leash and the cat trailing warily behind them as they survey the neighborhood. She would often come into the sun porch to plan some new dinner or party with Michelle, advice on gardening, and regale us with her particular, delightful brand of whimsy.

And in early April Ray York died, my tennis partner and dear friend for half a century. U. VA captain, Virginia State champion, ace stock picker, hilarious trash talker, generous patron of jazz. He was cheerful until the end and questioned me closely in our last call on this season's first shad roe sighting at the Oyster Bar, one of our many traditions. More than one friend has called it the end of an era, echoing Treddy's old phrase. But we have to go on.

Coming on to the 140th anniversary year of the IOW, what should have been a celebratory season was blindsided by the COVID-19 virus and the ensuing lockdown of our lives, not to mention most of our economy. Many families chose to shelter in their IOW homes, which provided company, at a distance. Lauren Burke got the virus but has recovered. Later several

Madsens and Caroline Williamson were felled as well. Nancy Blackford was, as usual, undaunted and organized a paper Easter egg hunt in which house-holders attached posters of eggs to their houses, and the youngsters sought to identify as many as they could. The response was overwhelming, over thirty houses participated and over 100 eggs were displayed. Some 70 young people sought them, and the Reitler boys, Andrew and Gregory, won the contest.

Peter Brooks came down with COVID-19 but quarantined successfully as did the others with whom he had come into contact. The summer progressed almost normally with kids biking to the Junior Sports Program. James Heaney won the men's Club tennis championship again, and Claire Minnis not only won the Coleman Cup for Junior girls but played a strong final in the Ladies Championship against repeat winner Maya Byrnes Clark.

There was a minor amusing kerfuffle when Steve Madsen reported a car had been driving into his driveway at 3:30 a.m. in the morning on succes-sive nights and suspected it could be a car thief. Warning emails went out along with reminders to lock all cars and suggestions to hire a security guard. Several days later Steve reported that the culprit was in fact his *Wall Street Journal* newspaper delivery man!

Severe drought conditions intensified in the American West and presaged increasing difficulties for all as climate change accelerates.

Mayor Edelman, who has proven himself a staunch friend to the Isle of Wight, benefitted from IOW support in a landslide re-election victory against an opponent with a potentially destructive agenda. Socially distanced Hallowe'en trick-or-treating went on enthusiastically, and, when much of Lawrence was declared a hot spot for coronavirus after heightened infections in the Orthodox communities, the back of Lawrence and the IOW were mercifully excluded.

Rhoads and Kerry Graham arrived in early November to clean out the house, which has been bought by Andriy Falenchuk and his wife Oksana, and for three days Bibi and we excavated the accumulations of a quarter century, the best of which is now relocated into Texas. We wish the Falenchuks as much joy as we were lucky to have had.

The year ended with more than 75 million COVID cases worldwide. The first ever Christmas tree lighting ceremony on the IOW ballfield included a blessing by Monsignor Paul Rahilly, carols led by Steve Madsen, and a Santa circling in a red convertible who, upon closer inspection, looked suspiciously like David Sherrill.

In his classic Irish country house memoir, *Woodbrook,* David Thomson writes, "A battlefield remains sick land for many generations, and a garden made and kept with love does not lose its beauty after it goes wild."

In the last five years on Stable Lane Michelle cooked her meals for family and friends and kept her little garden with the tenderest love. My hope and prayer is that, *that* love, the love of Lanie, Bibi and my children, and all the other wonderful times the family enjoyed on Stable Lane, will infuse the house with warmth and laughter so long as it still stands, and that the Isle of Wight will remain a place apart and an enchanted refuge for many generations to come.

# Index

# About the Author

**James P. MacGuire** was born in New York, grew up on Long Island, and was educated at Johns Hopkins and Cambridge. After serving as country program director for Catholic Relief Services in Burundi, he has worked at Time Inc., Macmillan, the Corporation for Public Broadcasting, and the UK Catholic Herald. His poetry, fiction and journalism have appeared in many national publications.

Jamie MacGuire is the author or co-author of fifteen books, the father of two beloved sons, Pierce and Rhoads, and is the proud grandfather of Patterson James and Walker. He lives in New York with the sublime Michelle Coppedge.